HEMINGWAY: LIFE AND WORKS

HEMINGWAY: LIFE AND WORKS

Gerald B. Nelson and Glory Jones

Facts On File Publications
460 Park Avenue South
New York, N.Y. 10016

Hemingway:
Life and Works

Library of Congress Cataloging in Publication Data

Nelson, Gerald B.
  Hemingway, life and works.

  Bibliography: p.
  Includes indexes.
  1. Hemingway, Ernest, 1899–1961—Biography.
2. Novelists, American—20th century—Biography.
I. Jones, Glory.   II. Title.
PS3515.E37Z7455   1983   813'.52   82-12070
ISBN 0-87196-709-X

Printed in the United States of America

10   9   8   7   6   5   4   3   2   1

Contents

General Introduction to the Chronology Series

The aim of this series is to provide an accurate, succinct, in-depth account of the central figure's life and ideas and the impact he had on the events of his day. Personal details are included when they shed light on character and personality. The subject's own writings are the main source of information, but letters and the opinions of his contemporaries are used when they add a useful extra dimension to the study. An attempt has been made only to record verifiable facts and to provide a reliable, up-to-date account of the subject's activities and influence. The main events of the time are included so as to set the person in historical perspective and to provide a rational context for his ideas and actions. Bibliographical references are given so as to permit readers, should they so desire, to follow up the quotations; a detailed bibliography of works by and about the subject is also included.

1899–1914

1899 (July 21): Ernest Miller Hemingway is born in the family home at 439 Oak Park Avenue, Oak Park, Illinois, to Dr. Clarence Edmonds Hemingway (1871–1928), a general practitioner, and Grace Hall Hemingway (1872–1951), a housewife and music teacher. Ernest is the second child. The first, Marcelline, was born on January 15, 1898, in Oak Park.

1899 (October 1): On the Hemingways' third wedding anniversary, Ernest is baptized at the First Congregational Church in Oak Park.

1900 (June): Ernest spends his first summer at the family cabin, Windemere, at Bear Lake (renamed Walloon Lake in 1901), Michigan. Subsequent summers, until Ernest leaves home, are spent in Northern Michigan as well.

1904 (November 28): His sister, Madelaine, nicknamed "Sunny," is born in Oak Park.

1905: The Hemingway family purchases a 40-acre farm across the water from the cabin on Walloon Lake and names it Longfield Farm. Ernest begins school in September in Oak Park.

1906 (August): After returning from summer vacation in Michigan, the family moves into a new home at 600 North Kenilworth Avenue, Oak Park.

1910 (August 29): Ernest accompanies his mother on a trip to Nantucket Island, Massachusetts. They stay at a boarding house, located at 45 Pearl Street. On the way home from his first lengthy travel, Ernest visits Boston, Cambridge, Lexington, and Concord, Massachusetts.

1911 (April): Ernest and his sister Marcelline are confirmed at the Third Congregational Church in Oak Park on Easter Sunday, April 16. The following day, Ernest writes his first piece of fiction. The four-paragraph story, "My First Sea Vouge," [sic] incorporates a tale the boy has heard from his great-uncle Tyley Hancock and the locations he visited on his trip the previous summer.

1911 (July 19): His sister, Carol, is born at Walloon Lake, Michigan.

1912 (March–April): Ernest appears in a school production of *Robin Hood*. He also begins to sing in the Third Congregational Church Choir. On April 12, he composes a six-line poem, "The Opening Game."

1913 (June): Ernest and Marcelline graduate from Holmes Grammar School in Oak Park.

1913 (September): Ernest, along with Marcelline, enters the Oak Park and River Forest High School. His studies include Latin, algebra, general science, and English.

1914 (June–July): Archduke Francis Ferdinand, the heir apparent to Austria-Hungary is assassinated along with his wife by a Bosnian terrorist, Bavnilo Princip. Ferdinand's death on June 28 accelerates diplomatic tension between Austria and Serbia. Germany sides with Austria while Russia aligns with Serbia. On July 25, Serbia replies to a series of demands from Austria, but the Austrian government is not satisfied with Serbia's reply. Austria declares war on Serbia on July 28. Two days later, Russia decides on partial mobilization, which is met by a war warning from Germany. Ernest is now fifteen years old, spending another summer at Walloon Lake. He and his friend, Harold Sampson, work throughout the summer selling vegetables from their boat along the shoreline of Walloon Lake.

1914 (August–September): Germany declares war on Russia on August 1, on France on August 3, and begins an invasion of Belgium on August 4. Great Britain declares war on Germany the same day. World War I has now begun. A series of

1916 (September–November): Now in his senior year of high school, Ernest increases his writing for *The Trapeze*. He covers sports for the newspaper and is hailed as Oak Park High School's "Ring Lardner, Junior." Another short story, set in Michigan and told by an Ojibway Indian, appears in *The Tabula* in November. The story is titled, "Sepi Jingan." Other contributions to *The Tabula* in November are two untitled poems, one of which consists entirely of punctuation marks, and another called "How Ballad Writing Affects Our Seniors." Ernest, now just under six feet tall, plays on the high school first-string football team.

1916 (December): The Battle of Verdun ends on December 15. This was the longest battle of World War I, beginning on February 21, 1916, and resulting in the highest casualties of the war. French losses amount to 500,000, and German losses to 400,000 soldiers. The battle ends with the Germans giving up their positions. Ernest is writing, on the average, one story each week for *The Trapeze* and working as alternate editor of the newspaper.

1917 (March 17): Three poems are published in *The Tabula* "The Worker," "Athletic Verse," and "The Inexpressible."

1917 (April): During a canoe trip along the Illinois River from April 2 through 6, Ernest and his friend, Ray Ohlsen, encounter soldiers guarding "Illinois" canal. The presence of the soldiers is the first evidence of the United States entry into World War I.

1917 (June): On June 11, Ernest graduates from Oak Park High School. He is selected as "Class Prophet" and his prophecy appears in the class yearbook, *The Senior Tabula*. Other activities listed in the yearbook are Class Day Speaker, *The Trapeze* staff, Burke Club, football team, track team manager, swimming team, orchestra, Boys' Rifle Club, Hanna Club, Boys' High School Club, Athletic Association, and Class Play. After graduation on June 17 Ernest addresses the Boys' Department of the First Congregational Church along with four other Oak Park graduates. The entire family goes to Northern Michigan during the third week of June.

1917 (July–September): Ernest spends the summer at the Hemingways' Longfield Farm in Michigan. A job has been arranged by his Uncle Tyler Hemingway at the *Kansas City Star* to begin in October. During the summer, Ernest seeks advice on writing from Trumball White, a retired journalist and former editor of *Everybody's Magazine*, who is now residing in Bay View, close to Petoskey. White tells him to write from personal experience and to learn more of the craft by practicing it. Ernest spends the summer months working on the family farm. His companions are Bill and Katy Smith and a new acquaintance, Carl Edgar, who lives in Kansas City. Edgar invites Ernest to share his apartment when Ernest moves to Kansas City in the fall.

1917 (October): On October 15, Ernest boards a train bound for Kansas City, Missouri. Dr. Hemingway sees his son off at the station. This scene is fictionalized in *For Whom the Bell Tolls*. During the trip, he crosses the Mississippi River for the first time in his life. Tyler Hemingway meets Ernest when he arrives in Kansas City and takes him to his home on Warwick Boulevard. The following day, Ernest goes to the editorial offices of the *Kansas City Star* at 1800 Grand Avenue. He first meets Harry Haskell, the chief editorial writer, is then introduced to the city editor, George Longan, and is offered a job as a reporter at $15 per week. Ernest is not given a byline during his employment at the *Star*. Ernest moves out of the house of his Uncle Tyler and Aunt Arabella towards the end of October. He is now living with Carl Edgar in an apartment on Agnes Street, but begins to stay overnight often at the Hotel Muehlbach's pressroom, which is closer to the newspaper office.

1917 (November–December): As a reporter on a city daily newspaper, Ernest is exposed to a rougher kind of life. Kansas City, with its population of 300,000, provides a stark contrast to the life he had known in Oak Park and Ernest becomes more worldly. The October Revolution in Russia now comes to an end. On November 6 and 7, the provisional government is overthrown. On November 8 and 9, Nikolai Lenin, (Vladimir Illitch Ulianov), the leader of the new Soviet government, the Council of People's Commissar, declares an end to his country's participation in World War I. (A formal peace agreement between

Germany and Russia is not signed until March 18, 1918.) Lenin's cabinet members include Joseph Stalin as commissar for national minorities and Leon Trotsky as commissar for foreign affairs. During November, Theodore Brumback joins the editorial staff of the *Star*. He had spent four months in France driving ambulances for the American Field Service. By Christmas, Ernest, Ted Brumback and Wilson Hicks make a pact to apply to the Red Cross as ambulance drivers after New Year's Day. Ernest is now living alone in an attic apartment in Kansas City. His unsigned articles for the *Star* include "Have Plenty of Coal Now," on December 3, "Note Hints at Suicide," on December 5, and "Kerensky, the Fighting Flea," on December 16. Hemingway later writes three sketches drawn from experiences in Kansas City during this winter. One of them is an early form of his story, "God Rest You Merry, Gentlemen."

1918

Numerous articles for the *Kansas City Star*
"Al Receives Another Letter" (article)

January: On January 6, "Battle of Raid Squads" appears in the *Star*. This article is attributed to Hemingway, but there is debate whether or not it is his work. "At the End of the Ambulance Run," a group of unsigned vignettes published on January 20 are credited to Hemingway.

February 18: "Throng at Smallpox Case," an unsigned article appears in the *Star*.

March 6: The *Star* publishes Hemingway's unsigned article, "Laundry Car Over Cliff."

April: On April 17, "Big Day for Navy Drive" and "Six Men Become Tankers," both unsigned, appear in the *Star*. The next day, "Would Treat 'Em Rough," "Recruits for the Tanks," and "Navy Desk Jobs to Go" are run. On April 21, two more unsigned articles, "Mix War, Art And Dancing" and "Dare Devil Joins Tanks," attributed to Ernest are published in the newspaper. Ernest draws his last paycheck from the Kansas City *Star* on April 30. He and Ted Brumback leave Kansas City to join the Red Cross Ambulance Service overseas.

May: Ernest and Ted Brumback stop over in Oak Park to visit with the Hemingway family for one night. The two continue on to Horton Bay, Michigan for a fishing trip before going overseas. Ernest receives notice from the Red Cross to report for a physical in New York by May 8. During his first visit to New York, Ernest stays at the Hotel Earle on Waverly Place. Passing the physical with a "B" rating, Ernest ignores the Red Cross doctor's recommendation for eyeglasses. (Poor vision is what prevented Hemingway from being accepted into the regular division of the armed services.) On May 24, he and Ted Brumback leave New York aboard the French Line ship, *Chicago*, bound for Bordeaux, France. Ernest befriends Howell Jenkins, another Red Cross volunteer, while sailing on the *Chicago*.

June: Upon arrival at Bordeaux, Hemingway takes the night train to Paris. During the stopover in Paris, while awaiting orders from the Red Cross, Ernest stays at a hotel near the Madeleine, the Church of Saint Mary Magdalen. It is in Paris that Hemingway first witnesses combat. German artillery is in the city's streets. After his first sight of battle, Ernest departs via train for Italy. When he arrives in Milan, he and other Red Cross ambulance drivers set up a makeshift mortuary at the site of a blown-up munitions factory near Milan. Ernest is then assigned to the American Red Cross Ambulance Unit, Section Four, and transported to Schio, located in the foothills of the Dolomites, 24 kilometers from the town of Vicenza. The Red Cross quarters are referred to as "The Schio Country Club." Ernest writes a humorous article called "Al Receives Another Letter" for the June 18 issue of *Ciao*, the monthly newsletter published by the American Red Cross Ambulance Unit. He is also listed as one of the newcomers to the Service in this issue. Ernest meets another ambulance driver in Dolo, who is on his way to Paris to join the Ambulance and Medical Corps of the United States Army. His name is John Dos Passos. Among other drivers assigned with Ernest to Section Four are Ted Brumback, Howell Jenkins, Fred Spiegel, and Bill Horne.

under, offers him a full year's stay in Italy with all expenses paid. Ernest declines.

December: Hemingway takes a trip to Treviso to visit Agnes von Kurowsky. His limp is still visible, and further ambulance driving is not a genuine possibility. Ernest decides to return home. Through the rest of the month he stays in Milan. Eric "Chink" Dorman-Smith is on hand for a series of preholiday parties and another to celebrate Ernest's discharge from the hospital. Hemingway spends Christmas Day with a group of friends at the Cova. He leaves the city to spend a week in Southern Italy before returning home to America.

1919

January: On January 4, Hemingway begins his journey home aboard the *S.S. Guiseppe Verdi*. He arrives in New York 17 days after leaving Genoa. He is met and interviewed by a reporter from the *New York Sun* when his ship docks. This first article on Hemingway, which appears on January 22 in a New York newspaper, is riddled with misinformation. The newspaper story gives an incorrect account of Ernest's wounding and claims that he spent October and November in combat. After a one-day stopover in New York, Hemingway travels to Chicago by train where he is met by his father Dr. Clarence Hemingway and his sister Marcelline.

February: Ernest passes the time by corresponding with Agnes von Kurowsky, whom he misses. He is honored with an article which appears in his hometown newspaper, *The Oak Parker* on February 1. He also enjoys the praise bestowed upon him by a group of Italian-Americans in Chicago at several celebrations in honor of his efforts for Italy in the war.

March: This is a rather inactive period for Hemingway. He is living in his parents' home. On March 14, Ernest speaks at an assembly at the Oak Park High School on his war experiences. At the end of the month, Hemingway receives a letter from Agnes von Kurowsky in which she informs him that she has fallen in love with an Italian soldier. Ernest's first love affair leaves him hurt and embittered.

April–May: Hemingway is beginning to write short stories again. He composes an unpolished piece called "The Passing of Pickles McCarty, or the Woppian Way." His Horton Bay friend, Bill Smith, pays Ernest a visit in Oak Park. Bill's brother, Y. K. Smith, is now living in Oak Park.

June–July: Ernest leaves Oak Park in early June for Horton Bay, Michigan. He stays with Bill Smith at the farm owned by Smith's aunt, Mrs. Joseph Williams Charles. Ernest seeks medical help from Dr. Guy Conkle in Boyne City, Michigan, because fragments of metals continue to surface in his legs. He receives another letter from Agnes von Kurowsky. She tells him that her affair has ended. Ernest claims that his bitterness has subsided and that he sympathizes with Agnes. His injuries are healing once more and Hemingway goes on a week's fishing trip. His family arrives at Windemere in early July. By this time, Ernest has written a number of stories. He contacts Edwin Balmer, a former *Chicago Tribune* reporter and a novelist, who is staying at Walloon Lake for the summer. Balmer gives Ernest the names of editors at the *Saturday Evening Post*, *Everybody's Magazine*, *Popular Magazine*, *Red Book*, and *Blue Book*. World War I is officially over with the signing of the Treaty of Versailles on June 28. Germany is defeated. The final agreement is signed at the Peace Conference of Paris, convened on January 18, 1919. In attendance is the "Council of Four," Georges Clemenceau, the premier of France and president of the peace conference; David Lloyd George, the British prime minister; United States President Woodrow Wilson; and Vittorio Emanuele Orlando, the prime minister of Italy. The treaty is signed on the fifth anniversary of Archduke Ferdinand's assassination. (The United States refuses to ratify the agreement and will sign a separate treaty with Germany on August 25, 1921.) The Treaty of Versailles brings about the League of Nations, the reshaping of Germany's borders and colonial territories, German disarmament, and provisions for war reparations. The Peace Conference of Paris closes on January 21, 1920.

August–October: Howell Jenkins and Larry Barnett, both friends from the Red Cross ambulance service, come to Michigan to join Ernest and Bill Smith on a fishing trip. Another camping trip, this time with his Oak Park friend, Jack Pentacost, and another companion, Al Walker, takes Hemingway into the Upper Peninsula of Michigan. En route, the three pass through a ghost town called Seney. The setting for this trip, about twenty miles from Lake Superior, will be used in "Big Two-Hearted River." Ernest befriends Marjorie Bump, a high school girl who works as a waitress at the Dilworths' Pinehurst Cottage. She is later fictionalized in "The Three-Day Blow" and "The End of Something." In September and part of October, Hemingway works the potato harvest near Petoskey. Ernest becomes romantically involved with another waitress from Pinehurst Cottage. He will write an account of their brief romance in 1921 in the story "Up in Michigan." After the potato harvest, Ernest returns to Oak Park on October 6. He stays until the end of the month when he returns to Petoskey. He moves into a boarding house owned by Evva Potter and located at 602 State Street. He intends to concentrate on writing. His friends in Petoskey at this time are Marjorie Bump, Grace Quinlan, "Dutch" Pailthorp, and Luman Ramsdall.

November–December: Among the stories Ernest writes is "Wolves and Doughnuts." Drawing from his own experience as he has been advised to do, Ernest writes about the Arditi as well as about Chicago. During December, Hemingway addresses the Ladies' Aid Society in Petoskey. Present at the talk is Harriet Gridley Connable, whose husband Ralph is in charge of the chain of F. W. Woolworth's variety stores in Canada. The Connable children are Dorothy, six years older than Ernest, and Ralph, Jr., 19 years old and lame from birth. After meeting the entire family, Ernest is asked to be Ralph, Jr.'s companion in Toronto while Mr. and Mrs. Connable winter in Palm Beach, Florida. Ernest accepts the position. Hemingway returns to Oak Park for the holidays. During this time, he goes to Chicago for a reunion of 15 of the "Schio Country Club" members and hears Tito Ruffo sing at the Chicago Opera. Back in Oak Park for the remainder of the year, Ernest befriends Isabel Simmons.

1920

Numerous articles in the *Toronto Star Weekly*
An unsigned article in the *Toronto Daily Star*
Numerous articles in the *Co-operative Commonwealth*

January: Ernest leaves Oak Park and takes the train to Toronto on January 8. The Connables' mansion, where he will live for the next five months, is located at 153 Lyndhurst Avenue. Ralph Connable, Sr. arranges a meeting between Hemingway and Arthur Donaldson, in charge of advertising layout for the *Toronto Daily Star* and the *Star Weekly*. In addition, Ernest meets the features editor, Greg Clark and the cartoonist, Jimmy Frise. After these introductions in mid-January, Hemingway begins to frequent the *Star*'s editorial offices at 20 King Street. By the end of the month, an arrangement is made for Ernest to write for the newspaper. The name "Ernest M. Hemingway" is published in book form for the first time in Charles M. Bakewell's *The Story of the American Red Cross in Italy*. Ernest is listed under the Ambulance Service, Section Four. An asterisk is placed by his name to indicate that he was awarded an Italian decoration, the Silver Medal. While working in Toronto as Ralph Connable, Jr.'s companion, Ernest spends time with Dorothy Connable, Ernest Smith, and "Dutch" Pailthorp.

February–March: Ernest's first article appears in the *Toronto Star Weekly* on February 14. (J. H. Cranston is the editor of both editions of the *Toronto Star*.) The article, "Circulating Pictures a New High-Art Idea in Toronto," carries no byline and is run in the newspaper's magazine section. Edwin Balmer, the novelist Ernest met at Walloon Lake, Michigan, during the previous summer, responds encouragingly to a letter and stories from Ernest. Balmer tells Hemingway that he thinks some of his work will sell. "Taking a Chance for a Free Shave," Hemingway's first signed article in the *Star Weekly*, is published on March 6. Other articles written this month are "Sporting Mayor at Boxing Bouts" and "How to be Popular in Peace Though a Slacker in War," which appear on March 13. The former is run in the news section, the latter in the magazine section. Ernest divides his time between hanging around the newspaper office, writing, attending boxing and hockey matches, and occasionally dating a Toronto girl named Bonnie Bonnell. Dr. Clarence Hemingway writes his son that his mother, Grace, is having emotional problems and requests that Ernest pay a visit to Oak Park before going to Northern Michigan for the summer. The Connables return from Florida. Ernest stays on at their house and the friendship deepens among him and Harriet and Dorothy. Ernest now receives the *Croce de Guerra* for his service in Italy.

April–May: Contributions to the *Toronto Star* increase during this period. Hemingway writes one unsigned article for the *Daily Star* on April 26, "Buying Commission Would Cut Out Waste." Others, both with and without a byline, are published in the *Star Weekly*. "Are You All Set for the Trout?", "Tooth-pulling Not a Cure-for-All," and "Lieutenants' Mustaches the Only Permanent Thing We Got Out of War" appear on April 10: and "Stores in the Wilds Graveyards of Style" and "Fishing for Trout in a Sporting Way" on April 24. "Keeping Up with the Joneses/the Tragedy of the Other Half" is printed on May 1, "Toronto Women Who Went to the Prize Fights Applauded the Rough Stuff" on May 15, "Galloping Dominoes Alias African" on May 22, and "Prices for 'Likenesses' Run from 25 Cents to $500 in Toronto" and "Canadian Fox-Ranching Pays since the Wild-cats Let the Foxes Go" on May 29. Ernest's job with the Connables ends. He stops over in Oak Park for a short visit during the last week of May.

June–July: A backlog of Ernest's work is printed in the *Toronto Star Weekly*. "Canuck Whiskey Pouring Into the U.S." appears on June 5, "It's Time to Bury the Hamilton Gag/Comedians Have Worked It to Death" is run on June 12 and "When You Camp Out Do It Right" on June 26. Ernest drives to Horton Bay with Bill Smith on June 3. His uncertainty about his future is evident in their discussions. Among possibilities Ernest talks about is shipping out of San Francisco and working on a ship bound for Japan, China, or India. Ernest begins a four-month stay in Northern Michigan. He celebrates his twenty-first birthday with his family, Bill Smith, and his friend from the *Kansas City Star* and ambulance service in Italy, Ted Brumback. He and his mother have a falling out two days later.

Ernest and Ted Brumback are blamed for a late-night picnic his sisters and a group of friends attend without permission. The rift between Ernest and his mother, who is still emotionally troubled, will continue for several weeks.

August–September: Two articles by Hemingway are published in the *Toronto Star Weekly*. "When You Go Camping Take Lots of Skeeter Dope and Don't Ever Lose It" appears on August 7 and "The Best Rainbow Trout Fishing in the World is at the Canadian Soo" on August 28. On August 8, Ernest tells his friend, Grace Quinlan, that he feels homeless because of having been kicked out by his mother. He leaves on a fishing trip with Ted Brumback, Howell Jenkins, and Dick Smale. His relationship with his mother improves somewhat when he returns although friction is still noticeable. Without a job, Hemingway passes his time with companions Katy Smith and Carl Edgar. Occasional money is earned picking apples and planting seed clover near Petoskey.

October–December: At the beginning of October, Ernest earns a small income picking apples in Mrs. Joseph Charles's orchard in Michigan. He decides to go to Chicago to look for work. Ernest stays at a communal apartment on 100 East Chicago Avenue, which belongs to Mr. and Mrs. Y. K. Smith. Katy Smith, Edith Foley, Bill Horne, and Donald Wright also live in this apartment on the north side of Chicago. Ernest meets Hadley Richardson through their mutual friend, Katy Smith. The young women had gone to the Mary Institute in St. Louis together. Hadley will become the first Mrs. Ernest Hemingway in 1921. Ernest is writing for the *Toronto Star Weekly* on a sporadic basis. His contributions during October are "The Average Yank Divides Canadians into Two Classes—Wild and Tame" on October 9 and "Carpentier Sure to Give Dempsey Fight Worth While" on October 30. "The Wild West Is Now in Chicago" and "No Danger of Commercial Tie-Up Because Men Carry Too Much Money" appear on November 6 and "A Fight With a Twenty-Pound Trout" on November 20. Hadley Richardson returns to St. Louis in the middle of November. She and Ernest begin to correspond. Hemingway writes freelance advertising copy for Firestone Tires. He moves from the Smiths' apartment to a room at 1230 North State Street, which is rented and paid for by Bill Horne. Ernest visits his family in Oak Park on most Sundays. In December, he begins to work as a writer and assistant editor of the *Co-operative Commonwealth*, a magazine published by the Co-operative Society of America. The editorial offices are located at 128 North Wells Street. During his tenure at the magazine Hemingway writes human-interest stories and some advertising copy. The only title that has survived is "Will You Let These Kiddies Miss Santa Claus?" published in the December 20 issue. Y. K. Smith's wife leaves Chicago and will be gone until May. Ernest, along with several other men, move into a new apartment, called "The Belleville" and located at 63 East Division, leased by Y. K. Smith. Hadley and Ernest continue to correspond and their romance flourishes. Hemingway's interest in boxing is rekindled with matches with Y. K. Smith, Nick Neroni, and a new acquaintance from the *Co-operative Commonwealth*, Krebs Friend. Captain Jim Gamble from the Red Cross again invites Ernest to visit him in Rome.

1921

Numerous articles in the *Toronto Star Weekly*
Numerous articles (lost) in the *Co-operative Commonwealth*

January–March: At the beginning of the year, Ernest begins work on a novel. The first sketchy attempts are dropped until his first winter in Paris. "Why Not Trade Other Public Entertainers Among the Nations as the Big Leagues Do Baseball Players?" appears in the *Star Weekly* on February 19. Ernest meets Sherwood Anderson during the spring through their mutual friend Y. K. Smith. Anderson is living near Ernest's Division Street apartment. Hadley and Ernest see more of each other in March. He visits her in St. Louis over a weekend beginning on March 11. Two weeks later, she comes to Chicago with her friends Ruth Bradfield and George and Helen Breaker. Ernest and Hadley plan to go to Italy in November.

April–June: Hadley sends money to Ernest on an ongoing basis to be invested in Italian lire for their trip. Hemingway becomes friendly with Sherwood Anderson. Now 45, Anderson has already published *Winesburg, Ohio* and *Poor White*. He advises the younger writer to go to Paris instead of Italy. Ernest visits Anderson's country house in Palos Park. Anderson and his wife, Tennessee, leave for Paris. Accompanied by their friend, Paul Rosenfeld, they plan to live among the expatriates on the Left Bank. Ernest publishes "Our Confidential Vacation Guide" in the *Toronto Star Weekly* on May 21, and "Gun-Men's Wild Political War On in Chicago" on May 28. He goes to St. Louis with Bill Horne to visit Hadley Richardson over Memorial Day weekend. Ernest and Hadley first make wedding plans while he is in St. Louis. Back in Chicago, Ernest is told by Krebs Friend that he also is interested in going to Paris. Ernest and Hadley's engagement is formally announced in the *St. Louis Post Dispatch*'s "Social Item" column with mistaken biographical information on Hemingway. Bill Horne, Y. K. Smith, and Ernest move back into the apartment at 100 East Chicago Avenue.

July–August: "Chicago Never Wetter Than It Is Today" is published in the *Star Weekly* on July 2. Ernest has begun to write poetry and considers submitting his work to *Dial* or *Poetry*. Hadley visits on the weekend of July 12. Hemingway turns 22 on July 21. Hadley gives Ernest a Corona typewriter for his birthday. She visits again in early August, enroute to Wisconsin to spend a month before the wedding. Ernest's article, "Condensing the Classics" appears in the *Toronto Star Weekly* on August 20. Ernest arrives in Horton Bay, Michigan, to spend three days before his wedding on a fishing trip along the Sturgeon River with Howell Jenkins and Charlie Hopkins.

September 3: Ernest Miller Hemingway and Elizabeth Hadley Richardson (1890–1979) are married in the afternoon at the First Presbyterian Church in Horton Bay, Michigan. Hadley's sister is her matron of honor and Helen Breaker, Ruth Bradfield, and Katy Smith serve as her other attendants. Ernest's best man is Bill Horne. The ushers are Howell Jenkins, Bill Smith, Carl Edgar, Jack Pentacost, and Art Meyer. Attending the wedding were the entire Hemingway family, "Dutch" Pailthorp, Luman Ramsdall, Ralph, Jr. and Harriet Connable, George Breaker, and the Dilworths. Pictures are taken in front of the Dilworths' Pinehurst Cottage after the ceremony with a dinner in the cafe following. Ernest will later incorporate details of this wedding day in a Nick Adams story. After a two-week honeymoon at Windemere cottage on Walloon Lake, the Hemingways return to Chicago. Their plans to live in the 100 East Chicago Avenue apartment are changed because of an argument with Y. K. Smith. The couple takes instead an apartment at 1239 Dearborn Street in Chicago.

October: Dr. and Mrs. Clarence Hemingway celebrate their twenty-fifth wedding anniversary on October 1. Ernest exacerbates the quarrel with Y. K. Smith by rescinding an invitation to his parents' anniversary celebration. After hearing rumors of the impending bankruptcy and dubious honesty of the Co-operative Society of America, Hemingway resigns his editorial position on the *Co-operative Commonwealth*. The only steady source of income for the couple is Hadley's trust fund.

November: "Cheaper Nitrates Will Mean Cheaper Bread" appears in the *Toronto Star Weekly* on November 12. Ernest and Hadley begin to make arrangements for their trip to Paris. Sherwood Anderson offers advice and gives the Hemingways letters of introduction to Gertrude Stein, Sylvia Beach, Lewis Galantière, and Ezra Pound. Anderson's letters are filled with praise for Ernest's talents as a writer.

December: Ernest submits an article to the *Toronto Star Weekly* called "On Weddynge Gifts" which includes a five-line free-verse poem. It is published on December 17. All arrangements for the trip to Paris are made by December 2. Ernest and Hadley arrive in New York on December 8. After a day's layover, they sail to Paris aboard the *Leopoldina*, a French Line vessel. During the third week of December, the ship passengers have a four-hour stopover in Vigo, Spain, which is Ernest's second visit to that country. While sailing, Ernest boxes in several matches, including one which is held as a benefit for a young French woman who has been deserted by her American husband. Ernest and Hadley arrive in Paris around December 23. They move into the Hotel Jacob et d' Angleterre, located in the Latin Quarter at 44 rue Jacob. The Hemingways meet Sherwood Anderson's friend, Lewis Galantière, the Paris secretary for the International Chamber of Commerce. Lewis and Ernest have a friendly boxing match after dinner, and overdoing it a bit, Ernest breaks Galantière's eyeglasses. On December 28, Ernest goes to Sylvia Beach's bookshop, Shakespeare and Company. Without using the letter Sherwood Anderson has given to him, Hemingway and Beach become friends. Ernest begins to use her lending library. He will also use 12 Rue de l'Odeon, the bookstore's address, as his mailing address, becoming one of many artists who is allowed by Beach to receive their mail through the shop. Others are James Joyce, George Antheil, Sherwood Anderson, Robert McAlmon, and Stephen Vincent Benet. On his first trip to Shakespeare and Company, Ernest borrows James Joyce's *Dubliners*. Two days later, he takes out Thomas Hardy's *Jude the Obscure*, Robert Louis Stevenson's *Dr. Jekyll and Mr. Hyde*, and Joyce's *Portrait of the Artist as a Young Man*. He borrows Walt Whitman's *Leaves of Grass*, a book on the Metahysical poets, and the prologue to *The Canterbury Tales* on December 31.

1922

Numerous articles for the *Toronto Star Weekly*
Numerous articles for the *Toronto Daily Star*
"A Divine Gesture" (fable)
"Ultimately" (poem)

January: The Hemingways move to an apartment at 74 Rue du Cardinal Lemoine on January 9. Their home is near a square named the Place de la Contrescarpe and above a dance hall called the Bal Musette. Ernest and Hadley travel to Switzerland. During a two-week trip, they stay in Chamby in the mountains above Montreux. After returning to Paris, Hemingway rents a room to work in in a hotel located at 39 rue Descartes. He is writing short impressionistic pieces and also continuing his work in journalism. He makes an agreement with the *Toronto Star Weekly* to write thirty articles by March. He sends the first to editor John Bone late in the month.

February: "Tourists Are Scarce at the Swiss Resorts" and "A Canadian with One Thousand a Year Can Live Very Comfortably in Paris" appears in the *Star Weekly* on February 4. Ernest meets Ezra Pound. After their meeting, Hemingway writes a satirical sketch of Pound. He shows it to Lewis Galantière and tells him that he wants to submit it for publication in *The Little Review*, edited by Jane Heap and Margaret Anderson. Galantière dissuades Ernest and the sketch is destroyed. Later in the month, Pound takes six of Hemingway's poems to send to the *Dial* literary magazine and accepts one for publication in *The Little Review*. Ernest teaches Ezra Pound to box. Hemingway's "Builder, Not Fighter, Is What France Wants," an article on Georges Clemenceau, is run in the *Toronto Daily Star* on February 18. The *Star Weekly* publishes "At Vigo, in Spain, Is Where You Catch the Silver and Blue Tuna, the King of All Fish" on the same day. "Influx of Russians to All Parts of Paris" appears in the *Daily Star* on February 25 when "Exchange Pirates Hit by German Export Tax" is run in the *Star Weekly*.

March: Ernest meets Gertrude Stein and Alice Toklas at their apartment at 27 rue de Fleurus. Stein comes to the Hemingway apartment and reads Ernest's poems, novel fragment, and a story he has written within the last two months, "Up in Michigan." Stein's reaction to his work is mixed. She likes the poems, dislikes the novel, and approves of all but the seduction scene in his short story. Ernest meets a newspaper correspondent from the *Brooklyn Daily Eagle* named Guy Hickok. Hemingway writes 12 articles for the Toronto newspapers. "Try Bob-Sledding if You Want Thrills" appears in the *Daily Star* on March 4. On the same day, "Behind the Scenes at Papal Election" and "Queer Mixture of Aristocrats, Profiteers, Sheep and Wolves at the Hotels in Switzerland" are published in the *Star Weekly*. On March 11, "Poincaré Making Good on Election Promises" runs in the *Daily Star* while "Wives Buy Clothes for French Husbands" and "How'd You Like to Tip Postman Every Time?" appear in the *Star Weekly*. "Sparrow Hat Appears on Paris Boulevards" and "Flivuer, Canoe, Pram and Taxi Combined is the Luge, Joy of Everybody in Switzerland" are published in the *Star Weekly* on March 18. One week later, the *Daily Star* prints "The Mecca of Fabers is the French Capital." The *Star Weekly* on that day runs "Prizewinning Book Is Centre of Storm" (a book review, and likely Hemingway's first, of René Moran's *Batonola*, winner of the Goncourt Academy Prize for 1921), "American Bohemians in Paris a Weird Lot," and "Wild Night Music of Paris Makes Visitor Feel a Man of the World."

April: Three articles appear in the *Daily Star* early in April. "Much Feared Man Is Monsieur Deibbler" and "95,000 Now Wearing the Legion of Honour" appear on April 1 and "Anti-Alcohol League Is Active in Paris" on April 8. Ernest is asked by the *Daily Star* to cover the Conferenza Internazionale Economica di Genova (Genoa). He is in Genoa by the end of the first week of April. The conference is attended by 34 nations. Between April 10 and 22, he writes 13 articles, some cabled to Toronto, for the *Daily Star*. "Tchitcherin Speaks" and "Must Work for Peace" are printed on April 10, "Tchitcherin at It Again, Wants Jap Excluded" on April 11, "Picked Sharpshooters Patrol Genoa Streets on April 13, "French Politeness" on April 15, "Regarded by Allies as German Cunning" and "Barthou Refuses to Confer with Russians and Germans" on April 18, "Two Russian Girls the Best Looking at Genoa Parley" and "Barthou, Like a Smith Brother, Crosses Hissing Tchitcherin" on April 24, "Strongest Premier at Parley Is Stambouliski of Bulgaria" on April 25, "Schober of Austria, at Genoa, Looks Every Inch a Chancellor" on April 26, "Russian Delegates at Genoa Appear Not to Be of This World" on April 27, and "German Delegation at Genoa Keeps Stinnes in Background" on April 28. While in Genoa, Ernest meets Bill Bird of the Consolidated Press and George Slocombe of the *London Daily Herald*. Hemingway receives superficial cuts when a water heater explodes while he is bathing in his hotel. Max Eastman of *The Masses* is in Genoa for the conference. He and Hemingway meet and Eastman reads his sketches. He takes copies from Ernest to send off to Claude McKay and Mike Gold for possible publication. Hemingway also meets journalist Lincoln Steffens and is asked to join a group that gathers in the evenings in a cafe in Genoa. George Seldes, Sam Spewack, and sculptor Jo Davidson are among the others who meet at the casual gatherings. As the conference is nearing its close, Ernest goes to Rampallo,

Italy, with Max Eastman and George Slocombe. The three visit British caricaturist Max Beerbohm.

May: After returning to Paris from the conference, Ernest concentrates on writing his poetry and prose. His journalism appears this month only in the Toronto *Daily Star* and his output for the newspaper is diminished. "Getting a Hot Bath an Adventure in Genoa" is published on May 2, "Russian Delegation Well Guarded at Genoa" on May 4, "German Journalists a Strange Collection" on May 8, and "All Genoa Goes Crazy over New Betting Game" on May 13. The *Double Dealer* publishes a fable by Hemingway entitled "A Divine Gesture." This is the first American publication (aside from his high school literary magazine) to publish fiction by Ernest Hemingway. The issue containing the fable is dated May 22, 1922. Ernest submits six poems to Harriet Monroe, editor of *Poetry: A Magazine of Verse*. The poems are accepted but will not appear until January 23, 1923. In mid-May, Ernest and Hadley begin a month-long trip to Switzerland and Italy. Eric "Chink" Dorman-Smith meets the Hemingways in Chamby, Switzerland. During the stay in Switzerland, Ernest climbs the 7000-foot Cap au Moine. The three travel to Bourg St. Pierre on May 31 and continue on to hike in Italy.

June: An article, "There Are Great Fish in the Rhode Canal," which Ernest wrote while still in Geneva on May 22 appears in the *Toronto Daily Star* on June 10. While in Milan, Italy, Ernest shows Hadley the Red Cross Hospital in which he convalesced. Ernest also interviews Benito Mussolini there and witnesses the growth of the Fascist Party in Italy. The interview appears under the title "Fascisti Party Now Half-Million Strong" in the *Daily Star* on June 24 along with "Pot-Shot Patriots Unpopular in Italy." Ernest and Hadley depart from Milan on June 13 and travel on to Schio, where Ernest was stationed as a Red Cross ambulance driver. Arriving on a dismal day, the disappointed Ernest finds that the town has changed. The Hemingways go to Lago di Garda by automobile and then to Mestre by train. Ernest hires a car to take them to Fossalta to revisit the site of his wounding. Afterwards, the Hemingways begin their journey home to Paris. Ernest makes another advance in getting his work published. His poem, "Ultimately," appears alongside William Faulkner's poem, "Portrait," in the June 22 edition of the *Double Dealer*. (The two will be reprinted together in 1932 in *Salmagundi* by William Faulkner *and a Poem by Ernest Hemingway*.)

July: Ernest is now writing each morning in Paris. John Dos Passos and Hemingway have lunch together at Lipp's Brasserie. This is their first meeting as writers. Their previous meeting in Italy during World War I was forgotten by Dos Passos. At this time, Dos Passos has already published his novel, *Three Soldiers* (1921). Hemingway contacts Harriet Monroe to send a brief biography to be included when her magazine, *Poetry*, publishes his poems. Ernest meets Ernest Walsh in Paris. Hemingway writes about his recent trip to Fossalta, Italy. The article appears in the *Toronto Daily Star* on July 22 under the headline, "A Veteran Visits Old Front/Wishes He Had Stayed Away."

August: Along with working on fictional sketches, Ernest writes six articles for the newspapers this month. "Expecting Too Much in Old London Town" appears in the *Star Weekly* on August 5 and "Latest Drink Scandal Now Agitates Paris" on August 12. "Did Poincaré Laugh in Verdun Cemetery" and "Rug Vendor Is Fixture in Parisian Life" are published in the *Daily Star* on August 12. The *Star Weekly* also runs "Old Order Changeth in Alsace-Lorraine" and "Takes to the Water/Solves Flat Problem" on August 26. In mid-August, Ernest and Hadley leave for a fishing and hiking trip through the Black Forest in Germany. The first airplane flight for both takes them to Strasbourg, France, where they are joined by Bill and Sally Bird and Lewis Galantière and his fiancée, Dorothy Butler. The group stays at a guesthouse in the town of Strasbourg and then travels on by train to Triberg. While fishing in the Kingdom of Baden, Ernest falls and sustains a minor injury to his back.

September: Hadley and Ernest stay in Germany through most of the month. Ernest sends in articles during his travels. "Germans Are Doggedly Sullen or Desperate Over the Mark" appears in the *Daily Star* on September 1 and the following day

"Once Over Permit Obstacle, Fishing in Baden Perfect" is published. Other *Daily Star* articles are "German Inn-keepers Rough Dealing with 'Auslanders,'" published on September 5, "A Paris-to-Strasbourg Flight Shows Living Cubist Picture" on September 9, and "Crossing to Germany Is Way to Make Money" on September 19. The Hemingways go to Cologne to meet Eric "Chink" Dorman-Smith, who is at the British Occupation Garrison. Ernest mails two articles to the *Star Weekly*. One, a light-hearted feature, is titled "Hubby Dines First Wifie Gets Crumbs." The other, in a more serious vein, is the story of a street mob that kills a German policeman. It appears under the headline, "Riots Are Frequent Throughout Germany." Both stories are published on September 30. Ernest is ordered to go to Constantinople by John Bone, managing editor of the *Toronto Star Weekly* after he and Hadley return to Paris in the third week of the month. (War between Greece and Turkey had broken out in late August. The Turks had mounted an offensive to remove the Greeks from Anatolia. The action had peaked with the Turkish occupation and burning of the Port of Smyrna. A neutral zone had been established by the Allies to protect the Straits from the Black Sea in the north to the Dardanelles in the south. It was anticipated that the Turkish Kemal Pasha would take over the neutral zone as well as occupying Constantinople.) Hadley Hemingway is opposed to Ernest's taking the assignment. Despite her objections, Ernest leaves Paris on September 25. He arrives in Constantinople on September 29 and cables his first dispatch the following day. It appears on the same date in the *Daily Star* and is called "British Strong Enough to Save Constantinople." Without the knowledge of his editor at the *Star*, Hemingway makes a secret agreement with Frank Mason of Hearst's International News Service to cover the war. While in Constantinople, Ernest stays at the Hotel de Londres, which proves to be bug-infested, and at the Hotel Montreal. He contracts malaria. Ernest conducts an interview with French Premier Georges Clemenceau in which the leader makes some very unflattering remarks about Canada. Hemingway submits the piece and it is rejected by John Bone because of the comments about Canada. This episode, now difficult to pinpoint, takes place sometime between September and November.

October: "Turk Red Crescent Propaganda Agency," cabled by Ernest from Constantinople, makes the first page of the *Daily Star* on October 4. Two days later, John Bone begins to notice duplication of the stories Hemingway is sending in and those appearing over the wire services. Ernest must also contend with a city overrun with lice and the problem of censorship. Newsmen are barred from the Conference of Mudaria, which cedes Thrace to the Turks and orders the Greek army to leave within three days. An interview by Hemingway, "Hamid Bey Wears Shirt Tucked in When Seen by *Star*," runs in the *Daily Star* on October 9. Ernest is still troubled by malaria. Following the Conference of Mudaria, attention is focused on Thrace. On October 14, Ernest leaves for Muradli. Three days later, he takes a train to Adrianople. On October 18, Hemingway witnesses the evacuation of the Christian population in Thrace and boards the Orient Express for a four-day trip to Paris. He arrives home on October 21. Not quite a week later, Ernest replies to John Bone's queries about his dispatches duplicating wire service reports. Ernest explains that his stories had been stolen by the International News Service. Hemingway's other articles for the *Daily Star* are "Balkans Look Like Ontario, a Picture of Peace, Not War," published on October 16, "Constantinople, Dirty White, Not Glistening and Sinister," on October 18, "Constantinople Cut-Throats Await Chance for an Orgy" on October 19, "A Silent, Ghastly Procession Wends Way from Thrace" on October 20, "Russia to Sport the French Game with Kemalists" on October 23, "Turks Beginning To Show Distrust of Kemal Pasha" on October 24, "Censor Too 'Thorough' in Near East Crisis" on October 25, "'Old Constan' in True Light Is Tough Town" on October 28, and "Kemal Has Afghans Ready to Make Trouble for Britain" on October 31. Hemingway ends the month by resting in bed from exhaustion and malaria.

November: The remaining articles by Hemingway from Thrace and Bulgaria are printed in the *Daily Star* at the beginning of the month. They include "Betrayal Preceded Defeat, Then Came Greek Revolt" on November 3, "Destroyers Were on Lookout for the Kemal's One Submarine" on November 10, and "Refugee Procession Is Scene of Horror" on November 14.

Ernest receives $400 from the *Star* for his work in the Middle East. He returns to work on his fiction. It is probable that he writes his story, "My Old Man," at this point. Plans for publication of *Three Stories and Ten Poems* begin to be made. The book will be a part of a series by Ezra Pound called "an inquest into the state of contemporary English prose." The series will be published by William Bird's Three Mountains Press, 29 Quai d'Anjou on the Ile St.-Louis. On November 16, Hemingway writes to Harriet Monroe asking for a publication date for his poems in *Poetry* and requests her permission to include them in the upcoming book Bill Bird will publish. Ernest writes more private, satirical sketches of acquaintances. Those he satirizes include Ernest Walsh, Ford Madox Ford, and Dave O'Neil, a former American businessman who is in Paris writing poetry. The Lausanne Peace Conference, to settle territorial questions between Greece and Turkey, opens on November 20. Ernest arrives in Switzerland on November 22 to cover the conference for the *Toronto Daily Star*, the International News Service, *and* the Universal News Service. The meetings take place at the Chateau Ouchy. While covering the conference, Hemingway sees Lincoln Steffens and shows him a copy of "My Old Man." The older journalist, liking the story, sends it to Ray Long of *Cosmopolitan* magazine. Steffens also admires Hemingway's journalism. Ernest is introduced to William Bolitho Ryall, the European correspondent for the *Manchester Guardian*. During the conference Hemingway spends quite a bit of time with Ryall and his sophistication in the realm of international politics greatly increases. Hemingway encounters Mussolini once again at Lausanne. He expresses the opinion that the Italian Fascist leader is a bluff.

December: Hadley, who has remained in Paris while Ernest went to cover the peace conference, takes a train to meet him in Switzerland. Mrs. Hemingway brings along most of her husband's manuscripts. All of his work, except "Up in Michigan," "My Old Man," and "Paris, 1922," is packed into a valise, which is stolen from Hadley on the train. Ernest returns to Paris to look for carbons of the lost work. His trip is unsuccessful. After a night alone, Ernest lunches with Gertrude Stein and Alice Toklas the next day. He then returns to Lausanne to resume his work on the conference. His job with the wire service ends on December 16. The Hemingways leave Lausanne for a skiing trip with Eric Dorman-Smith at Gangwisch.

1923

Wanderings (six poems)
In Our Time (later used as chapters one through six of *in our time*)
"They All Made Peace—What Is Peace?" (poem)
Three Stories and Ten Poems
Numerous articles in the *Toronto Daily Star*
Numerous articles in the *Toronto Star Weekly*

January: The Hemingways stay in Switzerland through most of the month. Eric Dorman-Smith leaves on New Year's Day and Isabel Simmons, Ernest's friend from Oak Park, Illinois, arrives. "Wanderings," a collection of six poems, is published in *Poetry: A Magazine of Verse* on January 23. "Mitrailliatrice," "Oily Weather," "Roosevelt," "Riparto D'Assalto," "Champs d'Honneur," and "Chapter Heading" comprise the collection. The poems will be included in *Three Stories and Ten Poems*. The Toronto *Daily Star* runs Ernest's article, "Mussolini, Europe's Prize Bluffer More Like Bottomley Than Napoleon," on January 27.

February: "Gaudy Uniform is Tchitcherin's Weakness/A 'Chocolate' Soldier" appears in the *Daily Star* on February 10. The Hemingways leave Switzerland by train for Italy. Hadley is now pregnant. Upon arrival the Hemingways check into the Hotel Splendide. Henry "Mike" Strater and Dorothy and Ezra Pound are also in the Meditteranean town. Pound is working on the Malatesta Cantos. Ernest intends to write while he stays in Rapallo. The Pounds leave three days after Ernest and Hadley arrive. Mike Strater paints a portrait of Ernest (the second he has painted, the first having been done in November 1922). Ernest is getting very little writing done. Hemingway meets Edward O'Brien, who is gathering material for *The Best Short Stories of 1923*. He accepts Ernest's short story, "My Old Man," for inclusion in the collection. Another new acquaintance who proves helpful to Hemingway's literary career is Robert Menzies McAlmon. With his own funds, McAlmon has just started Contact Editions, serving as editor and publisher. Sylvia Beach's bookstore is used as the small publishing company's mailing address. McAlmon will publish Ernest Hemingway's first book. Ernest's creative output during this month is five pages outlining the first chapter of "The Bull Ring," a fragment on cats, and an account of Mike Strater. Hemingway notifies his editor at the *Daily Star* that he wants to return to work in Toronto in September.

March: Dorothy and Ezra Pound return to Rapallo. Ernest reads T. S. Eliot's newest effort, *The Wasteland.* He begins a rough draft on a story about himself, Hadley, and the Hotel Splendide entitled "Cats in the Rain." The Hemingways and the Pounds take a walking tour through Italy, traveling through Pisa, Siena, Piombino, and the site of General Malatesta's battle, Onbetello. The general, whom Pound wrote about, was a patron of the arts as well as a soldier. The Pounds and the Hemingways part in the town of Sirmoine. Ernest and Hadley travel on to Cortina d' Ampezzo, located in the Dolomites, north of Venice. They stay at the Hotel Bellevue. Ernest divides his time between skiing and writing. He is working on sketches for the *Little Review* and completes six. These pieces will be used as the first six chapters of *in our time.* Included in the collection is a sketch on bullfighting. Since Hemingway has still not seen the sport, his is a second-hand account. John Bone, editor of the *Daily Star*, contacts Ernest late in the month. The newspaper wants him to cover Franco-German relations in the Ruhr. Ernest leaves for the assignment alone. He stops in Paris to interview French politicians and then goes to Germany. He travels through Offenburg, Ortenburg, Dusseldorf, and Essen.

April: Ernest stops in Cologne, Germany, to see Eric Dorman-Smith. On April 8, Dorman-Smith arranges for a safe-conduct pass for Ernest's trip back to Paris. By mid-April, Hemingway is in Cortina, Italy. The *Toronto Daily Star* begins to print Hemingway's series of articles at this time. "Will France Have a King Again?" appears on April 13, "A Victory Without Peace Forced the French to Undertake the Occupation of the Ruhr" on April 14, "French Royalist Party Most Solidly Organized" on April 18, "Government Pays for News in French Papers" on April 21, "Ruhr Commercial War Question of Bankruptcy" on April 25, and "A Brave Belgian Lady Shuts Up German Hater" on April 28. The series continues through May and runs about 20,000 words in length. In Italy, Hemingway is working on a new short story called "Out of Season" which is the longest piece of fiction he has written since the loss of his manuscripts. The sketches Ernest wrote in March are published in the Spring 1923 edition of the *Little Review*, edited by Jane Heap, Margaret Anderson, and Ezra Pound. Also included in the publication is a poem of Hemingway's entitled "They All Made Peace—What Is Peace?"

May: Hemingway's Franco-German series continues in the *Toronto Daily Star*. Articles include "Getting into Germany Quite a Job, Nowadays" on May 1 and 2, "Quite Easy to Spend a Million, If in Marks" on May 5, "Amateur Starvers Keep Out of View in Germany" on May 9, "Hate in Occupied Zone, a Real, Concrete Thing" on May 12, and "French Register Speed when Movies Are on Job" on May 16. Ernest is back in Paris at his apartment at 74 Rue du Cardinal Lemoine. He goes to Spain with Bill Bird and Robert McAlmon. Hemingway sees his first major bullfight during the Feast of Corpus Christi in Seville. He also travels to Ronda and Granada. Ernest is put off by the way Robert McAlmon, who is financing the trip, reacts to the bullfights. He will discuss the matter in *Death in the Afternoon* in 1932. A leaflet is distributed announcing the plans Contact Series has to publish Ernest. Other authors in the series are William Carlos Williams, Mina Loy, Marsden Hartley, and Robert McAlmon. Ernest has returned to Paris by the end of the month.

June: The publication of *in our time* continues in the planning stages. Publisher Bill Bird suggests including the six stories from the *Little Review* along with twelve new ones. The Hemingways begin to make arrangements for another trip to Spain. At Gertrude Stein's recommendation, they decide to go to Pamplona for the Feast of San Fermín.

July: Hadley and Ernest arrive in Pamplona on July 6. The Hemingways are most impressed with bullfighters Nicanor Villalta from Aragon and Manuel Garcia, who is called Maera. The couple decides to name their child for Nicanor if it is a boy. There is a very unproductive time for Ernest when the couple returns to Paris after the fiesta. Hadley is sick and Ernest must care for her. His domestic duties leave little time for writing. His impending fatherhood and the plans for return to Canada are making the young writer unhappy. He begins to work again late in the month. Along with six stories, Ernest writes an unpublished sketch on housework.

August: Hemingway completes the stories by the middle of the month. His stories are based on the events he has just seen in Pamplona. Ernest fictionalizes accounts of both Manuel Garcia and Nicanor Villalta. Another story is drawn from his experience with Agnes von Kurowsky. Shortly before the Hemingways are to sail to Montreal, Ernest receives proof pages for his first book, *Three Stories and Ten Poems**. Ernest and Hadley board the Cunard Line, *Andania* on August 17. They arrive in Canada on August 27.

September: Hemingway begins work on the *Toronto Daily Star* on September 10. There is a new city editor, Harry Hindmarsh, and tension begins immediately between the two. Hindmarsh will not give Ernest a byline on his stories and decides to send him out of town on assignments. Ernest is sent to Kingston, Ontario, to cover a story on an escaped convict. Hadley, now eight months pregnant, stays alone in Toronto at the Selby Hotel on Sherbourne Avenue. Hemingway is next sent to Sudbury, Ontario, on a mining story. While in the town, he

---

*The actual publication date of Ernest Hemingway's first book is not known. His bibliographer, Audre Hanneman, lists July, 1923, as the probable publication date. Since Hemingway did not receive final proof pages until August it is likely that the book came out sometime between late August and October. *Three Stories and Ten Poems* was published by Robert McAlmon/Contact Publishing Company in Paris, France. "Up in Michigan," "Out of Season," and "My Old Man" were the stories included in the collection. The poems were "Mitrailliatrice," "Oklahoma," "Oily Weather," "Roosevelt," "Captive," "Champs d' Honneur," "Riparto d' Assalto," "Along with Youth," and "Chapter Heading."

stays at the Nickel Range Hotel. The Hemingways move into an apartment in Cedarvale Mansions, 1599 Bathurst Street, at the end of the month. The *Star Weekly* publishes "King Business in Europe Isn't What It Used to Be" on September 15. "Search for Sudbury Coal a Gamble, Driller Tells of What He Has Found," "Anthraxolite, and Not Coal, Declares Geologist Again," and "Tossed about on Land Like Ships in a Storm" appear in the *Daily Star* on September 25.

October: Ernest is sent by the *Daily Star* to New York to cover the visit of the British prime minister, Lloyd George. Hadley is left in the care of the Connable family. Ernest's articles about the prime minister appear in the *Daily Star*. "He's a Personality, No Doubt, but a Much Maligned One" is printed on October 4, "Lloyd George Willing to Address 10,000 Here" and "Lloyd George Up Early as Big Liner Arrives" on October 5, "Little Welshman Lands/Anxious to Play Golf," "Wonderful Voice Is Chief Charm of Lloyd George," "Miss Megan George Makes Hit 'A Wonder' Reporters Call Her," and "Cope Denies Hearst Paying Lloyd George" on October 6, and "A Man of the People, Will Fight for People" on October 8. "Lloyd George Attends Theatre in New York" is published in the *Star Weekly* on October 6. It has been claimed that the interview with Megan George, the prime minister's daughter, was actually conducted by Ernest's friend from Oak Park, Isabel Simmons, who was in New York attending Barnard College. Hemingway misses a speech given by the deputy mayor of New York on England's sins. The *Toronto Daily Star* is scooped and the publisher of the newspaper wants Hemingway taken off the story. His request is moot because Ernest has already boarded Lloyd George's train and is on his way back to Toronto. On October 10, while Ernest is still enroute home, John Hadley Nicanor Hemingway is born. Ernest arrives seven hours after his first child has been delivered. The fact that Hemingway missed the birth of his child because of having been sent on assignment by Hindmarsh further aggravates the relationship between them. Ernest writes his last article for the *Daily Star* on October 15. It appears under the headline, "Hungarian Statesman Delighted with Loan." He continues to write for the *Star Weekly*. "Bullfighting Is Not a Sport—It Is a Tragedy" is published on October 20 and "World's Series of Bullfighting a Mad, Whirling

Carnival" on October 27. The *New York Tribune*'s "Social and Literary Notes" column, written by Burton Rascoe, mentions Hemingway and his book *Three Stories and Ten Poems*. The writer has not yet read the book, so there is no critical assessment. Rascoe also notes that Edmund Wilson had called his attention to Hemingway's work in the *Little Review*. Burton Rascoe's item about Ernest's work is probably the first in an American newspaper. Aside from Rascoe's column of October 21, there is no critical response to Hemingway's first book.

November: "More Game to Shoot in Crowded Europe than in Ontario/Forests and Animals Are Really Protected Over There" appears in the *Toronto Star Weekly*. On November 11, Ernest writes to Edmund Wilson for advice about getting his book reviewed. He asks Wilson for five names of possible reviewers to whom he should send a copy of his book. Edmund Wilson offers, in his reply, to include a note on Hemingway in the "Briefer Mentions" section of *Dial*. Hemingway begins to use the pen name "John Hadley" sporadically in the *Star Weekly*. The first instance is with the article, "Cheer Up! The Lakes Aren't Going Dry/High Up and Low Down Is Just Their Habit," which is run on November 17. "Trout Fishing All Across Europe/Spain Has the Best, Then Germany" appears on the same day. Ernest's other articles for the *Star Weekly* this month are "Wild Gastronomic Adventures of a Gourmet, Eating Sea Slugs, Snails, Octopus, Etc. for Fun" (Hemingway assumes another pen name for this article, used only once, of "Peter Jackson"), "General Wolfe's Diaries Saved for Canada," "Tancredo Is Dead," and "Learns to Commune with the Fairies, Now Wins the $40,000 Nobel Prize." The above articles and two vignettes, "The Sport of Kings" and "The Big Dance on the Hill," are published on November 24. Responding to Edmund Wilson's offer, Ernest suggests that Wilson wait until *in our time* and *The Best Short Stories of 1923* are published before mentioning his work in *Dial*. The *Paris Tribune* runs a favorable review of *Three Stories and Ten Poems* on November 27.

December: The publication date of *in our time* was set for this month. It appears that because of a printing error the book is not completed until March 1924. Ernest and Hadley begin to make preparations for their return to Paris. Hemingway, in the meantime, is kept quite busy at the *Star Weekly*. His articles include "Fifty-ton Doors Laugh at Robbers' Tools/Bank Vaults Defy Scientific Cracksmen" on December 1, "German Marks Make Last Stand as Real Money in Toronto's 'Ward'" and "Lots of War Medals for Sale/but Nobody Will Buy Them" on December 8, "Night Life in Europe a Disease/Constantinople's Most Hectic" and "Dose Whole City's Water Supply to Cure Goitre by Mass Medication" on December 15, "The Blind Man's Christmas," "Christmas on the Roof of the World" (a three-part autobiographical series set in the Swiss Alps, Paris, and Italy), "Toronto 'Red' Children Don't Know Santa Claus," and "W. B. Yeats—A Night Hawk Kept Toronto Host Up" on December 22, "Toronto Is the Biggest Betting Place in North America," "Weird, Wild Adventures of Some of Our Modern Amateur Imposters," and "Wild New Year's Eve Gone Forever/Only Ghost of 1914 Party Remains" on December 29. Hemingway submits his resignation to John Bone on December 27, effective January 1, 1924. Although three of his articles appear in January, Ernest goes off the payroll of the *Toronto Star Weekly* on December 31. Gertrude Stein's poem, "Hemingway: A Portrait" is published in *Ex Libris*.

1924

in our time
The Best Short Stories of 1923 and the Yearbook of the American Short Story ("My Old Man")
The Best Poems of 1923 ("Chapter Heading")
Three articles for the *Toronto Star Weekly*
"Work in Progress" (later titled "Indian Camp"; short story)
The Soul of Spain with McAlmon and Bird the Publishers, parts one and two (poems)
"The Earnest Liberal's Lament" (poem)
"Mr. and Mrs. Elliot" (short story)
"The Doctor and the Doctor's Wife" (short story)
Articles in the *transatlantic review*

January: *The Best Short Stories of 1923*, which anthologizes "My Old Man," is dedicated to Hemingway and is the first book published in America to contain his work. A subsequent British edition is published in 1924 as well. The book is edited by Edward J. O'Brien, published by Small, Maynard and Company in Boston. "My Old Man" is reprinted from *Three Stories and Ten Poems* (1923). Ernest and Hadley stay in Toronto until January 12. The Connables hold a farewell party for them. The Hemingways arrive in New York on January 13 and stay until their ship sails on January 19. Ernest's last articles appear in the *Star Weekly* while he is in transit. They are "Skiers Only Escape from Alpine Avalanche Is to Swim! Snow Slides Off Mountain as Fast as Off Roof of House" on January 12, and "So This Is Chicago" and "Must Wear Hats Like Other Folks if You Live in Toronto" on January 19. Ernest, Hadley, and John Hadley sail to Paris aboard the Cunard Line, *Antonia*. They arrive on January 29 and move into an apartment at 113 rue Notre Dame Des Champs. Madame Henri Rohrbach is hired to help with their child, John, who is now nicknamed "Bumby."

February: Ernest meets Ford Madox Ford through Ezra Pound. Ford is publishing a new literary magazine, *transatlantic review*. Pound had suggested that Ernest work on the editorial staff. Ford takes Pound's recommendation and Ernest will be a "sub-editor" of the review, which is located behind Bill Bird's Three Mountains Press at 29 Quai d' Anjou. Ernest is not paid for his work on the *transatlantic review*, and Hadley learns of bad investments which have been made with her trust. The Hemingways are experiencing financial strain. Ernest proposes serializing Gertrude Stein's *The Making of Americans*, written in 1911, in the review. He discusses the idea in a letter to Stein on February 17. Hemingway meets another American living in Paris, Harold Loeb, who is editor of *Broom*. He is introduced to Loeb's fiancée, Kitty Cannell.

March: "Bumby" is christened on March 10 at St. Luke's Episcopal Chapel. Gertrude Stein is named as godmother and Eric "Chink" Dorman-Smith as godfather. *in our time* is published. The actual publication date is difficult to determine, but is probably March 24. The book includes 18 short, untitled chapters. The first six had appeared in the *Little Review* in slightly different form in the spring of 1923.

April: Hemingway's poem "Chapter Heading" is reprinted in *The Best Poems of 1923*, which is published by Small, Maynard and Company in Boston. The poem had appeared in *Poetry* in January 1923. *Three Stories and Ten Poems* and *in our time* are reviewed in the April issue of *transatlantic review* (first reviews for both books). Ernest's work continues on the *review*. He is on a regular schedule of writing each morning and then taking care of his son, Bumby. Hemingway earns extra money by sparring with heavyweight fighters in a gymnasium in the rue Pontoise. He receives about ten francs per round. He is very active physically during this time. He also boxes for sport with Harold Loeb, George O'Neill, and Paul Fisher. His afternoons are usually spent attending prizefights or going to Sylvia Beach's bookstore. John Dos Passos is a frequent visitor to Paris and Ernest sees him often. Hemingway meets poet Dr. William Carlos Williams and rekindles his friendship with Donald Ogden Stewart. A story, written since his return to Paris, appears under the heading "Work in Progress" in the April 24 issue of *transatlantic review*. Later called "Indian Camp," the short story will be included in *In Our Time* (note: Liveright edition, 1925). "Indian Camp" marks the first appearance of Hemingway's character Nick Adams. Ernest contributes a series of 16 short items about artists, writers, boxers, and bullfighters entitled "And to the United States" to the same issue of the *review*.

May–June: Hemingway is working on a second short story, "Big Two-Hearted River," using Nick Adams as the central figure. By May, Ernest has received 150 francs for his work on the *transatlantic review*. He continues to incorporate those people he dislikes into fiction, but uses the form of the short story rather than fragmented sketches. In June, Hemingway writes an unflattering story based on Ford Madox Ford and his wife, Stella Bowen. Ford leaves Ernest in charge of the next issue of *transatlantic review* while he goes to New York to search for more financial backing for the magazine. Ernest's choices for the editorial content of the August *review* are stories by John Dos Passos and Nathan Asch, a nonfiction article by Guy Hickok, and an excerpt from Gertrude Stein's *The Making of Americans*. Hemingway's cousin, Frank Hines, visits him in Paris. Ernest and Hadley leave for Spain at the end of June and leave Bumby in the care of Madame Rohrbach.

July–August: The Hemingways are joined by Eric Dorman-Smith, Sally Bird, John Dos Passos, Don Stewart, Robert McAlmon, and George O'Neil in Pamplona for the bullfights. (Ernest will include Sally Bird and Dorman-Smith's reactions to the bullfights in *Death in the Afternoon* in 1932.) Hemingway takes part in the amateur bullfights during the fiesta. Ernest and Hadley leave Pamplona on July 14 to meet Bill and Sally Bird in Burguete, a Basque mountain village, for a fishing trip. They spend a day along the Irati River fishing. Ernest turns 25 on July 21. On July 28, John Quinn, *transatlantic review*'s patron, dies of cancer in New York. After Ford Madox Ford returns to Paris, he and Ernest have a disagreement over the choice of editorial content in Ford's absence. Ford includes a note in the issue about the matter. The strife between the two blows over quickly. Hemingway suggests Krebs Friend, his associate from the *Co-operative Commonwealth*, as successor to John Quinn as financial backer of the *transatlantic review*. Friend has married a wealthy woman and is now living in Paris. An agreement is reached that Friend will give the magazine $200 each month for a period of six months. Krebs Friend is, in turn, named president of the *transatlantic review* on August 15. Ernest finishes writing "Big Two-Hearted River," which has turned into his longest story. He has written eight other stories since his return to Paris from Toronto at the end of January. They are "Indian Camp," "The Doctor and the Doctor's Wife," "Soldier's Home," "The End of Something," "The Three-Day Blow," "Cross-Country Snow," "Cat in the Rain," and "Mr. and Mrs. Smith." "And Out of America," an unsigned article by Hemingway criticizing the works of Tristan Tzara, the so-called father of the Dada movement, as well as those of Gilbert Seldes and Jean Cocteau, appears in the August issue of the *transatlantic review*.

September–October: A favorable review of "My Old Man" is run in the September 3 issue of *The Nation*. The critic, Johan Smertenko, refers to the author of the story as "Ernest Hemenway." John Dos Passos and Don Stewart urge Hemingway to submit his work for American publication. Ernest sends his nine new stories, the prose portion of *Three Stories and Ten Poems*, and the miniatures from *in our time* to Stewart, who is in New York, to pass along to American publishers. Hem-

ingway meets Hans von Wedderkop, the Paris representative
of *Der Querschnitt* (The Cross-Section). The literary magazine
is published in Germany by Alfred Flechtheim. Four of Ernest's
bawdy poems are purchased by the magazine. "The Soul of
Spain with McAlmon and Bird the Publishers," part one, and
"The Earnest Liberal's Lament" are published in *Der Querschnitt*'s Autumn issue. (Parts one and two of "The Soul of
Spain..." and "The Earnest Liberal's Lament" are reprinted
in *Das Querschnittbuch* in 1924.) Hemingway is introduced by
Harold Loeb to Leon Fleischman, the literary scout for publishers Boni and Liveright in New York. *Doodab*, Loeb's novel,
is being published by Boni and Liveright. Ernest is at work on
his story, "The Undefeated." Edmund Wilson reviews *Three
Stories and Ten Poems* and *in our time* in the October issue of
Dial magazine. With some reservations, Wilson is quite com-
plimentary about Hemingway's work. Ernest adds to his collection of unflattering sketches about acquaintances. He writes
"An Appreciation of Joseph Conrad" (a special section on Conrad is included in the magazine this month because of his recent
death) and "Pamplona Letter" for the October *transatlantic
review.*

November–December: Tension between Ford Madox Ford
and Ernest flares over the Joseph Conrad article. Hemingway
had made disparaging remarks about T. S. Eliot in order to
praise Conrad by contrast. Ford prints an apology in the November issue of the *review*. Hemingway is angry at Krebs Friend
as well as at Ford Madox Ford. "The Soul of Spain with McAlmon
and Bird the Publishers," part two, appears in *Der Querschnitt*
in November along with "The Lady Poets with Foot Notes."
Ernest completes "The Undefeated" on November 20. He meets
John Herrmann and his fiancée, Josephine Herbst, in early
December. Another new acquaintance is Archibald MacLeish.
Hemingway will become close friends with Archibald and his
wife, Ada. Ernest rekindles a friendship with Ernest Walsh
and Ethel Moorehead, who are starting a new publication named
This Quarter. Janet Flanner, who will remain as a lifelong
friend, and Ernest meet in Paris. She is a journalist with *The
New Yorker*. Robert McAlmon buys "Soldier's Home" on December 10 for publication in his *Contact Collection of Contemporary Writers*. While revising "Big Two-Hearted River," Ernest

him by Harold Loeb. Duff and Ernest become friends and meet often in the following months. "The Undefeated" is rejected by *Dial*. Hemingway mistakenly believes that Gilbert Seldes played a part in the rejection. He submits the story to Ernest Walsh at *This Quarter*. Hemingway sends the signed contracts to Horace Liveright on March 31. A review of Sherwood Anderson's *A Story-Teller's Story*, written by Ernest, appears in *Ex Libris* during the month.

April: Ernest Walsh accepts "The Undefeated" for *This Quarter*. On April 4, Hemingway resigns his unpaid position with Walsh's magazine and suggests that Bill Smith be given a paid editorial job. Walsh rejects the idea, which upsets Hemingway. He develops a grudge against Ethel Moorehead and Ernest Walsh. Two important relationships begin at this time. Maxwell Perkins, an editor with the New York publishing firm, Charles Scribner's Sons, writes Hemingway to express interest in reading his work. (F. Scott Fitzgerald first recommended that Perkins contact Hemingway on October 18, 1924.) The letter never reaches Ernest. Perkins sends another, dated February 26, which reaches Hemingway in mid-March, by which time he had already signed with Boni and Liveright. Hemingway responds to Perkins in a letter dated April 15 and explains the terms of his agreement with Horace Liveright. His contract stipulates that Boni and Liveright has options on Hemingway's next three books. The agreement will be void, however, if the second book is rejected within 60 days of receiving the manuscript. Ernest's letter of April 15 begins the correspondence between him and Perkins that will continue until the editor's death in 1947. The first mention of his idea for a book on bullfighting is made in the letter to Perkins. (This will develop into *Death in the Afternoon* and be published in 1932.) The Hemingways have been back in their apartment at 113 rue Notre Dame Des Champs since mid-March. F. Scott and Zelda Fitzgerald are visiting Paris. The two writers first meet at the Dingo Bar in rue Dalambre. (The exact date of their meeting is unknown, but it was either in the last few days of April or the first few days of May.) Fitzgerald was quite famous by this time, having already published two collections of short stories, a play, and three novels. During their meeting, Fitzgerald expressed enthusiasm for Hemingway's Nick Adams stories.

May–June: Hemingway and Fitzgerald meet again just days after their original introduction. Fitzgerald is eager for Hemingway to read his newest novel, *The Great Gatsby*. During the second week in May, Hemingway goes to the Fitzgeralds' apartment at 14 rue de Tilsitt. Ernest dislikes Zelda from his first meeting with her. In the middle of May, Hemingway receives his $200 advance from Horace Liveright. On May 22, with all revisions completed, he sends the galley proofs of *In Our Time* to Boni and Liveright in New York. The first issue of *This Quarter*, dedicated to Ezra Pound, appears in May. Ernest's story "Big Two Hearted River" (published originally without a hyphen in the title), and his article "Homage to Ezra" are included in the premier issue. (The article will be reprinted in *Ezra Pound* by Peter Russell in 1950.) In June, Hemingway writes 27 pages of a novel entitled *Along with Youth*. Using Nick Adams as his central figure, Ernest draws on his experiences in Italy during World War I. He will put aside this work in the preliminary stage. The Hemingways begin to make plans for another trip to Pamplona, Spain, for the Fiesta of San Fermín. In his last editorial act for *This Quarter*, Ernest makes arrangements for a portion of James Joyce's *Finnegan's Wake* to be printed in the magazine before he leaves for Spain. He and Hadley go to Burguete, Spain, on June 25 with Bill Smith. The fishing trip is a disappointment. The first appearance (and first translation of Hemingway's work) of "The Undefeated" is in *Der Querschnitt* in June. The story, carrying the German title, "Stierkamp," appears in two parts and is translated by B. Bessmertny. *Contact Collection of Contemporary Writers* is published by William Bird and Robert McAlmon, Three Mountains Press, in Paris. Hemingway's "Soldier's Home" is included under the title of "A Story." Other writers in the collection are James Joyce, Djuna Barnes, Ford Madox Ford, Ezra Pound, William Carlos Williams, and Gertrude Stein.

July–August: The Hemingways leave Burguete on July 2 for Pamplona, where they stay at the Hotel Quintana. Bill Smith, Donald Stewart, Harold Loeb, Lady Duff Twysden and her companion, Pat Guthrie, are with them. The trip to the Fiesta of San Fermín proves less satisfactory than in the past. Tension exists between Harold Loeb and Ernest. Ernest is again taking note of the reactions of those in his group to the bullfights.

Ernest and Hadley are impressed by a new bullfighter, Cayetano Ordoñez. The tension between Loeb and Hemingway, at least in part caused by Loeb's relationship with Duff Twysden, erupts into a fight between the two on July 12. Before leaving the group the following day, Ernest gives a note of apology to the innkeeper to be handed to Loeb. Ernest and Hadley travel on to stay at the Pension Aguilar in the Calle San Jerónimo in Madrid for eight days. They visit the Prado and the bullfights to see the bullfighters, Belmonte and Ordoñez. Ernest begins working on a novel called *Fiesta*. It is possible that he began it while still in Pamplona. The novel includes the recent events which took place during the festival between Hemingway and his friends. The characters are modeled on the group. Lady Brett Ashley resembles Lady Duff Twysden, Mike Campbell like Pat Guthrie, Robert Cohn like Harold Loeb, and Pedro Romero like Ordoñez. Jake Barnes shares character traits of Hemingway and Bill Bird. Ernest and Hadley leave Madrid and arrive in Valencia on July 21. Ernest is 26 years old. He begins another draft of *Fiesta* on July 23 and finishes the first one and a half chapters by August 3. The Hemingways make a brief trip back to Paris and then return to the Pension Aguilar in Spain on August 5. They continue on to the Hotel Suizo in San Sebastian and stay through August 9, arriving at the Hotel Grand in Hendaye, France, on August 10. Hadley returns alone to Paris on August 12. Ernest stays on in Hendaye and works on his novel. On August 19, he goes back to Paris to join his family. The rest of the month is spent working on *Fiesta*. The only piece of Hemingway's work published during this period is the second part of "Stierkampf" ("The Undefeated") in *Der Querschnitt*'s July issue.

September: "The Undefeated" is first published in English in the Autumn-Winter issue of *This Quarter*. The story will later be included in *Men Without Women* (1927). Bill Smith is planning to return to New York along with Harold Loeb. The two have become close friends. A party is given before their departure on September 4. The tension between Hemingway and Loeb is apparent at the gathering. Ernest works on his novel through most of the month and completes it on September 21. The last line reads, "It's nice as hell to think so." On the 21st, he changes it to "Isn't it nice to think so." After completing

Fiesta, Ernest considers travelling to Italy. Family responsibilities and a fear of Mussolini's government prevent the trip. He goes to Chartres instead and takes his manuscript along with him. In Chartres, he writes a foreword which explains a title he is considering for the novel. "The Lost Generation" is a phrase coined by an automobile mechanic in a conversation with Gertrude Stein. Ernest makes a list of other possible titles for *Fiesta*. They include "River to the Sea," "Two Lie Together," "The Old Leaven," and "The Sun Also Rises." Hemingway returns to Paris and begins work on his story, "Ten Indians." The manuscript, which is dated September 27, involves Nick Adams and his Indian girlfriend, Prudence Mitchell.

October: *In Our Time* is published by Boni and Liveright in New York on October 5. The collection contains the short chapters from *in our time* placed as interchapters between the short stories "Indian Camp," "The Doctor and The Doctor's Wife," "The End of Something," "The Three-Day Blow," "The Battler," "A Very Short Story," "Soldier's Home," "The Revolutionist," "Mr. and Mrs. Elliot," "Cat in the Rain," "Out of Season," "Cross Country Snow," "My Old Man," "Big Two-Hearted River," parts one and two, and "L'Envoi." Sherwood Anderson, Edward J. O'Brien, John Dos Passos, Waldo Frank, and Gilbert Seldes contribute dust jacket "blurbs" for Hemingway's first book published in America. The *New York Times* and the *World Review* run favorable reviews on October 18. The previous day, the *Literary Review* of the *New York Evening Post* published another favorable review by Herschel Brickell, which bothers Ernest in that it compares his writing (once again) to Sherwood Anderson's. Ernest writes "Fifty Grand," his short story about a welterweight champion fight that took place in the New York Hippodrome on June 26, 1922. Since he first arrived in Paris, Hemingway has held a borrower's card for Sylvia Beach's lending library at Shakespeare and Company. During this month, he borrows Upton Sinclair's *Mammonart*, *Sentimental Education* by Gustave Flaubert, and *A Lear of the Steppes*, *A Sportsman's Sketches*, and *The Torrents of Spring* by Ivan Turgenev.

November: Ernest borrows *The Travel Diary of a Philosopher* by Hermann Alexander from Shakespeare and Company on November 9 and, one week later, checks out Donald Ogden

will be changing publishers. Hemingway meets with Max Perkins for the first time on February 10 at the Scribner's office on Fifth Avenue. Perkins offers him an advance of $1500 on *The Torrents of Spring* and *The Sun Also Rises* in addition to a 15 percent royalty rate. Ernest decides to sign a contract with Charles Scribner's Sons. Publisher Alfred Harcourt of Harcourt, Brace is interested in publishing Hemingway's work. They meet and Ernest explains his prior arrangement with Perkins. After his business is taken care of, Ernest spends the rest of his stay in New York looking up old friends and making new acquaintances. He sees Robert Benchley, Dorothy Parker, Ernest Boyd, Madeleine Boyd, John Herrmann, Josie Herbst, his friend from Chicago, Bobby Rouse, and from Oak Park, Isabel Simmons. At the end of February, he sails back to Paris aboard the *Roosevelt.* Also on board are *New Yorker* writers Dorothy Parker and Robert Benchley.

March–April: Ernest stays in Paris for a few days before rejoining Hadley and his son, Bumby, in Schruns, Austria. He spends most of his time with Pauline Pfeiffer while in Paris. During his brief stay, he also sees Zelda and Scott Fitzgerald. He returns to Schruns on March 10. John Dos Passos and Gerald and Sara Murphy join the Hemingways in Austria for a week after his return. Ernest receives a rejection notice for his story "Fifty Grand" from *Collier*'s magazine. He notes in a journal that he would like to write a picaresque novel set in America. He also records some early thoughts on suicide and death. During the last weeks of March, Hemingway revises the last five chapters of *The Sun Also Rises.* The Hemingways return to Paris at the end of March. Ernest has the completed manuscript of *The Sun Also Rises,* now 90,000 words, professionally typed to send on to Max Perkins. "L'invincible," the French translation of his story, "The Undefeated," appears in the March issue of *Navire d' Argent.* "Banal Story," which will be included in *Men Without Women* in 1927, makes its first appearance in print in the Spring-Summer issue of the *Little Review.* Hadley Hemingway takes a trip through the Loire Valley with her friends, Virginia and Pauline Pfeiffer. The holiday is tension-filled. Hadley becomes suspicious about Pauline's relationship with Ernest. In the middle of April, Hemingway is contacted by Curtis Browne who wishes to act as his agent for continental and British publishing. Browne tells Ernest that Jonathan Cape, the London publisher, wants to bring out an English edition of *In Our Time* and that a German publisher is interested in his work. Ernest relays the information and his approval of the arrangement to F. Scott Fitzgerald in a letter dated April 20. Four days later, Hemingway mails *The Sun Also Rises* to Maxwell Perkins in New York. Borrowings from the library at Shakespeare and Company this month include *Along the Road* by Aldous Huxley, *Strait Is the Gate* by Andre Gide, *Selected Poems* by Carl Sandburg, *Early Poems and Stories* by William Butler Yeats, and *An Outcast of the Islands* by Joseph Conrad. At the end of April, Hadley confronts her husband with her suspicions about his affair with Pauline Pfeiffer. Ernest responds in anger and expresses the opinion that she was wrong to mention the matter.

May: Ernest completes his story "An Alpine Idyll" and, on May 5, sends it to Max Perkins for submission to *Scribner*'s magazine. On May 13, Hemingway travels to Madrid alone. While staying at the Pension Aquilar, Ernest revises two short stories, "Ten Indians" and "The Killers" (the latter had been called "The Matadors"), and a one-act play. Hadley and Bumby are at Cap d'Antibes on the French Riviera with Gerald and Sara Murphy, Zelda and Scott Fitzgerald, and Archibald and Ada MacLeish while Ernest is in Spain. Hadley and her son, who has contracted whooping cough, move into the Villa Paquita when the Fitzgeralds move into larger quarters. Ernest's reading during this month includes *Egoists: A Book of Supermen* and *Steeplechase* by James Gibbons Huneker, *Thus Spake Zarathustra* by Friedrich Nietzsche, *Knock, Knock, Knock and Other Stories*, *The Two Friends and Other Stories*, and *On The Eve* by Ivan Turgenev. On May 21, Hemingway writes to Sherwood Anderson to tell him about his upcoming book which parodies Anderson's writing. *The Torrents of Spring*, subtitled "A Romantic Novel in Honor of the Passing of a Great Race," is published by Charles Scribner's Sons, New York, on May 28.

June–July: Ernest joins Hadley and Bumby on the French Riviera on June 5. Scott Fitzgerald's behavior upsets Hemingway when he first arrives. Ernest gives his newest manuscript to Fitzgerald to read and follows his advice to remove the first one and a half chapters of *The Sun Also Rises*. *Scribner*'s Magazine rejects "An Alpine Idyll." The critical response to *The Torrents of Spring* is mainly positive. Sherwood Anderson is angry with Hemingway when he reads the book. Pauline Pfeiffer joins the Hemingways on the French Riviera. She moves into the Hotel de la Pinède in Juan-les-Pins with them. The group stays in the hotel through the end of June. *Today Is Friday*, Hemingway's one-act play, is published by The As Stable Publications in Englewood, New Jersey. The play is number four of the company's The As Stable Pamphlets. The Hemingways, the Murphys, and Pauline Pfeiffer go to the bullfights in Pamplona in early July. The group splits up after the Fiesta of San Fermín. Pauline, Gerald, and Sara depart for Bayonne, while Ernest and Hadley go to stay at the Hotel Suizo at San Sebastian and afterwards at the Pension Aguilar in Madrid. In late July, the Hemingways travel on to Valencia, Spain.

August: By the middle of the month, on their return to Paris, Ernest and Hadley Hemingway agree to a separation. Hadley moves into the Hotel Beauvoir. Ernest stays at a studio, which belongs to Gerald Murphy, at 60 rue Froidevaux. He spends a great deal of time with Archibald and Ada MacLeish. Hemingway borrows Ford Madox Ford's *A Mirror to France* from Shakespeare and Company. Proofs of *The Sun Also Rises* arrive in Paris. After proofreading them Ernest returns them and the book's dedication to Max Perkins. His book is sent back to America aboard the *Mauretania* on August 27. The dedication of *The Sun Also Rises* reads: "This book is for Hadley and for John Hadley Nicanor."

September: Hadley writes an agreement which stipulates that if Pauline and Ernest stay away from each other for 100 days she will give Ernest a divorce. Ernest signs the agreement. Gerald Murphy writes a letter to Hemingway on September 4 in which he includes a $400 check and advice on his personal life. (The advice, which Ernest resents, is said to be the basis for his attack on the Murphys years later in *A Moveable Feast*.) On September 10, Ernest borrows *A Sportsman's Sketches* by Ivan Turgenev and *Paul Cezanne* by Ambroise Vollard from Shakespeare and Company's lending library. "The Killers,"

Ernest's short story, is accepted by *Scribner*'s magazine. He receives $200 for publication of the story. Pauline Pfeiffer sails to New York aboard the *Pennland* on September 24. She and Ernest decided that their enforced separation would be more tolerable if they were on different continents. The British edition of *In Our Time* is published by Jonathan Cape in London during this month.

October: Hemingway and Archibald MacLeish travel to Zaragaza, Spain, to attend the bullfights. On October 7, Ernest's paternal grandfather, Anson Hemingway, dies. A new short story, "A Canary for One," is submitted to *Scribner*'s magazine. The story is a fictional account of Ernest's and Hadley's return trip to Paris shortly before their separation. A very distraught Hemingway helps Hadley move into her new apartment at 35, rue de Fleurus. D. H. Lawrence's translation of *Mastro-Don Gesualdo* by Giovanni Verga and *The Life, Work and Evil Fate of Guy de Maupassant* by Robert Sherard are among the books Ernest reads this month. *The Sun Also Rises* is published by Charles Scribner's Sons in New York on October 22.

November: Hemingway borrows Gertrude Stein's *Composition as Explanation* from the lending library at Shakespeare and Company on November 4. "A Canary for One" is accepted by *Scribner*'s magazine on November 11. On the following day, Ernest writes a letter to Pauline Pfeiffer in which he talks about his current depression and his suicidal thoughts. Hadley Hemingway takes a trip to Chartres and leaves Bumby in Ernest's care in Paris. On November 18, Ernest tells Hadley that he is assigning all royalties from *The Sun Also Rises* to her. The following day, he writes his editor, Max Perkins, and encloses an article, most likely the satirical sketch "My Own Life," which appears in *The New Yorker* on February 13, 1927. Ernest explains his intentions in writing *The Sun Also Rises* in the letter to Perkins. The novel, he writes, is intended to be a tragedy, not a satire laced with bitterness. Hemingway submits his story "In Another Country" to *Scribner*'s magazine on November 22.

December: *Scribner*'s notifies Hemingway that they are accepting his story on December 4. Ernest discusses his plans for a book on bullfighting in a letter to Max Perkins on December 6. Hemingway receives a letter from his mother, Grace, in which she asks about rumors of Hadley and Ernest's separation and attacks the subject matter of *The Sun Also Rises* as being profane. The book, despite Grace Hemingway's feelings, is selling extremely well. Almost 7000 copies have sold within the first two months of its publication. The models for the characters in Ernest's novel have mixed reactions to the book. It is reported that Harold Loeb is puzzled over what he'd done to deserve shoddy treatment by his friend, Ernest. Duff Twysden, as Ernest explains to F. Scott Fitzgerald at a later date, is only angry initially. John Peale Bishop passes along the information to Ernest that Edmund Wilson thinks *The Sun Also Rises* is the best novel of any writer in Hemingway's generation. Dodd, Mead and Company publish *The Best Short Stories of 1926 and the Yearbook of the American Short Story* in New York this month. Editor Edward J. O'Brien has selected Hemingway's story "The Undefeated" for the collection.

1927

Contemporary Short Stories (Chapter VIII of *in our time* included under the title "A Separate Peace")

Samples: A Collection of Short Stories ("My Old Man" is anthologized)

"My Own Life" (parody)

"The Killers" (short story)

"Neothoemist Poem" (poem; title contains typographical error)

"In Another Country" (short story)

"A Canary for One" (short story)

"Indianisches Lager" (German translation of short story, "Indian Camp")

"Der Boxer" (German translation of short story, "The Battler")

"Italy - 1927" (article, later retitled as short story, "Che Ti Dice La Patria?")

"Das Ende von Etwas" (German translation of short story, "The End of Something")

Fiesta (British edition of novel, *The Sun Also Rises*)

"Fifty Grand" (short story)

"Hills Like White Elephants" (short story)

"Cinquante mille dollars" (French translation of short story, "Fifty Grand")

The American Caravan: A Yearbook of American Literature (short story, "An Alpine Idyll," included in the collection)

Men Without Women (collection of short stories)

"The Real Spaniard" (article)

January–February: Harper Publishing Company in New York includes Chapter Eight of *in our time* in its *Contemporary Short Stories*, edited by Gordon Hall Gerould and Charles Bayley, Jr. The story is retitled "A Separate Peace." A school text edition is published simultaneously. The story "My Old Man" is anthologized in *Samples: A Collection of Short Stories*, which is published by Boni and Liveright in New York. The book is compiled by Lillie Ryttenberg and Beatrice Lang for the community workers of the New York Guild for the Jewish Blind. Pauline Pfeiffer returns to Paris. She and Ernest, accompanied by Virginia Pfeiffer, go to Gstaad, Switzerland, in mid-January. They stay at the Hotel Rossli. John ("Bumby") Hemingway joins them for two weeks. At the publisher's request, Ernest submits his story "An Alpine Idyll" for publication in *The American Caravan* on January 21. An unfavorable review of *The Sun Also Rises* appears in the January 27 issue of *Dial* magazine. On the same day, Ernest and Hadley Richardson Hemingway's divorce is final. They had been married for six years and seven months. Max Perkins writes Hemingway and suggests he assemble a new collection of stories to be published by Scribner's. The letter is dated January 28. Pauline Pfeiffer and Ernest spend the entire month of February in Gstaad. The *Atlantic Monthly* purchases Hemingway's story "Fifty Grand" for $350.00 The sales of *The Sun Also Rises* now total 12,000 copies. On February 5, Ernest writes to his parents, Grace and Clarence Hemingway, to tell them of his divorce from Hadley. He does not mention his affair with Pauline. He responds to Perkins's suggestion for a new book of stories by sending him a list of possible choices for the content on February 14. (All of Ernest's selections will be included in the book except for "Up in Michigan.") Ernest reports in a letter to Perkins, dated February 19, that he has received requests for stories from

Vanity Fair, Harper's Bazaar, The *New Yorker*, and the Hearst Publishing Company.

March: Hemingway is one of 162 signers of a letter to the editor of the *New York Herald Tribune* book section protesting the pirating of James Joyce's *Ulysses*. The letter is dated February 2, but not published until March 6. Bumby visits his father and Pauline in Gstaad for ten days. In mid-March, when he leaves, Ernest travels through Fascist Italy with Guy Hickok. Their route takes them through central France and the Riviera. By March 20, Ernest and Guy are in Rapallo, Italy. While in this town, Hemingway encounters Don Giuseppe Bianchi, the priest who had anointed him when he was wounded in Italy in 1918. After a stopover in Pisa, Hickok and Hemingway travel through Florence, the Apennines, and Rimini. While in the Adriatic town of Rimini, Ernest receives a letter from Pauline Pfeiffer in which she discusses their wedding plans and the new apartment she has found for them at 6'rue Férou, located near the Church of St.-Sulpice. Pauline would like to be married by a Catholic priest. She explains that this will be possible because Ernest was baptized as Catholic in 1918 and his marriage to Hadley, performed outside the Church, is not recognized by the Catholic church. Ernest and Guy Hickok continue their trip, travelling through northern Italy. The towns of Forlì, Imola, Bologna, Piacenza, and Genoa are on their route. Hemingway's depressed state has been evident during the trip, according to his travelling companion. After ten days in Italy, Hemingway and Hickok spend the last night of their trip in Menton, France. "The Killers" is published in the March issue of *Scribner*'s magazine. This is the first appearance of a Hemingway short story in an American magazine. The story will be included in his collection *Men Without Women*, published later in the year. Ernest's "Neo-Thomist Poem" is published in the spring in *Exile*, no. 1. A typographical error turns the name into "Neothoemist Poem."

April: Now back in Paris, Ernest writes "Italy—1927," an account of his trip through Italy with Guy Hickok. He submits it to Edmund Wilson at the *New Republic*. "Indianisches Lager" and "Der Boxer," German translations of Hemingway's stories, "Indian Camp" and "The Battler," are published in the *Frank-*

furter Zeitung on April 10 and 17. On April 16, Hadley and Bumby leave for the United States. Ernest sees them off as they sail. Two more stories, "In Another Country" and "A Canary for One," appear in *Scribner*'s magazine in April. Hemingway continues to work on his new collection of short stories, *Men Without Women.*

May: Ernest is working on two new stories, "Hills Like White Elephants" and "Now I Lay Me," in the beginning of the month. Donald Friede, a partner at Boni and Liveright, comes to Paris to woo Hemingway back to his publishing company. He offers Ernest $3000 as an advance on any novel, $1000 on any book of short stories, and an additional 15 percent royalty rate for any book published by the firm. Friede also explains that Boni and Liveright would buy the reprint rights to *The Sun Also Rises* and *The Torrents of Spring* from Charles Scribner's Sons and reissue them, along with *In Our Time*, in a uniform edition. Donald Friede leaves without signing Hemingway, but a friendship develops between the two. Another new acquaintance, painter Waldo Pierce, will become a close friend of Hemingway's as well. Ernest and Pauline Pfeiffer are married on May 10. The ceremony takes place at L'Eglise de St.-Honoré d'Eylau at 9 Place Victor Hugo in the 16th arrondisement. Afterwards, a luncheon is held for the Hemingways by Ada and Archibald MacLeish. (Pauline Pfeiffer (7/22/1895–10/1/1951) was born in Parkersburg, Iowa. She, along with her family, later moved to Piggott, Arkansas where her father became wealthy through ownership of timberland.) After his marriage to Pauline, Ernest considers himself to be a Catholic. The baptism, which allowed the church ceremony, is not documented. The newlyweds take a three-week honeymoon trip to Grau du Roi, France. Hemingway completes the two stories he began earlier in the month and sends them to his editor, Max Perkins, on May 27. It is also during his honeymoon that Ernest cuts his foot and becomes infected with anthrax. Back in Paris, Ernest borrows St. John Irvine's *Parnell* from Shakespeare and Company's lending library. "Italy-1927" is published in the *New Republic* on May 18. The recounting of his trip through Fascist Italy will be included in *Men Without Women* under the title "Che Ti Dice La Patria?" (What Do You Hear from Home?), as a story, and reprinted in the November 22, 1954 issue of the *New Republic*. "Das Ende von Etwas," the German translation of "The End of Something," appears in the *Frankfurter Zeitung* on May 22.

June: Pauline and Ernest stay in Paris through the month. Ernest is still sick with the anthrax infection for the first ten days after their arrival home. He reads Ring Lardner's *The Story of a Wonder Man*. *Fiesta*, the British edition of *The Sun Also Rises*, is published by Jonathan Cape in London on June 9. This edition omits the quotes from Gertrude Stein and Ecclesiastes included in the American version of the book.

July–August: The Hemingways return to Pamplona, Spain, for the Fiesta of San Fermín. During the second week of July, they travel to San Sebastian. By the next week, they are in Valencia and stay at the Hotel Inglés until July 31. Ernest is reading proofs of *Men Without Women*. Ernest's story "Fifty Grand" is published in the *Atlantic*'s July issue. It will be included in his new book of short stories. "Cinquante mille dollars," the French translation of "Fifty Grand," is printed in the *Nouvelle Revue Francaise* on August 1. Hemingway's translator is Ott de Weymer, a pseudonym for Georges Duplaix. Ernest and Pauline stay at the Penson Aguilar in Madrid from August 1 through 4 and then travel to La Coruna. By mid-August, they are in Santiago de Compostela where they will remain through the end of the month. "Hills Like White Elephants," included in *Men Without Women*, makes its first appearance in print in the August number of *transition*. On August 31, Hemingway writes to Max Perkins and mentions that Hadley will be in New York and will check with the editor about royalties on *The Sun Also Rises*. Ernest notes that to date he has never received royalties from any of his writing.

September: Ernest and Pauline leave for Valencia on the first day of the month and travel on to Hendaye, France, where they stay for two weeks. Ernest writes his father on September 14 to tell him about his marriage to Pauline. In the letter, Hemingway tells his father that he and Pauline did not commit adultery. He discusses Bumby, whom Clarence Hemingway had recently met for the first time. Ernest also addresses his father and mother's attitude towards his work. Hemingway begins work on a new novel, which carries the working title, *Jimmy Breen and A New Slain Knight*, set in Chicago and New York. The Hemingways return to Paris after the middle of the month. Ernest borrows Glenway Wescott's *The Grandmothers* from Shakespeare and Company.

October: *Men Without Women* is published on October 14 by Charles Scribner's Sons in New York. The collection of stories contains "The Undefeated," "In Another Country," "Hills Like White Elephants," "The Killers," "Che Ti Dice La Patria?", "Fifty Grand," "A Simple Inquiry," "Ten Indians," "A Canary for One," "An Alpine Idyll," "A Pursuit Race," "To-day Is Friday," "Banal Story," and "Now I Lay Me." Max Perkins forwards a negative review to Hemingway written by Virginia Woolf in the *New York Herald Tribune*. Ernest is angry about the reviews and asks Perkins to hold back on sending others until after Christmas. There are other bad notices of the book. Pauline is now pregnant. Ernest is working on his new novel and experimenting with the third-person narrative. He calls the book a modern *Tom Jones*. During the month, he meets Sinclair Lewis while on a six-day trip to attend bicycle races in Berlin. Late in October, Hadley and Bumby return to Paris. Ernest and Pauline begin to make plans to return to the United States. *Time and Western Man* by Wyndham Lewis and *Barnum's Own Story* by Phineas Taylor Barnum are among the books Ernest reads during the month. An article "The Real Spaniard" appears in the *Boulevarder* in October. Hemingway claims the piece was rewritten by editor Arthur Moss. Sales of *The Sun Also Rises* now stand at 23,000.

November–December: Hemingway has written 23 chapters, about one-third of the planned length, of his new novel. During November, he borrows Thornton Wilder's *The Bridge of San Luis Rey* from Shakespeare and Company. On December 7, he takes Feodor Dostoyevsky's *The Gambler and Other Stories* and *The Insulted and The Injured* from the lending library. Pauline, Ernest, and Bumby leave Paris for Switzerland on December 12. An accident occurs during the first night. While being helped in the bathroom, Bumby sticks his finger into Ernest's eye and cuts the pupil with his fingernail. Hemingway's vision, now defective in both eyes, is quite blurred. The following day, the three arrive in Gstaad where Ernest will remain through the end of January, 1928. At the end of the year, sales figures for *Men Without Women* stand at 15,000 copies. A one-sentence excerpt from Chapter Four of *The Sun Also Rises* appears in the *Golden Book* magazine in December.

1928

Prose Models: For Use with Classes in English Composition ("Big Two-Hearted River," Part One, included)

Anthologie de la poésie américaine (French translation of EH's "Montparnasse" is included)

Short Story Writing ("The Killers" is reprinted)

O. Henry Memorial Award Prize Stories of 1927 (second-prize winner, "The Killers," is included)

Le Batailleur (French translation of short story, "The Battler")

Cinquante mille dollars (French translation of "Fifty Grand" and five other short stories)

Fiesta (German translation of *The Sun Also Rises*)

Men Without Women (British edition of collection of short stories)

"Soldaten Zu Hause" (German translation of short story, "Soldier's Home")

"Le village indien" (French translation of short story, "Indian Camp")

January–February: Ernest is in Gstaad until January 31. Bumby and Pauline are with him through most of his stay. Ernest's work is appearing in various formats including textbooks and anthologies. Translations of his work are increasing. Generally, his German translator is Annemarie Horschitz, who translates *The Sun Also Rises* for Rowohlt publishers in Berlin. His French translators include Ott de Weymer (a pseudonym for Georges Duplaix) and Jean Georges Auriol. The collection of short stories (*Cinquante mille dollars*) is translated by the former and published by Editions de la Nouvelle Revue Francaise. The poetry anthology, which includes "Montparnasse," is published by Simon Kra in Paris and edited by Eugene Jolas. Hemingway's British publisher is Jonathan Cape. Two nonfiction works published this year include discussions of Hemingway's work. The first is *Paris, Salons, Cafés, Studios: Being Social, Artistic and Literary Memories* by Sisley Huddleston, published by Lippincott in Philadelphia (under the title *Bohemian Literary and Social Life in Paris*, by Harrap in London).The second is *By Way of Art: Criticisms of Music, Literature, Painting, Sculpture and the Dance* by Paul Rosenfeld, published by Coward McCann in New York. Hemingway's story "The Battler" appears in a translation by Jean Georges Auriol in the January-February issue of *Revue Européene*. In a letter to James Joyce on January 30, Hemingway discusses his recent eye injury and tells Joyce that for ten days he had impaired vision, which enabled him to sympathize with Joyce's plight. The following day, Pauline and Bumby return to Paris while Ernest goes on a short skiing trip to Lenk and Adelboden. He rejoins his family in Paris in early February. Upon his return, he finds the water pipes frozen in their apartment. After living without heat for a week, Ernest becomes ill. He tries, unsuccessfully, to work on a short story. During February, he reads *Lawrence and the Arabs* by Robert Graves, *The Torrents of Spring* by Turgenev, *Recollections of the Irish War* by Darrell Figgis, *The Riddle of the Irish* by John Chartres Maloney, *The Emperor Jones* by Eugene O'Neill, and *The Magic Mountain* by Thomas Mann. These books are borrowed from the lending library at Shakespeare and Company.

March: In the early days of March, Hemingway begins working on a short story about his war experiences in 1918. (This will develop into *A Farewell to Arms*.) He stops his work on the story and returns to the abortive Jimmy Breen novel. After having written 22 chapters, totalling approximately 45,000 words, Ernest puts aside the novel and returns to the story he began earlier in the month. He borrows, from Shakespeare and Company, *The Wonder Book of the Wild*, edited by Harry Golding on March 3 and Emil Ludwig's *Genius and Character*, in translation, on March 8. Within a few days, Hemingway is taken to the American Hospital at Neuilly for treatment of injuries caused when the skylight in his bathroom falls on his head. Nine stitches are necessary for head injuries. Pauline and Ernest begin to discuss leaving Paris again. John Dos Passos has told Ernest about the Florida Keys. The Hemingways book passage and sail to Havana aboard the *R.M.S. Orita* in late March.

April–May: After their arrival in Havana, Ernest and Pauline board a boat for the 100-mile trip to Key West, Florida. They make arrangements to stay at the Trevor and Morris apartment building on Simonton Street for six weeks. Ernest begins a schedule of writing in the morning and fishing in the afternoon. He is working on *A Farewell to Arms*. New acquaintances include fishing guide Bra Saunders; Josie Russell, the owner of Sloppy Joe's bar on Green Street in Key West; machinist J. B. Sullivan, a bartender called Skinner; and Charles Thompson, who owns a fishhouse, a cigarbox factory, a ship's chandlery, an icehouse, a hardware store, and a tackle shop. Ernest becomes closest to Thompson. To economize, Ernest exchanges the fish he catches for bait and gasoline to continue fishing. By mid-April, 19,000 copies of *Men Without Women* have been sold, but Ernest receives little income from his writing. Pauline's wealthy uncle, Gus Pfeiffer, helps the Hemingways financially. Dr. and Mrs. Clarence Hemingway visit Pauline and Ernest in Key West. It is their first meeting with the new Mrs. Hemingway. His father's ill health is apparent to Ernest during their visit. On April 20, Jonathan Cape publishes the British edition of *Men Without Women* in London. Ernest continues his work on *A Farewell to Arms*. The Hemingways are visited by John Dos Passos, Waldo Pierce, and Bill Smith in mid-May. The three guests stay at the Overseas Hotel in Key West. On a fishing trip with guide Bra Saunders, Ernest hears the story of a Spanish liner, the *Val Banera*, which ran aground in quicksand near Key West during a hurricane on September 9, 1919. Saunders found the ship first and tried to break the porthole glass to get at the valuables aboard. Five hundred passengers had been aboard; there were no survivors. Ernest will use the incident in his story "After the Storm," written four years later. Towards the end of May, the Hemingways leave for Pauline's hometown, Piggott, Arkansas. Ernest gets on well with his mother-in-law, but dislikes the town of Piggott.

June–July: "Le village indien," a translation of Ernest's story "Indian Camp" by Ott de Weymer (Georges Duplaix) appears in the June 1 issue of *Nouvelle Revue Francaise*. Ernest contacts his father about using the family cabin in Northern Michigan. His father advises that he and Pauline go to Kansas City or St. Louis instead until their child is born. The Hemingways decide to take Dr. Hemingway's advice and travel to Kansas City, where they stay with Malcolm and Ruth Lowry in their home on Indian Lane. By mid-June, Ernest has completed 311 manuscript pages of *A Farewell to Arms*. He is considering going west to finish the novel after the child's birth. Patrick Hemingway, Ernest's second son, is born on June 28 in the Research Hospital in Kansas City, Missouri. The delivery, by Caesarian section, is difficult for Pauline. She will stay in the hospital for 20 days. In the third week of July, after Pauline's release from the hospital, the three Hemingways travel to Piggott, Arkansas. By July 23, Ernest reports to Max Perkins that he is on page 468 of his novel. Two days later, Hemingway leaves for Kansas City, where he meets with Bill Horne for the drive to Wyoming. On July 28, he and Horne leave for Wyoming and arrive in the western state two days later. Upon arrival, Horne and Hemingway check into the Folly Ranch, located near the Bighorn mountains. The dude ranch is too commercial for Ernest's tastes.

August–September: Ernest leaves the Folly Ranch on August 3 and drives to Sheridan, Wyoming. After staying at the Sheridan Inn for four days, he moves to Eleanor Donnelley's Lower Ranch near the town. He establishes a pattern of writing in the morning and drinking each night. On August 18, Pauline joins her husband at the ranch. Patrick stays with his grandparents in Piggott, Arkansas. Ernest writes his friend Waldo Pierce on August 23 and tells him that he has completed the first draft of his novel. The manuscript is 600 pages long. Ernest takes Pauline to meet a French family living in Sheridan, who make and sell wine. They are Charles and Alice Moncini and their children, August and Lucien. Ernest will include the family in his story "Wine of Wyoming" in 1930. Pauline and Ernest move to the Spear-O-Wigwam dude ranch, which is located close to Sheridan and by a Crow Indian Reservation. The ranch is owned by Willis Spear. The Hemingways leave Sheridan and travel through the state. One of their stops is to see Owen Wister, author of *The Virginian*, in Shell. Wister had read and admired *The Sun Also Rises* prior to their meeting. Ernest and Pauline travel through the Grand Tetons, the Snake River, Jackson Hole, and Casper before beginning their return trip to Piggott to pick up Patrick. After a stop in Kansas City, the Hemingways continue on to Piggott, Arkansas, where they remain for a month. Ernest receives a royalty check for $3700, which he acknowledges in a letter to Max Perkins on September 28.

October–November: Ernest and Pauline stay in Piggott through most of October. Ernest is physically active but is not writing. Both begin to feel homesick for Europe and the Florida Keys. They make plans to spend winter in Key West and have Bumby join them. On October 11, Ernest makes a statement to Perkins about his feelings towards Zelda and Scott Fitzgerald. Scott's trouble, he asserts, is mainly due to Zelda. The two writers are still close at this time and maintain a steady correspondence. Towards the end of October, Pauline and Ernest go to Chicago. They plan to return to Piggott in mid-November to pick up Patrick and return to Key West. Their agenda includes visits to Chicago, Massachusetts, and New York. The Hemingways stay at the Whitehall Hotel in Chicago during the last week of October. For the first time in five years, Ernest visits his family in Oak Park, Illinois. While at the Art Institute of Chicago, Ernest is struck by the paintings of Winslow Homer. Ernest receives an offer from Max Perkins for serial rights to the new novel. Sight unseen, *Scribner*'s magazine offers to pay Hemingway $10,000 to serialize his new work, beginning in the spring of 1929. This is the largest amount of money Ernest has yet made from his writing. While in the eastern United States, Ernest and Pauline visit Archibald and Ada MacLeish at their farm in Conway, Massachusetts. In New York, Hemingway sees painters Waldo Pierce and Mike Strater and Max Perkins. On November 17, Ernest and Pauline attend a Princeton–Yale football game with Mike Strater and Zelda and Scott Fitzgerald. The following day, the Hemingways board a train, the *Spirit of St. Louis*, bound for Chicago. After a stop in Piggott, Arkansas, to retrieve their son, they drive home to Key West. By the end of the month, they are settled into a rental house at 1100 South Street.

December: Ernest returns to New York to meet his son, Bumby, who will be spending the winter in Key West. In New York, he sees writers Lincoln Steffens and Ring Lardner. Ernest and Bumby board the *Havana Special* on December 6. In Trenton, New Jersey, a telegram from Ernest's sister, Carol, is waiting for him. It carries the news that his father, Clarence Edmonds Hemingway, died that morning. Ernest leaves Bumby in care of a porter on the train headed south. He wires Max Perkins, F. Scott Fitzgerald, and Mike Strater, asking that $100 be wired to the North Philadelphia train station. Fitzgerald responds first and has the money waiting for Ernest by evening. Ernest leaves from the station aboard an all-night train to Chicago. On December 7, when he arrives in Oak Park, he learns that his father shot himself. Mrs. Hemingway, her son Leicester, and the family's cook, Louise, were in the house when the shooting occurred. Illness and financial worries appear to have been Mr. Hemingway's reason for suicide. A letter from Ernest to his father, written on his way to New York, in which he tried to boost his father's spirits, was never seen by Dr. Hemingway. Grace Hemingway knew how to contact her son only after reading the letter. Dr. Clarence Hemingway's funeral is held on December 8. Now the head of the extended Hemingway family, Ernest feels obligated to help ease his mother's financial strain. In a letter to Max Perkins on December 16, Hemingway explains his new responsibility to his editor and tells him that his father was the one he cared about most. Ernest ends the year in Key West working on revisions of his new novel. He decides on the title, taken from a poem by George Peel: *A Farewell to Arms.*

1929

The Dance of the Machines: The American Short Story and the Industrial Age (Chapters VI and VIII of *in our time* included)

Present-Day American Short Stories ("The Undefeated" reprinted)

Männer (German translation of *Men Without Women*)

Og solen går sin gång (Norwegian translation of *The Sun Also Rises*)

Och solen går sin gång (Swedish translation of *The Sun Also Rises*)

"Valentine" (poem)

A Farewell to Arms (novel; published in book form in America and England, and serialized)

"Les Collines sont commes des elephants blancs" (French translation of short story, "Hills Like White Elephants")

"Drei Tage Sturm" (German translation of short story, "The Three-Day Blow")

January–February: Hemingway is in Key West working on revisions of *A Farewell to Arms*. In a letter to Max Perkins on January 22, he notes that he has completed the manuscript. Critical attention is increasing. Mention of Ernest's work is made in four books this year. They are *Essay Reviews* by Schuyler Ashley, published by Lowell Press in Kansas City, Missouri; *Contemporary American Literature: Bibliographies and Study Outlines* by Edith Rickert and John Matthews Manly, published by Harcourt, Brace in New York; *An Hour of the American Novel* by Grant Overton, published by Lippincott in Philadelphia; and *A Bookman's Daybook* by Burton Rascoe, published by Liveright in New York. Translations of Hemingway's work appear in Norwegian (translated by Gunnar Larsen for Gyldendal in Oslo, Norway) and Swedish (translated by Bertel Gripenberg for Swedish publisher, Holger Schildt) as well as in French and German. Also rising is the number of anthologies which include Hemingway's fiction. Along with his story "The Killers," a letter on his writing habits in Paris and Madrid, written by Ernest on January 16, 1928, appears in *Creating the Short Story: A Symposium-Anthology*, with an introduction by Henry Goodman, published by Harcourt, Brace in New York in February. Max Perkins stays in Key West from February 2 through 9. On a working vacation, he reads *A Farewell to Arms*. Although Perkins is enthusiastic about the novel, he has apprehensions about serializing it in *Scribner*'s magazine because of the profanity. After returning to New York, Perkins cables Hemingway with the news that Robert Bridges of *Scribner*'s has decided to serialize the book. Bridges, who doesn't find the language objectionable, will pay Hemingway $16,000 for first serial rights, the largest sum the magazine has yet paid for such rights.

March–April: Ernest receives opinions on *A Farewell to Arms* from his visiting friends, Mike Strater, Waldo Pierce, and John Dos Passos. The three, including Dos Passos, who Ernest felt would be his harshest critic, agree on the high quality of the novel. Ernest writes his mother on March 11. He encloses $100 and explains that he will send that amount on a regular basis along with particular tax payments as they come due. He expresses his view that his uncle George had helped to kill his father and should help Grace financially as a form of reparation for the premature death. He warns his mother that he has not yet written stories about the family, but just might do so now that his father is dead. Ernest's friend from Michigan and later Chicago, Katy Smith, is visiting him in Key West. During her visit, Ernest opens a crate from his mother at Katy's prodding. Among the contents are the gun which his father has used to shoot himself and paintings by Grace, which she would like Ernest to sell when he returns to Paris. Ernest has previously requested the gun. On April 4, the four Hemingways and Ernest's sister, Madelaine (called "Sunny"), sail for Paris from Havana aboard the North German liner *York*. After docking at Boulogne on April 21, they move back into their apartment at 6 rue Ferou. Ernest begins to correct the proofs of *A Farewell to Arms*. After hearing that the Fitzgeralds are returning to Paris, Hemingway asks Max Perkins not to give them his address. Ernest will see Scott in public places but does not want Scott in his home because of his drunkenness. This is the first sign that the friendship between the two writers is deteriorating. Ernest begins to use the lending library at Shakespeare and Company once more. He borrows Lord Alfred Bruce Douglas' autobiography and Matthew Josephson's *Zola and His Time*.

May–June: The first serial installment of *A Farewell to Arms* appears in the May issue of *Scribner*'s magazine. Portions of the novel run in the magazine through October. Towards the end of May, Ernest makes final revisions on the last three paragraphs of *A Farewell to Arms*. Ernest is upset when he learns that Owen Wister, author of *The Virginian*, was allowed to read proof pages of the novel and that he has suggested revisions. He is also annoyed at Robert Bridges' changes in the serialized version in *Scribner*'s. "Valentine," a poem addressed "For a Mr. Lee Wilson Dodd and Any of His Friends Who Want It," is published in the final issue of the *Little Review* in May. Dodd had previously written a negative review of *Men Without Women*. This poem will be reprinted in *The Little Review Anthology*, edited by Margaret Anderson, in 1953 and included in an edition of Hemingway's *Collected Poems*. Borrowings from Shakespeare and Company's library in May include *The Diary of Dostoyevsky*'s *Wife* by Anna Dostoyevsky and *Life in the Middle Ages*, Volumes I—III, edited by George Gordon Coulton. Canadian writer Morley Callaghan and his wife Loretto come to Paris. (Callaghan and Hemingway first met while they were writing for the *Toronto Star* in 1920.) The two writers begin to compete in boxing matches. It is during June that a match, timed by F. Scott Fitzgerald, occurs. Engrossed in watching the two fight, Fitzgerald lets the round run for four minutes. This incident will be exaggerated in later accounts and cause friction between Fitzgerald, Hemingway, and Callaghan. Hemingway corresponds with Max Perkins about the profanity in *A Farewell to Arms* on June 7. He suggests using dashes with specific letters to imply the meaning of a possibly objectionable word rather than simply deleting the word. Ernest borrows, from the lending library at Shakespeare and Company, *A Bookman*'s *Daybook* by Burton Rascoe, *Three Lives* by Gertrude Stein, *Contemporary Russian Literature, 1881–1925* by Dmitrii Svyatopolk, *Round the Green Cloth* by Samuel Beach Chester, and *Politicians and the War, 1914–1926* by William Aitken Beaverbrook. Ernest and Pauline leave for Spain at the end of the month.

July–August: The Hemingways attend the Fiesta of San Fermín in Pamplona in early July. They visit Ernest's friend, painter Joan Míro, in Montroig during the following week and continue on to follow the bullfights in Huesca, Lérida, and Tarragona. Ernest is 30 years old on July 21. He is having trouble writing. Ernest and Pauline arrive in Valencia on July 25. They stay at the Hotel Regina until August 3. On July 26, Hemingway writes Max Perkins that he intends to dedicate *A Farewell to Arms* to Pauline's uncle, Gus Pfeiffer, who had helped smooth relations between Ernest and Pauline's parents before their marriage and has assisted him financially. An agreement is reached on the use of dashes in place of obscene words to prevent the censorship of *A Farewell to Arms*. Ernest receives news that his friends Katy Smith and John Dos Passos have been married recently in Ellsworth, Maine. After a stopover in Santiago, the Hemingways leave for Madrid to see a new bullfighter from Brooklyn, New York, named Sidney Franklin.

September: During the first two weeks of the month, the Hemingways are in Madrid where they watch and befriend Sidney Franklin. (The New York bullfighter had made his debut in Seville in June. Ernest had been hearing about him since that time.) On September 4, Hemingway writes to F. Scott Fitzgerald and urges him to finish his new novel (*Tender Is the Night*). Ernest and Pauline arrive in Hendaye, France, on September 13 and after staying a week return to Paris. Ernest drives Morley and Loretto Callaghan to Chartres and visits the cathedral on September 25. *A Farewell to Arms* is published by Charles Scribner's Sons in New York on September 27. A limited edition of 510 numbered copies is published simultaneously with the first edition. The book is banned in Boston. Reviews, however, are the most favorable in Hemingway's writing career. Shortly after its publication, Hemingway meets Allen Tate at Sylvia Beach's Shakespeare and Company and gives him a copy of *A Farewell to Arms*. (Tate will praise the novel as Hemingway had hoped.) Borrowings from Sylvia Beach's lending library this month include the privately published edition of D. H. Lawrence's *Lady Chatterly's Lover*, Ludwig Renn's *War*, Turgenev's *A Sportsman's Sketches* and *On the Eve*, a volume on Sir Walter Raleigh, and Dostoyevsky's *The Idiot*. Hemingway's story "Hills Like White Elephants" is translated into French by Alice Turpin. It is published under the title "Les Collines sont comme des elephants blancs" on September 20 in *Bifur*.

October–December: The American stock market crashes on October 29. By mid-month, sales of *A Farewell to Arms* stand at 28,000. Save the effects on sales after the Wall Street disaster, Hemingway is virtually untouched by the crash. The British edition of *A Farewell to Arms*, now a bestseller in America, is published by Jonathan Cape on November 11. Ernest and Guy Hickok go to Berlin to attend bicycle races in the middle of the month. After his return, Hemingway begins to work on an article on the bullfights for Henry Luce's new magazine, *Fortune*. He is to be paid $1000 for the 2500-word article. Archibald MacLeish is now an editor with *Fortune*. Ernest becomes furious when he reads the November issue of *Bookman* which carries an article attacking his work. The piece, written by Robert Herrick, draws an angry response in writing from Hemingway in which he threatens to spank the editor for printing it. A quite flattering profile of Ernest appears in the November 30 issue of *The New Yorker*. Dorothy Parker, the author of the article, erroneously intimates that Gilbert Seldes was responsible for rejecting Ernest's early work submitted to *Dial*. Annemarie Horschitz translates Hemingway's story "The Three-Day Blow" into German. It appears in the November issue of *Europaissche Revue*. (Horschitz is the translator of the German edition of *Men Without Women*, published by Rowohlt publishing company in Berlin in 1929 and titled *Männer*.) The story appears in the *Revue* under the name "Drei Tage Sturm." December is a tumultuous time for Ernest in relation to his friends. At a dinner with F. Scott Fitzgerald on December 9, Ernest learns that Robert McAlmon is spreading rumors about him. Ernest vows to retaliate physically. The *Denver Post* and the *New York Herald Tribune* print the story of the boxing match between Morley Callaghan and Hemingway and report that Ernest was knocked out during the round. Callaghan insists the *New York Herald Tribune* print a retraction. The newspaper agrees but in the meantime Hemingway convinces Fitzgerald, the timekeeper of the match, to send a collect cable to Callaghan demanding an apology. Writer Harry Crosby shoots himself on December 10 in New York. Although Hemingway was not close to Crosby, he is quite upset by his suicide. He writes a friendly letter to Fitzgerald and dismisses the whole episode of the Callaghan fight as being trivial. John and Katy

Dos Passos visit the Hemingways in Paris in mid-December. Towards the end of the month, the Dos Passoses, the Hemingways, Gerald and Sara Murphy, and Dorothy Parker go on a skiing trip to Switzerland.

1930

Kiki's *Memoirs* (pamphlet)

Great Short Stories of the War: England, France, Germany, America (short story, "In Another Country," included)

Armageddon: The World War in Literature (Chapter XXX of *A Farewell to Arms* reprinted under the title, "The Retreat from the Isonzo")

Great Modern Short Stories (Chapter IV of *in our time* and "The Three-Day Blow" included)

Je vous salue marie (French translation of story, "Now I Lay Me")

In einem andern Land (German translation of *A Farewell to Arms*)

Bu-ki yo, saraba (Japanese translation of *A Farewell to Arms*)

Farvel til våpnene (Norwegian translation of *A Farewell to Arms*)

"Bullfighting, Sport and Industry" (article)

Schluss damit Adieu Krieg! (serialized version of *A Farewell to Arms*, in German)

"Abenteuer in sommer" (German translation of story, "My Old Man")

"Wine of Wyoming" (short story)

"Modern Writers at Work" (excerpt on writing prose)

January–February: Discussions of Hemingway and his work appear in five books during the year. Prime among these are *My Thirty Years' War: An Autobiography* by Margaret C. Anderson, founder of the *Little Review*; *The Nineteen-twenties: Literature and Ideas in the Post-War Decade* by A. C. Ward; and *Moderne amerikansk Litteratur: 1920–1930* by Frederick Schyberg (published in Copenhagen, Denmark, by Gyldendalske Boghandel). On January 4, Ernest writes a note of apology to Morley Callaghan for the boxing-match mishap. (Despite this letter, the friendship between the two remains damaged.)

Hemingway writes an introduction to the memoirs of Kiki of Montparnasse, an artist's model. The Hemingways leave Paris on January 10, sailing aboard *La Bourdonnais* for the United States, where they will remain through the year. After a two-day stopover in New York, Ernest and Pauline continue on to Key West. In early February, they move into a rental house on Pearl Street. Ernest extends invitations to Archibald and Ada MacLeish, Mike Strater, John and Josephine Herrmann, and Max Perkins for a fishing trip in the Tortuga and the Marquesa islands. All but the MacLeishes accept.

March–April: The fishing trip takes place during mid-March. Accompanying Ernest are Max Perkins, Mike Strater, and John Herrmann. Bra Saunders acts as the group's guide. (It is reputed that Max Perkins, much taken with the area, asks Ernest why he doesn't write about it. Perkins plants the idea to do so in Ernest's mind.) The fishing party becomes stormbound 70 nautical miles from Key West for 17 days. Towards the end of this period, they encounter Eldridge Johnson, an executive with the Victrola Corporation, and have dinner aboard his yacht. Hemingway's article "Bullfighting, Sport and Industry" appears in the debut issue of *Fortune* magazine in March. The feature on the economics of the sport is illustrated with color and black-and-white reproductions of work by Goya, Manet, and Zuloaga and carries an appendix with notes on bullfighting. Ernest learns that *A Farewell to Arms* has been added to the United States presidential library in April. His article in *Fortune* rekindles the idea of writing a book on bullfighting. Ernest begins to make plans for a safari in Africa. Gus Pfeiffer, Pauline's uncle, has offered to finance the trip. On April 6, Ernest accepts the post of honorary vice president of the Mark Twain Society. John and Katy Dos Passos visit the Hemingways in Key West in mid-April. They bring news that Sidney Franklin has been badly gored in a bullfight in Madrid. Ernest and Pauline and the Dos Passoses go to the Tortugas. Captain Louis Henry Cohn, a bookseller from New York, approaches Hemingway to write a foreword or epilogue for a bibliography he has compiled of Ernest's work. Cohn offers to pay Hemingway $350 for his addition to the book. On April 23, Ernest replies to Cohn that he must see the bibliography before making his decision.

May–July: The *Frankfurter Zeitung* runs the first installment of "Schluss damit Adieu Krieg!" on May 8. The serialized
version of *A Farewell to Arms*, translated into German by Annemarie Horschitz, appears in the magazine through July 16.
Ernest has begun to work on his bullfighting book and on May
20 reports to Mike Strater that he has completed 74 manuscript
pages. Ernest's writing slackens while Archibald MacLeish is
visiting in Key West. He writes the story, "Wine of Wyoming,"
towards the end of the month and sends it to Max Perkins on
May 31. *Kiki's Memoirs*, published by Edward Titus/At the Sign
of the Black Manikin Press in Paris and including an introduction by Hemingway, appears in June. It is barred from the
United States on the grounds of obscenity. "Wine of Wyoming"
is accepted for publication in *Scribner's* magazine. Ernest receives this news and that he will be paid $600 for the story on
June 3. "Abenteur im sommer," the German translation of "My
Old Man," is published in the *Berliner Tageblatt* on June 8.
Late in the month, the Hemingways leave Key West. Pauline
and Patrick stay in Piggott, Arkansas, while Ernest continues
on to meet his son, Bumby, in New York. During his brief stay
in New York, Hemingway consults Lewis Galantière about the
French he uses in "Wine of Wyoming." Ernest and Bumby leave
for Piggott on June 24. On the same date, Hemingway notifies
Captain Cohn that he does not wish to write the foreword for
the upcoming bibliography on his works, nor does he want to
have any further dealings with the project. After a week's stay,
Ernest, Pauline, and Bumby drive to Wyoming. Patrick is left
behind with his grandparents. The three check into the Nordquist Ranch on July 13. Located just inside the Wyoming state
line, the ranch is situated twelve miles from Cooke City, Montana, near the Clarks Fork of the Yellowstone River. The ranch
is owned by Lawrence and Olive Nordquist. Ernest meets Floyd
Allington, Ivan Wallace, and Leland Stanford "Chub" Weaver.
(The last will appear as a character in *For Whom the Bell Tolls*
in 1940.)

August–September: Ernest is working on the bullfight book
(Death in the Afternoon). He divides his time between writing
and a new interest—bear hunting. He and Ivan Wallace begin
to set traps for bears that have been killing local cattle. Bill
Horne and his wife, Frances, referred to as "Bunny," come to

Wyoming for their honeymoon. They stay at the Nordquist Ranch with the Hemingways from August 8 through 22. While the Hornes are visiting, Ernest is going back over *In Our Time*. Charles Scribner's Sons is planning to reissue the collection of short stories, with a preface by Edmund Wilson. On August 12, Hemingway writes to Max Perkins and tells him that he has written 40,000 words on *Death in the Afternoon*. Ernest has an accident while horseback riding and goes to Dr. True-blood in Cody, Wyoming, for treatment for a long gash on the left side of his chin. The following day, Ernest kills the bear he and Ivan Wallace have been baiting. "Wine of Wyoming" appears in the August issue of *Scribner*'s magazine. A prefatory note explains that it is the first short story written by Hemingway since *A Farewell to Arms*. During September, Laurence Stalling's stage adaptation of *A Farewell to Arms* opens and closes after a three-week run. Pauline and Bumby leave for New York on September 13. Ernest begins a hunting trip through Squaw and Timber creeks, near Pilot Mountain, that will last until September 28. The length of his manuscript is now 200 pages. John Dos Passos notifies Ernest that he will be coming to Wyoming to see him. *Modern Writers at Work*, published by the Macmillan Company in New York in September, contains an excerpt written by Hemingway on writing prose, a facsimile manuscript page from *A Farewell to Arms*, and a reprint of the story "Cat in the Rain."

October: Still working on *Death in the Afternoon*, Ernest is staying alone in Wyoming. He and Ivan Wallace hunt around Crandall Creek on October 14, and Ernest sees his first grizzly bear. He also encounters John Staib, a German who lives alone in the woods. (Staib will be alluded to in *Green Hills of Africa* in 1935.) John Dos Passos arrives in Billings, Montana, on October 21. Ernest meets him there and on the following day they go on a hunting trip. Dos Passos's eyesight renders him a poor hunter. Nevertheless, the trip through Crandall and Timber creeks and in the wilderness surrounding the Crazy Lakes lasts ten days. Floyd Allington, Dos Passos, and Ernest leave for the Clarks Fork Valley, the first leg of the trip which will end in Key West. They spend the last night in October sleeping outdoors in Yellowstone Park. *In Our Time* is issued by Charles Scribner's Sons in New York on October 24.

November–December: Hemingway is injured in an automobile accident 20 miles outside of Billings, Montana, on November 1. He suffers a spiral fracture three inches above the
elbow and is taken to St. Vincent's Hospital in Billings, run
by the Sisters of Charity of Leavenworth. Ernest stays in Room
422. John Dos Passos wires Pauline Hemingway. She arrives
by train from Piggott, Arkansas two days before surgery is
performed on Ernest. The break near the elbow requires bind-
ing with kangaroo tendons. Dos Passos stays on in Billings
until after the surgery is completed. Hemingway has to put
his writing aside. Pauline offers to take dictation so Ernest can
continue working on *Death in the Afternoon*. Hemingway declines because he does not feel able to write without seeing the
words on paper. (Pauline takes dictation for all of Hemingway's
correspondence through his hospital stay.) The manuscript,
which Ernest had hoped to finish by Christmas, stands at close
to two hundred and fifty pages. Also affected are the plans
Hemingway has made for an African safari. The trip with Archibald MacLeish, Mike Strater, and Charles Thompson will
have to be postponed. On November 5, Sinclair Lewis is awarded
the Nobel Prize. Ernest is upset that the award was not given
to James Joyce or Ezra Pound instead. (He discusses the matter
in a letter to Guy Hickok on December 5 and takes consolation
in the fact that the award at least did not go to Theodore
Dreiser.) During the last week in November, Hemingway reads
Edmund Wilson's introduction to Scribner's reissue of *In Our
Time* and although the content is favorable and accurate, he
is angry. The worsening American economy is reflected in the
diminishing sales of Hemingway's books. The first sale of film
rights to one of his works helps to offset the drop in book sales.
In a letter to Guy Hickok on December 5, Ernest reports the
details of the sale of *A Farewell to Arms* to Hollywood. The
outright film rights brought in $80,000. After taxes and agent's
fees, Ernest realizes only $24,000. (Additionally, this year he
had received $750 for the rights to adapt the novel to the stage.)
Despite his negative response to Sinclair Lewis's receiving the
Nobel Prize, Ernest hears that upon notification, Lewis had
cabled Scribner's to congratulate the firm for publishing two
of the most superb novels in recent years. Lewis names the
two: Thomas Wolfe's *Look Homeward, Angel* and Ernest Hem-

ingway's *A Farewell to Arms*. During his hospital stay, Ernest befriends Earl Snook, an associate of western artist Will James, and Sister Florence, a nurse at St. Vincent's. It is from the stay that Ernest gathers material for his short story "The Gambler, the Nun, and the Radio." Archibald MacLeish flies out to Billings at Pauline's request during the month of December. Hemingway's response is to accuse his friend of coming out to witness his death. Ernest is released from the hospital on December 21. He and Pauline travel to Piggott, Arkansas. On December 28, Hemingway writes a letter to Max Perkins in which he praises Archibald MacLeish's writing and urges the editor to sign him. MacLeish, however, will eventually sign an agreement with Houghton Mifflin Publishing Company. The Hemingways stay in Piggott, Arkansas, through the end of the year.

1931

Great American Short Stories ("Fifty Grand" and "My Old Man" included)

Les Romanciers américains (French translation of short story, "Now I Lay Me," included)

The Twenty-five Finest Short Stories ("My Old Man" included)

Best Short Stories of the War ("In Another Country" included)

Back to Montparnasse: Glimpses of Broadway in Bohemia (First reprint of "Neo-Thomist Poem." In this book by Sisley Huddleston, the title of the poem is spelled incorrectly, just as it had been in its original publication in *Exile*, Number 1, in 1927.)

Omnibus: Almanach auf das Jahr 1931 (Includes the first chapter of *A Farewell to Arms* which is printed in English)

Pozegnanie z broniq (*A Farewell to Arms* translated into Polish by Zbigniew Grabowski)

"They All Made Peace—What Is Peace?" (poem reprinted in article by Louis Zukofsk)

The New Yorker Scrapbook (Contains reprint of article "My Own Life: After Reading the Second Volume of Frank Harris's 'My Life'")

"The Sea Change" (short story)

January–February: Seven books containing critical appraisal, biographical material, or bibliographical information on Hemingway are published during the year. Victor Llona's *Les Romanciers américains* couples an essay on Ernest with the French translation of his story "Now I Lay Me." Critical mention of Hemingway's work is made by Aldous Huxley in his book *Music at Night and Other Essays* and Lincoln Steffens recounts their association in the 1920s in his autobiography. Edward J. O'Brien, who has included Ernest's short stories in several anthologies, discusses his contribution to the form in *The Advance of the American Short Story. Checklists of Twentieth-Century Authors* by Paul Romaine and Harry Schwartz contains a listing of Hemingway first editions through 1931. *Living Authors: A Book of Biographies*, edited by Dilly Tante (Stanley V. Kunick), includes a biographical sketch of Hemingway. Louis Henry Cohn publishes *A Bibliography of the Works of Ernest Hemingway* in August. On January 3, the Hemingways leave Piggott, Arkansas, and return to Key West, Florida. The family moves into a rental house on the corner of United and Whitehead streets. A steady stream of visitors and a still-ailing arm prevent Ernest from writing. Guests include Carol and Grace Hemingway, Virginia Pfeiffer, Leland Stanford "Chub" Weaver, Lawrence and Olive Nordquist, and John and Josie Herrmann. "They All Made Peace—What Is Peace?" is reprinted in *Poetry: A Magazine of Verse* on February 23 in an article by Louis Zukofsk. The poem first appeared in the *Little Review* in the Spring 1923 issue.

March–April: Ernest spends most of March fishing in the Dry Tortugas. On one trip he is joined by Maxwell Perkins, John Herrmann, and new acquaintances, Pat and Maude Morgan. It is during this trip that Hemingway meets Gregorio Fuentes. During April, Pauline learns of her second pregnancy. The child is expected in November. Plans are made for a trip to Europe in the summer, followed by travel to Kansas City, Missouri, for the birth. Pauline's uncle, Gus Pfeiffer, purchases the house at 907 Whitehead Street as a gift to her. The deed is dated April 29, 1931.

May–September: Ernest sails alone from Havana aboard the *S.S. Volendam* bound for Vigo, Spain. Patrick and Pauline will sail from New York and meet Hemingway in Paris. While sailing, Ernest encounters seven Spanish priests who have been exiled from Mexico. Thus begins his interest in the developing revolution in Spain. After arriving in Vigo, Hemingway continues on to Madrid where he is reunited with bullfighter Sidney Franklin. The political climate in the city offers little or no indication of the impending revolution. Ernest travels to Paris to meet Pauline and Patrick. While there, signs of the crippled American economy and its effect on Left Bank writers are evident to Hemingway. The Depression has yet to affect Ernest, however. Towards the end of May, the Hemingways return to Madrid. During their stay in the city, they reside at the Hotel Biarritz in the Calle Victoria, which is frequented by matadors. Among new acquaintances are Spanish painter Luis Quintanilla and *Chicago Tribune* reporter Jay Allen, both of whom are concerned with the upcoming Spanish revolution. In mid-June, 23,000 Carlists riot in Pamplona. On June 26, Hemingway writes to John Dos Passos and reports the unrest in Spain and discusses the elections which are to be held on June 28. Bumby joins his father and stepmother in Pamplona in early July for the fiesta. Ernest is working on the glossary and lexicography for *Death in the Afternoon* during August. During the same month, the first bibliography of his work is published by Random House in New York. Along with the listing of his writing, *A Bibliography of the Works of Ernest Hemingway* by Louis Henry Cohn, contains a facsimile of the manuscript of "Death of the Standard Oil Man" and a quote from Ernest in which he expresses his view on listing his early newspaper articles. In mid-September, the Hemingways return to Paris. Ernest has by this time written 18 chapters and the glossary for *Death in the Afternoon*. The book is not yet finished. During his stay in Paris, Ernest visits Sylvia Beach's Shakespeare and Company and borrows D. H. Lawrence's *The Virgin and the Gypsy* and a book on paganism. The Hemingways depart Europe aboard the *Ile de France*. Other passengers include Don and Bertha Stewart, who introduce the couple to Jane Mason, the wife of a Pan American Airways official, who resides in Cuba and will become a close friend of Ernest's. Pauline and Ernest arrive in New York on September 29.

October–December: Early in October, the Hemingways go to Conway, Massachusetts, to stay with Archibald and Ada MacLeish. During their stay, the four meet Waldo Pierce at a Harvard football game and Ernest is introduced to Professor Charles Townsend Copeland of the university. The Hemingways return to New York and Ernest meets with Maxwell Perkins to give the editor photographs from Spain for *Death in the Afternoon*. Another business meeting takes place with Louis Cohn, the bibliographer, who informs Hemingway that he has acquired the corrected typescript of *The Sun Also Rises* (this version of the novel still carries the opening section on Brett Ashley, Mike Campbell, and Robert Cohn that was eventually cut in the final form). Pauline and Ernest leave New York aboard the *Spirit of St. Louis* train for Kansas City, while Patrick is sent to stay with his grandparents in Piggott, Arkansas. Upon arrival in Kansas City, Missouri, in November, the Hemingways stay with Mr. and Mrs. Malcolm Lowry briefly. Shortly afterwards, the two move into the Riviera Apartments, located at 229 Ward Parkway, where Ernest begins to revise the first 18 chapters of *Death in the Afternoon*. Gregory Hancock Hemingway, Ernest's third son, is born on November 12, 1931. *The New Yorker Scrapbook*, published in November by Doubleday, Doran, and Company, includes a reprint of "My Own Life: After Reading the Second Volume of Frank Harris' 'My Life.'" The article first appeared in *The New Yorker* on February 12, 1927. On December 1, Ernest travels to Piggott, Arkansas, for a week of quail hunting. By the time he returns to Kansas City, Ernest has finished the final chapter of *Death in the Afternoon*. The Hemingways arrive home in Key West on December 19. Many distractions, including minor illnesses in the family, prevent Ernest from writing through the rest of the year. A short story, "The Sea Change," appears in *This Quarter*'s December issue which is edited by Edward W. Titus. The story is included in *Winner Take Nothing* in 1933.

1932

Salmagundi by William Faulkner and a Poem by Ernest Hemingway (reprint of poem, "Ultimately")

"After the Storm" (short story)

Death in the Afternoon (nonfiction book)

20 Best Short Stories in 20 Years as an Editor ("Fifty Grand" and letter from Hemingway included)

Americans Abroad: An Anthology (contains "Big Two-Hearted River")

Modern American Short Stories ("The Undefeated" reprinted)

Profile: An Anthology Collected in MCMXXXI (This collection, edited by Ezra Pound, includes "Neothomist Poem.")

The Omnibus of Sport ("The Undefeated" included)

Omnibus: Almanach auf das Jahr 1932 (contains poem, "Advice to a Son," in English, dated September, 1931; German publication)

L'adieu aux armes (*A Farewell to Arms* translated into French by Maurice-Edgar Coindreau. Deletions which appear in Scribner's edition are filled in by Hemingway in this Gallimard edition.)

In unserer Zeit (*In Our Time* translated into German by Annemarie Horschitz)

Farvel till vapnen (*A Farewell to Arms* translated into Swedish by Louis Renner)

"Mord på bestallning" ("The Killers" translated into Swedish)

A Farewell to Arms (first film adaptation of work by Hemingway)

January–February: Critical appraisal of Hemingway's fiction appears in six books during the year. Among these are *The Twentieth-Century Novel: Studies in Technique*; *The Little World: 1914 and After*; *The Story of American Literature*; *Scrittori anglo-americani d'oggi* (published in Milan); *At landvind* (published in Stockholm); and *American Literature: 1880–1930* (published simultaneously in New York and London). On January 5 and 6, Ernest writes to Max Perkins about having John Dos Passos and Archibald MacLeish work on the proof pages of *Death in the Afternoon* as a means of checking the Spanish spellings. Revisions on the book are completed by Hemingway on January 13. The following day, Ernest wires Perkins that he has finished. The editor notifies Hemingway that he has received his manuscript on January 20. Ernest is contacted by William Lengel late in January about excerpting *Death in the Afternoon* in *Cosmopolitan*. Lengel, acting as an agent for the magazine, has read the book in manuscript form. Ernest decides against the proposition, but agrees to sell his story "After the Storm" to *Cosmopolitan*. Ernest begins work on short stories and on February 7 reports to Max Perkins that he has completed three. The number of stories grows to seven by February 24. Hemingway is working on the group of stories for a new collection to be published in 1933 (*Winner Take Nothing*). When not writing, Ernest spends time fishing in the Dry Tortugas and begins making plans for an African safari, which Gus Pfeiffer has offered to finance. Archibald MacLeish, Mike Strater, and Charles Thompson are to accompany Ernest on the trip. Philip Percival is recommended to Hemingway as the best white hunter in Africa.

March–June: The title *Death in the Afternoon* is decided on by Hemingway during the spring while he is working on the final prepublication details of the book. On March 26, Ernest writes to John Dos Passos and tells him that he has sold his story "After the Storm" to *Cosmopolitan*. The first sale to the Hearst-owned publication brings Ernest $2700. Dos Passos had written Hemingway after reading *Death in the Afternoon* and suggested that he cut some of the more philosophical portions. On the whole, however, he felt the book was excellent. Making a mildly retaliatory gesture, Hemingway criticizes parts of Dos Passos' *1919*. Hemingway also expresses his views about writers and political systems (e.g., communism which Dos Passos ascribes to) and about how the writer should keep his distance from politics so that his writing remained unencumbered and grounded in reality. Ernest is dividing his time between fishing and working on *Death in the Afternoon*. In the third week of April, Hemingway travels from Key West to Havana, Cuba, with Joe Russell, owner of Sloppy Joe's Bar and of the fishing boat the *Anita*. Ernest stays at the Ambos Mundo Hotel, where, when not fishing, he works on proofs (deciding at this time to accept Dos Passos's suggestions for revisions). During his stay in Cuba, Ernest tries marlin fishing for the first time. "Mord på bestallning," the Swedish translation of "The Killers," appears in *Bonniers Litterara Magasin* in April. Hemingway is in Cuba through the third week of June. During May, Pauline comes over from Key West for two separate week-long visits. While she is in Havana, they see their friend Jane Mason. Another introduction, which becomes quite significant later in Ernest's life, is to a Cuban commercial fisherman named Carlos Gutierrez. (He will become the prototype for Santiago in *The Old Man and the Sea*.) "After the Storm" is published in *Cosmopolitan* in May. The Casanova Press of Milwaukee, Wisconsin, publishes *Salmagundi by William Faulkner and a poem by Ernest Hemingway* during the same month. Hemingway's poem "Ultimately" appears on the back cover of the book. His poem had originally been published with "Portrait," a poem by Faulkner, in *The Double Dealer* in June 1922. Ernest decides to postpone his trip to Africa in June. During the month, he again expresses his feeling that writers should remain apolitical in a letter to Midwestern bookseller Paul Romaine. In the third week of June, Ernest contracts pneumonia after an extended bout with a marlin he hooked and that eventually got away. He returns to Key West and continues his work on the galleys of *Death in the Afternoon*. On June 26 and 27, Ernest corresponds with Maxwell Perkins about his anger over seeing the slug, "Hemingway's Death," which the typesetter had placed on the galleys of his book. Ernest's superstitious nature causes the upset.

July–September: On July 2, Ernest and his sister, Carol, begin their drive from Key West to Piggott, Arkansas, where they will meet Pauline and continue on to Wyoming. The Hemingways arrive at the Nordquist Ranch on July 12. Ernest finishes reading the page proofs of *Death in the Afternoon* on July 26. During August, correspondence continues between Hemingway and bookseller Paul Romaine, who has been trying to nudge Ernest to the left politically. On August 9, Ernest writes an insulting letter to Romaine in which he calls him a parasitic hanger-on and insinuates that the bookseller is not unaware of the monetary gains he can make by pursuing their correspondence. Hemingway submits a short story, "Homage to Switzerland," to William Lengel at *Cosmopolitan* on August 15 (the three-part story will be rejected by the magazine but

purchased by *Scribner*'s and published in April 1933). Angered
by an article in *Hound & Horn* (July–September issue), Ernest
writes a letter to the editor on August 27. Gerald and Sara
Murphy arrive at the Nordquist Ranch with their children,
Honoria and Baoth, in early September and stay until the middle of the month. Ernest meets his friend from Key West, Charles
Thompson, in Cody, Wyoming, on September 11. They begin
the month-long hunting trip Thompson has come north for.
Pauline leaves Wyoming on September 22, while Ernest is
away hunting with Charles Thompson, Ivan Wallace, and Chub
Weaver. *Death in the Afternoon* is published by Charles Scrib-
ner's Sons in New York and London on September 23, 1932.

October–November: While Ernest is hunting in Wyoming,
the reviews of *Death in the Afternoon* begin to appear. On October 4, he returns to the Nordquist Ranch to read the first
notices that have been sent to him. One of the two reviews,
both unfavorable, is a copy of Robert M. Coates's *New Yorker*
article. Coates has criticized Hemingway for making deroga-
tory remarks about William Faulkner in the book. The following day, Ernest writes a letter to the reviewer objecting to his
remarks being construed in this way. (Hemingway's letter appears in Coates's book column in a November issue of *The New
Yorker*.) Ernest returns to Pilot Creek to resume hunting for
another week. On October 10, upon his return to the ranch, he
receives word from Max Perkins that from a publisher's point
of view the reviews of *Death in the Afternoon* have been good.
Ernest ends his stay in Wyoming by spending the last five days
hunting in Pilot Creek. It is during his last days of hunting
that he kills a 500-pound bear. On October 16, Hemingway
begins his drive back to Key West. After a stopover in Piggott,
Arkansas, he arrives in Florida on October 29. A favorable
quotation by Hemingway appears in an advertisement in *Contact* magazine for John Herrmann's *Summer Is Ended* in October. Ernest's rebuttal to Lawrence Leighton's article, written
in September, is published in *Hound & Horn*'s October-Decem-
ber issue. Bumby visits his father for the month of November.
Pauline travels to Piggott with Patrick and Gregory because
the boys have whooping cough. Late in the month, Ernest and
Bumby drive to Arkansas to meet the other Hemingways for
the upcoming holidays. On November 21, Ernest sends a ten-

line tribute on Ezra Pound to Ford Madox Ford. His contribution is to be published in a testimonial issue of *Festschrift* to coincide with the publication of Pound's *A Draft of XXX Cantos* in January 1933. The upcoming film adaptation of *A Farewell to Arms* is an irritant to Hemingway because of the script changes which alter the original story and the pressure he is receiving from the movie studio to help boost his own status as a celebrity. Ernest notifies the studio, through Perkins, that he wishes to be left out of the publicity campaign.

December: The first screen adaptation of a work by Hemingway is released this month. Made by Paramount Studios, *A Farewell to Arms* is produced and directed by Frank Borzage. The script is written by Benjamin Glazer and Oliver H. P. Garrett. The cast includes Gary Cooper as Frederic Henry, Helen Hayes as Catherine Barclay, and Adolphe Menjou as Rinaldi. On December 6, the *New York Times* reports that Hemingway refused to attend the world premiere of the film, which was held in Piggott, Arkansas. By this time, most of the reviews of *Death in the Afternoon* have come in. Although the negative notices outweigh the favorable ones, Ernest is cheered when he learns that critic Allen Tate likes the book. On December 14, Hemingway travels from Piggott to Memphis, Tennessee, to meet Max Perkins for a duck-hunting trip. The two stay on a houseboat on the Watson River in Arkansas. From son Bumby's bout with influenza late in the month Ernest gets the idea for his short story "A Day's Wait." Arrangements are made during the month for Evan Shipman, a poet and friend from Hemingway's early days in Paris to become Bumby's tutor after Christmas. The Hemingways stay in Piggott, Arkansas, through the end of the year.

1933

Winner Take Nothing (collection of short stories)
"A Clean, Well-Lighted Place" (short story)
"God Rest You Merry, Gentlemen" (short story)
"Homage to Switzerland" (short story)

"Give Us a Prescription, Doctor" (short story, later retitled "The Gambler, the Nun, and the Radio")

"Marlin Off the Morro: A Cuban Letter" (article)

Joan Miró: Paintings (excerpt of article appears in folder)

The Cantos of Ezra Pound/ Some Testimonies by Ernest Hemingway, Ford Madox Ford, T. S. Eliot, Hugh Walpole, Archibald MacLeish, James Joyce and Others (Hemingway's ten-line tribute to the poet is included)

Twentieth-Century Short Stories ("The Undefeated" reprinted)

Capajon: Fifty-Four Short Stories ("Hills Like White Elephants," "The Killers," and "The Battler" included)

Great American Short Stories: O. Henry Memorial Prize Stories 1919–32 (contains reprint of "The Killers")

Creative America: An Anthology (excerpt from Chapter XXXVII of *A Farewell to Arms* published under the title "Escape")

American Omnibus ("The Killers" reprinted)

These Our Moderns (Includes excerpt from *A Farewell to Arms* under the section titled "Modern Soldiers Look at War")

Contemporary Trends: American Literature Since 1914 (reprint of "The Killers")

Pět Stováků (short stories translated into Czechoslovakian by Stasa Jilovska, first Czech translation)

Le Soleil se lève aussi (French translation of *The Sun Also Rises* by Maurice-Edgar Coindreau)

The Torrents of Spring (first British edition, published by Jonathan Cape in London)

"Ein Sauberes, gut beleuchtetes cafe" ("A Clean, Well-Lighted Place" translated into German by Annemarie Horschitz)

Active Anthology (Includes reprint of poem, "They All Made Peace—What Is Peace?")

"I conuigi Elliot" ("Mr. and Mrs. Elliot" translated into Italian by Achille Danieli)

January–February: Hemingway is discussed in five books published in 1933. Chief among these are *The Autobiography of Alice B. Toklas* by Gertrude Stein. Material on Hemingway also appears in the *Atlantic* in August, 1933 and in *It Was the Nightingale* by Ford Madox Ford (Hemingway's days as the sub-editor of the *transatlantic review* are covered by the author). Criticism of his work appears in *The Art of the Novel: From 1700 to the Present*; *The Great Tradition: An Interpre-*

tation of *American Literature*; and *World Panorama, 1918–1933*. At the beginning of January, Pauline and the three Hemingway boys leave for New York. Ernest drives by himself to Roanoke, Virginia, then entrains to New York. He arrives on January 7. Max Perkins arranges a meeting between Thomas Wolfe and Hemingway, both Scribner's authors. Ernest tries to intercede in his sister Carol's marriage plans. John Gardner, Carol's fiancée, meets with Ernest in New York to ask for his approval of the marriage. Hemingway not only denies the request but threatens Gardner physically. Bullfighter Sidney Franklin is also in New York and he and Ernest spend time together. Aside from business appointments with his editor, Max Perkins, and his lawyer, Maurice Speiser, Hemingway meets with Louis Henry Cohn and Arnold Gingrich. Cohn, his bibliographer, wants to publish a special edition of the story, "God Rest You Merry, Gentlemen," but Hemingway declines. Gingrich, introduced to Hemingway by Cohn, is the editor of *Apparel Arts*, a trade journal published in Chicago (and will become the founder and editor of *Esquire* magazine). After meeting with the two on January 20, Ernest leaves New York. He rejoins Pauline in Jacksonville, Florida, and the couple returns to Key West together. Evan Shipman arrives in Florida to begin his job as Bumby's tutor and to do some clerical work for Ernest at the end of the month. Adolf Hitler begins his rise to power in Germany, becoming chancellor of the country on January 30. During late January and early February, Ernest discusses possible solutions to Scott Fitzgerald's problems in letters to Max Perkins. Fitzgerald's salvation could come, Ernest asserts, from the development of stomach problems which would force an end to his drinking or from his wife Zelda's death. On February 10, Hemingway begins to work on plans for another nonfiction book, this one on the Gulf Stream. He is also working on a long story based on Joe Russell and a pirate named Morgan. He completes three chapters of the story by February 23. Late in the month, Arnold Gingrich contacts Hemingway and asks him to become a contributor to *Esquire*, a new magazine he is going to publish. *The Torrents of Spring* is published by Jonathan Cape in London on February 23.

March–April: Early in March Ernest makes a brief trip to New York to confer with film director Lewis Milestone on a proposed documentary on Spain. Ernest would serve as an advisor and location scout. During his stay, he meets and is fascinated by lion tamer Clyde Beatty who is appearing with Ringling Brothers at Madison Square Garden. Ernest's upcoming African safari has heightened his interest in large cats. Beatty allows Hemingway to watch his rehearsals. Back in Cuba by March 13, Ernest writes to Arnold Gingrich to tell him that he has decided to contribute articles to *Esquire*. Correspondence continues through the next three weeks while details of the business arrangement emerge. Hemingway will be paid $250 for brief nonfiction articles on hunting and fishing. Ernest tells Gingrich in his letter of March 13 that he has begun keeping new material stored for posthumous publication, and that he views the practice as a sort of insurance policy in the event of his death. Aside from the growing business relationship, a friendship begins to develop between the editor and writer. John Gardner cables Hemingway on March 17 to notify him of his upcoming marriage to Carol on March 25. Ernest vows to disown his sister. Hemingway reads advance copies of the *Atlantic* containing excerpts from Gertrude Stein's *The Autobiography of Alice B. Toklas*. Stein purports that Hemingway was created by Sherwood Anderson and that he learned to write, in part, by proofreading her book, *The Making of Americans* in 1924. She also calls Ernest a coward. Furious after reading Stein's work, Hemingway writes to John Dos Passos and first mentions writing his own memoirs at some time. "A Clean, Well-Lighted Place" is published in *Scribner*'s March issue. Adolf Hitler becomes president of Germany when the Enabling Act is passed through the Reichstag on March 23. On April 11, Ernest goes to Cuba and begins a two-month marlin-fishing trip aboard Joe Russell's boat, the *Anita*. Hemingway has chartered the boat and hired Carlos Gutierrez as his guide and advisor. As on his last trip in Cuba, Ernest spends his night at the Ambos Mundos Hotel. A first limited edition of *God Rest You Merry Gentlemen* is published by House of Books, Ltd. in New York. This is the story's first appearance in print. *Scribner*'s April issue carries "Homage to Switzerland." The three-part story includes "Portrait of Mr. Wheeler in Montreux," "Mr. Johnson Talks About It at Vevey," and "The Son of a Fellow Member at Territel."

May–July: In mid-May, while still on his fishing trip in Cuba, Hemingway learns that John Dos Passos has rheumatic fever and is in the Johns Hopkins Hospital in Baltimore, Maryland. On May 15, Ernest writes Dos Passos and encloses a check for $1000. Archibald MacLeish reads an advance copy of the June issue of the *New Republic* which contains an article by Max Eastman entitled "Bull in the Afternoon." MacLeish feels that Eastman is questioning Hemingway's virility. He writes a letter to the editor of the magazine and encloses a copy of it and the article and sends both to Ernest on May 31. "A Clean, Well-Lighted Place" is translated into German by Annemarie Horschitz and published in *Neve Rundschau* in May. *Scribner's* magazine contains "Give Us a Prescription, Doctor." The story later appears, with some revisions, in *Winner Take Nothing* under the title "The Gambler, the Nun, and the Radio." On June 2, Ernest is contacted by Morrill Cody, an American correspondent in Paris, about writing a preface to Jimmy Charters's autobiography. Charters had been a bartender in Paris in the 1920s. (Ernest writes the preface for the book, *This Must Be the Place*, later in the year.) On June 7, Max Eastman's "Bull in the Afternoon," critical of Hemingway's *Death in the Afternoon*, is published in the *New Republic*. (Four years later, this article will cause a fistfight in Max Perkins's office between Hemingway and Eastman). Ernest wires the title of his new collection of stories to Perkins on June 11. He has selected *Winner Take Nothing*. The following day, Hemingway writes an open letter to the *New Republic* responding to Eastman's attack and addressing the question of his sexual potency. On June 13, he writes to Max Perkins to notify him that he will sue Eastman if he attempts to publish his review in book form. On June 28, the magazine prints a letter from Max Eastman in which he denies making a personal attack on Hemingway in his review. On July 3, Hadley Richardson, Ernest's first wife, marries Paul Scott Mowrer in London. Still fishing in Cuba, Ernest catches a 750-pound marlin on July 6. After struggling for an hour and a half, the fish frees itself. On July 15, Hemingway writes to Max Perkins and tells him that he will not accept Max Eastman's apology and that he will get revenge. Ernest returns to Key West on July 20 and writes for *Esquire* "A Cuban Letter," his first piece of journalism in ten years. On

July 26, in a letter to Max Perkins, Hemingway discusses his plans to revise his story "The Tomb of My Grandfather." (The title is later changed to "Fathers and Sons.") Five days later, he wires Perkins to notify him about the ordering of the fourteen stories in the upcoming collection. Their correspondence on the best order of the stories continues through the next month.

August–November: After spending the first week of August in Key West, Hemingway leaves for Havana. The Cuban Revolution against dictator Gerardo Machado is underway by the time Ernest arrives on August 7. Ernest sails to Spain aboard the *Reina de la Pacífica* on the same date. Shortly after the ship sets sail, crowds gather in the Havana streets after a premature announcement that Machado has resigned and are dispersed forcibly by the dictator's police force. On August 12, Hemingway hears the news that Machado has been deposed and has fled Cuba. Dr. Carlos Manuel de Céspedes becomes the new provisional president of the country. Ernest arrives in Santander, Spain, in the latter part of August. He plans to stay in Spain for the next two months. His travel will eventually take him to Africa for his first safari. Archibald MacLeish and Mike Strater are no longer scheduled to join Hemingway in Africa. Charles Thompson, however, is still planning to meet him for the safari. After Ernest, Pauline, Bumby, and Virginia Pfeiffer arrive in Spain, the group parts company. All but Ernest continue on to Paris. Hemingway travels to Madrid and checks into the Hotel Biarritz, located at Calle Victoria 2. Ernest is unhappy with the changes he observes in the city. Bullfighting, he feels, has deteriorated and the three-year-old government is a conservative bureaucracy, which has resulted in increased poverty. In September, Ernest returns to work on the Harry Morgan story. Using Cuba as a backdrop for the first time in his fiction, he recounts the story of the street scene in Havana on the day he sailed for Spain. He completes the story in mid-September and titles it "One Trip Across" (it will appear in *Cosmopolitan* in April 1934). Ernest is also editing and rewriting a Spanish bullfight novel, *Currito de la Cruz*. The book, written by Alejandro Pérez Lugín, has been translated into English by Sidney Franklin. Through September and October Ernest makes visits to Paris. Most of his time during the two months, however, is spent in Madrid. *Winner Take Nothing*, Hemingway's fifth collection of short stories, is published by Charles Scribner's Sons in New York and London on October 27. Included in the book are "After the Storm"; "A Clean, Well-Lighted Place"; "The Light of the World"; "God Rest You Merry, Gentlemen"; "The Sea Change"; "A Way You'll Never Be"; "The Mother of a Queen"; "One Reader Writes"; "Wine of Wyoming"; "The Gambler, the Nun, and the Radio"; "Fathers and Sons"; and "Homage to Switzerland." The collection is dedicated to Archibald MacLeish. Also published this month is *Active Anthology*, which is edited by Ezra Pound and contains a reprint of "They All Made Peace—What Is Peace?" The poem had originally been published in the *Little Review*'s Spring, 1923 issue. "Mr. and Mrs. Elliot" is translated into Italian by Achille Danieli and published in the October–December issue of *Occidente* under the title "I coniugi Elliot." The critical response to *Winner Take Nothing* is mostly negative. Ernest has arrived in Paris by November 10 to await his departure to Africa. On that date, he borrows W. H. Auden's *The Orators*; *Sober Truths*, edited by Margaret Barton and Osbert Sitwell; *Discussions on Travel, Art and Life* by Osbert Sitwell; and Erik Linklater's *The Men of Ness* from Shakespeare and Company's lending library. The following day, Ernest meets with Morrill Cody and Jimmy Charters at the bookstore to discuss the preface he's going to write for Charters's book. By mid-November, *Winner Take Nothing* has sold 11,000 copies. On November 16, Hemingway writes to Max Perkins and complains about the lack of advertising for the book. Charles Thompson arrives in Paris. On November 20, he and Hemingway go on a day's shooting trip in Sologne with Ben Gallagher. The next day, the Hemingways meet James and Nora Joyce for dinner. Joyce expresses concern that his own writing is too suburban, that he hasn't seen enough of the world to benefit his work. On November 22, Ernest, Pauline, and Charles Thompson sail for Mombasa aboard the *S.S. General Metzinger*. Their route takes them through the Mediterranean to Port Said, the Suez Canal, the Red Sea, the Gulf of Aden, and the Indian Ocean.

December: After their arrival in Mombasa on December 8, the group stays with Charles and Katherine Fannin. On December 10, having completed a 300-mile road trip, the Hemingways and Charles Thompson check into the New Stanley Hotel in Nairobi where they will wait for Philip Percival, their white hunter. They next move on to Percival's farm at Potha Hill in Machakos and begin hunting in the Kapiti Plains for gazelle, kongoni, impala, and guinea fowl. On December 20, Ernest, Pauline, and Charles Thompson leave Nairobi with Philip Percival for a 200-mile trip to the south. On their first night they stay at the Athenaeum Hotel in Aruska. It is from this location that Hemingway gets his initial look at Mt. Kilimanjaro. The following day places the group in its first campsite, at M'Utu Umbi, and by December 23 they are settled in on the Serengeti Plain. They remain in this area until January 16. *Joan Miró: Paintings*, a folder written by Hemingway, is published in December by the Pierre Matisse Gallery in New York. The text is excerpted from an article which will be published in *Cahiers d'Art* in 1934. "The Killers" is reprinted in the *Golden Book Magazine* and "After the Storm" in *Lovat Dickson's Magazine*.

1934

"The Farm" (article)

"A Paris Letter" (article)

One Trip Across (short novel)

"a.d. in Africa: A Tanganyika Letter" (article)

"Shootism vs. Sport: The Second Tanganyika Letter" (article)

"This Must Be the Place/Memoirs of Montparnasse" (preface to James Charters's memoirs)

"Notes on Dangerous Game: The Third Tanganyika Letter" (article)

"Out in the Stream: A Cuban Letter" (article)

"Defense of Dirty Words" (article)

"Genio after Josie: A Havana Letter" (article)

Luis Quintanilla Catalogue (folder)

"Old Newsman Writes: A Letter from Cuba" (article)

"Ein Tag Warten" ("A Day's Wait" translated into German by Annemarie Horschitz)

"Die Veranderung" ("The Sea Change" translated into German by Annemarie Horschitz)

"My Old Man" (reprinted in *Golden Book Magazine*)
"The Friend of Spain: A Spanish Letter" (article)
International Short Stories ("Cat in the Rain" reprinted)
A Book of the Short Story (contains "Fifty Grand")
Editor's Choice (anthology edited by Alfred Dashiell, editor of
    Scribner's magazine; "The Gambler, the Nun, and the Radio"
    reprinted)
Modern English Readings (includes "The End of Something")
Modern American Prose ("The Killers" reprinted)
American Poetry and Prose (excerpt from *A Farewell to Arms*
    published under the title "The Retreat from Caporetto")
Amerikanskaya novella XX veka (contains "Alpiskaya idilliya,"
    the Russian translation of "An Alpine Idyll")
"Ubitsy" (Russian translation of "The Killers")
Smert' Posle Poludnya (selections from *Death in the Afternoon*
    and other Hemingway works translated into Russian, edited
    and introduced by Ivan Kashkin)

January–February: Eight books published during the year
contain discussions of Hemingway. A psychoanalytical critique
of his work, *Kjaerlighet og åndslov: Essays* by Trygve Braatoy
is published by Fabritius and Sonners in Oslo, Norway. *Modern
Art: The Men, The Movements, The Meaning* by Thomas Craven
and *Exile's Return* by Malcolm Cowley give evidence of Hemingway's growing impact on American literature. Gertrude
Stein's *Portraits and Prayers* includes a section entitled "He
and They, Hemingway." Max Eastman publishes *Art and the
Life of Action*, which contains a reprint of his *New Republic*
review, "Bull in the Afternoon." (Hemingway had threatened
to sue Eastman should he try to publish the article in book
form. No lawsuit is filed, yet Hemingway's anger continues
and will culminate in a fight in 1937.) On January 2, Ernest
sends his preface to *This Must Be The Place* to Morrill Cody.
Written in Africa, the preface contains his first public response
to Gertrude Stein's attack on him in *The Autobiography of Alice
B. Toklas*. During the first two weeks of January, Hemingway
is stricken with amoebic dysentery. The first lion killed on the
safari was slated to be Pauline's. Although there is doubt
whether Pauline or Ernest fired the fatal shot, a celebration
is carried out in honor of Mrs. Hemingway. This incident, viewed
as somewhat immoral by Ernest, coupled with his illness makes

for a period of disappointment for him. Soon afterwards, Hemingway's spirits are lifted when he kills his first lion and Philip Percival praises his shooting skills. In mid-January, Ernest is flown to Nairobi by rescue plane when his lower intestine collapses. During the flight, he gets a clear view of Mt. Kilimanjaro. Upon arrival in Nairobi, Ernest checks into the New Stanley Hotel and is placed under the care of a Nairobi physician named Anderson. On January 18, Hemingway writes "a.d. in Africa" for *Esquire*. In a letter to Arnold Gingrich on the same day, he writes that he will contribute 12 articles a year for the magazine. Sales figures, as reported to Ernest during the third week of January, on *Winner Take Nothing* stand at 12,500. *Cosmopolitan* magazine has agreed to purchase *One Trip Across*, Hemingway's short novel, for $5500. Ernest rejoins the safari near the Ngorongoro Crater. His improved health and ability to resume the trip make him jubilant. His reputation is boosted in Russia during January when "The Killers" is translated into Russian by "G. K. Kh" and published in *International Literatura*'s debut issue along with Ivan Kashkeen's (nee Kashkin) "Due novelly Khemingueya." The hunting party moves into the Rift Valley in early February to search for zebras. Ernest is displeased with the area and the type of hunting. Philip Percival tells Hemingway the story of a frozen leopard found by Reverend Dr. R. Reusch by the crater rim of Kibo Peak on Mt. Kilimanjaro. The leopard was found in September 1926. The evening fireside discussions the group holds will later influence Hemingway's story "The Short Happy Life of Francis Macomber." Courage is among the subjects they talk about. The safari travels through the area surrounding Babati, along the Cape-to-Cairo road, Kijungu (where new guides, including David Garrick, are hired), and Kibaya. By this time, Ernest has killed a rhinoceros and is seeking to add a kudu to his collection. On February 17, the group heads back to Kijungu when they hear the animals have been sighted there. Ernest kills two kudus in this area and spends the next two days hunting for sable. Hemingway's safari ends shortly afterwards in a coastal town called Tanga. The third week of February is spent fishing aboard a chartered boat, the *Xanadu*, on the Indian Ocean. Ernest's companions include Pauline, Charles Thompson, Philip Percival, and Alfred Vanderbilt (who had been introduced in mid-December at Percival's farm). The trip begins at Malindi and occupies the Hemingways' time until they are to sail back to Paris from Mombasa.

March–June: On March 3, Ernest, Pauline, and Charles Thompson depart from Mombasa aboard the *Gripsholm*. They sail through Port Sudan on March 9, through the Suez Canal on the 11th, and have a brief stopover in Haifa on the 12th. Lorine Thompson joins the three in Haifa and the group takes an afternoon's trip to see the Sea of Galilee. Six days later, the Hemingways and the Thompsons disembark at Villefranche and continue on to Paris by train. The Hemingways stay at the Paris-Dinaud in rue Cassette for nine days. While in France, Ernest becomes godfather to Alden Calmer, son of Ned and Priscilla. Hemingway had met Ned Calmer, a fiction writer and reporter for the *Paris Herald*, in November. At this time Ernest also pays for the Calmers' passage to New York so the family can be in the United States for the publication of Ned's first novel. On March 20, Hemingway cables Arnold Gingrich about two more articles on Africa and sends them to the editor within the next four days. A visit to Shakespeare and Company on the 24th results in another instance of Ernest's anger when criticized. Sylvia Beach shows Ernest a copy of Wyndham Lewis's essay, "The Dumb Ox." Furious after reading the piece, Hemingway breaks a vase in the shop and then offers to pay Beach to replace it. During a subsequent stop at the bookstore, Hemingway and writer Katherine Anne Porter meet. After a brief introduction, the two simply stare at one another and depart. The Hemingways sail for New York in the latter part of March. They meet actress Marlene Dietrich aboard the *Ile de France*. The friendship between Dietrich and Hemingway will continue throughout his life. On April 4, Ernest and Pauline arrive in New York. He is asked to tea by an unidentified woman who, having heard of his recent safari, offers to finance another African trip if she would be allowed to go along. Ernest declines the offer, but the incident serves as a catalyst for writing his story "The Snows of Kilimanjaro." F. Scott Fitzgerald is also in New York. His novel *Tender Is the Night* has been recently published. Hemingway expresses his dislike for the portrait of Gerald and Sara Murphy because he feels it's untrue. He also feels that the merging of characteristics of the Fitzgeralds and the Murphys into Nicole and Dick Diver does not work. Ernest also sees friends Waldo Pierce, Sidney Franklin, and Edwin Balmer. The day before he leaves New York, Ernest buys his boat, the *Pilar*, from the Wheeler Shipyards in Brooklyn. The purchase price for the 38-foot, diesel-powered boat is $7500. Ernest receives $3000 as an advance on future articles from Arnold Gingrich, which serves as the down payment for the *Pilar*. Despite having many visitors when he returns to Key West, Hemingway begins to work on a book about Africa. By the end of April he has written 50 pages of his book, which carries the working title "The Highlands of Africa" (subtitled "Hunters Are Brothers"). Thirty of these pages are destroyed by Ernest because he feels they are not good enough. When not writing, Ernest spends his time fishing with the stream of visitors, which includes Katy and John Dos Passos, Gerald and Sara Murphy, Ada MacLeish, and Charles and Lorine Thompson. *One Trip Across*, called "a complete short novel," appears in *Cosmopolitan* in April. (It will become, with minor revisions, Part One of *To Have and Have Not*.) Hemingway's article about amoebic dysentery, "a.d. in Africa: A Tanganyika Letter," is published in the April issue of *Esquire*. On May 1, Hemingway and John Dos Passos go to Havana for the May Day celebration under the new government. They see Carlos Gutiérrez and Manuel Asper and are told that the political climate is still not very good in the country. The two return to Key West. The *Pilar* arrives in Miami on May 9 while Ernest's brother, Leicester, is visiting. Hemingway's schedule in May is similar to that of April. Towards the end of the month, Ernest and Archibald MacLeish, who has joined the group in Florida, have a falling out during a fishing trip aboard the *Pilar*. Ernest appears to be still angry that MacLeish cancelled out on the African trip, and MacLeish feels that fame has had an adverse effect on Hemingway. Their friendship cools. On May 28, Hemingway writes to Scott Fitzgerald to explain his reactions to *Tender Is the Night*.

June–September: By June 20, Hemingway has written 150 pages of his African book. In correspondence to Fitzgerald, Hemingway asserts that he is beginning to think it better than he had originally. "Shootism vs. Sport: The Second Tanganyika Letter" appears in *Esquire* in June. In July, Hemingway hears from Carlos Gutiérrez that marlin are now in Cuba. He begins to make plans to take the *Pilar* over from Florida. Arnold Samuelson, a young writer who had come to interview Hemingway, is hired by him as a hand on the *Pilar*. Ernest nicknames him "Maestro," which is subsequently shortened to "Mice." The African manuscript stands at 200 pages, and Hemingway also writes during this period an article for *Esquire* entitled "Defense of Dirty Words." Ernest leaves for Cuba on July 18 and spends the remainder of the month there. He stays at the Ambos Mundo Hotel when not fishing. Companions during the Cuban trip are Jane and Grant Mason and new acquaintances Dick Armstrong and a Venezuelan sportsman named Lopez Mendez. Hemingway also meets Cuban painter Antonio Gattorno and scientists Charles Cadwalader and Henry W. Fowler. Working on the reclassification of all North American marlin, Fowler fishes with Hemingway and Cadwalader. "Notes on Dangerous Game: The Third Tanganyika Letter" is published in *Esquire* in July. "A Day's Wait" is translated into German by Annemarie Horschitz and published in July in *Die Sammlung* under the title "Ein Tag Warten." *This Must Be the Place/ Memoirs of Montparnasse* by Jimmy the Barman (James Charters), edited by Morrill Cody with an introduction by Ernest Hemingway, is published by Herbert Joseph Limited in London in July. Hemingway's introduction is dated Sarengetti Plains, Tanganyika, December 1933. Ernest turns 35 years old on July 21. During July and August while Ernest is fishing and writing in Cuba, Adolf Hitler is advancing his political control of Germany. A blood purge, which lasts from June 30 through July 2, results in the deaths of approximately 1000 of Hitler's political enemies. On July 25, Austrian chancellor Engelbert Dollfuss is assassinated in an attempt to exterminate the entire chancellery of the country in order to reunite Austria and Germany. Although Dollfuss is slain, the Nazis do not win control of Austria. Paul von Benecken Hindenburg, the president of Germany, dies on August 2, and Hitler's title is changed to Fuehrer and reich chancellor. An election is held on August 19 to approve Hitler's new position. The vote count is 45 million in favor of and 38 million opposed to Hitler's becoming Germany's leader. By August 20, Hemingway has written 23,000 words on his African book. "Out in the Stream: A Cuban Letter" is published in the August issue of *Esquire*. In early September, Ernest returns to Key West to have the *Pilar* cleaned and repaired. His writing pace increases and in a four-day period, from September 9 through 12, Ernest writes 72 pages on his manuscript. On September 13, he returns to Havana to resume his schedule of writing and fishing. "Defense of Dirty Words: A Cuban Letter" appears in *Esquire* in September.

October–December: Ernest remains in Cuba until October 26 when he returns to Key West. During the third week of the month, he sees 20 whales while aboard the *Pilar* and makes his first unsuccessful attempt at whaling. He will recount the incident in May 1936 in an *Esquire* article, "There She Breaches." "Genio after Josie: A Havana Letter" is published in *Esquire* in October. In the second week of November, Katy and John Dos Passos arrive in Key West. Tensions develop between the two writers as Ernest questions, jestingly at first, Dos Passos's integrity in writing the screenplay for a Marlene Dietrich film, "The Devil Is a Woman." Both Katy and John Dos Passos begin to share Archibald MacLeish's view that Hemingway is showing the ill effects of being a well-known writer. A more generous side of Ernest is evident in the assistance he is giving to new writers Prudencio de Pereda and Ned Calmer by reading and making editorial recommendations on their work. Irving Stone, who has just written a biography of Vincent Van Gogh entitled *Lust for Life*, is in Key West. The two writers meet and a discussion ensues on why Hemingway has not used the United States as a setting for a novel. Hemingway's response is that life in America is too dull. Ernest completes his African book on November 16. The manuscript is 492 pages long. The following day he returns to work on a short story and on the 18th writes "Notes on Life and Letters" for *Esquire*. In this article, he attacks Gilbert Seldes and William Saroyan's first book of short stories, *The Daring Young Man on the Flying Trapeze*. Ernest invites Arnold Gingrich to Key West on November 19. Gingrich suggests that he bring F. Scott Fitzgerald along with him. Fitzgerald, however, declines the offer. The *Luis Quintanilla Catalogue*, written by John Dos Passos and Hemingway, is published by the Pierre Matisse Gallery in New York for an exhibit which runs from November 20 through December 4. "The Sea Change" is translated into German by Annemarie Horschitz and published in *Die Sammlung* in November as "Die Veränderung." Dos Passos is still in

Key West by the time Arnold Gingrich arrives and the two meet for the first time. Hemingway and Gingrich try to convince Dos Passos that the Quintanilla article should appear in *Esquire* instead of in the *New Republic* as originally planned. Dos Passos notes that Hemingway manages his editor, Gingrich, as he would a marlin, yet one that doesn't put up a great fight. After Gingrich has left in December, Hemingway persuades Dos Passos to sell the Quintanilla article to *Esquire*. On December 18, Pauline, Patrick, and Ernest leave Key West for the drive to Piggott, Arkansas. They stop at the Hotel Peabody in Memphis, Tennessee, on the 22nd and arrive in Piggott on the following day. They stay through mid-January. "My Old Man" is reprinted in the *Golden Book Magazine* in December. *Esquire*'s December issue carries "Old Newsman Writes: A Letter from Cuba."

1935

"Notes on Life and Letters: Or a manuscript found in a bottle" (article)

"Remembering Shoot-Flying: A Key West Letter" (article)

"Program Notes" (article)

"Sailfish Off Mombasa: A Key West Letter" (article)

Gattorno (folder containing thirty-eight reproductions and commentary by Hemingway)

"The Sights of Whitehead Street: A Key West Letter" (article)

Green Hills of Africa (non-fiction book published and serialized)

"a.d. Southern Style" (article)

"On Being Shot Again: A Gulf Stream Letter" (article)

"The President Vanishes: A Bimini Letter" (article)

"He Who Gets Slap Happy: A Bimini Letter" (article)

"Notes on the Next War: A Serious Topical letter" (article)

"Who Murdered the Vets?" (article)

"The Malady of Power: A Second Serious Letter" (article)

"Million Dollar Fight: A New York Letter" (article)

"Death in the Afternoon Cocktail" (recipe and comment)

A Quarto of Modern Literature ("After the Storm" and "Retreat from Caporetto," excerpted from *A Farewell to Arms* reprinted)

The Great American Parade and *Study of the Short Story* (each contains reprint of "The Killers")

Short Stories for English Courses ("A Day's Wait" included)

The Short Story Case Book ("The Undefeated" reprinted)

The Third New Year ("Notes on the Next War" reprinted)

Great American Short Stories: O. Henry Memorial Prize Winners 1919–34 ("The Killers" included)

Fiyesta (*The Sun Also Rises* translated into Russian by V. Toper)

American Big Game Fishing (includes a revised version of article "Marlin off the Morro")

So Red the Nose (contains reprint of *Death in the Afternoon* cocktail)

"Kto ubil veteranov voiny vo Florida?" (Russian translation of article "Who Murdered the Vets")

January–March: Hemingway's work is discussed in four books published during 1935. They are *Redder Than the Rose* by Robert Forsythe (pseudonym for Kyle Crichton), *Banned Books: Informal Notes on Some Books Banned for Various Reasons at Various Times and in Various Places* by Anne Lyon Haight, *Creating the Modern American Novel* by Harlan Hatcher, and *Personal History* by Vincent Sheean. The Hemingways return to Key West from Arkansas in mid-January. Maxwell and Louise Perkins come to Florida for a working vacation. Perkins reads Ernest's African manuscript. Ernest turns down *Cosmopolitan*'s offer to serialize the book if he will shorten it. In February, Hemingway and Perkins correspond about *Scribner*'s magazine buying the serial rights to the book. Ernest, who wants $10,000 to $20,000 for the rights, sends an angry response to Perkins's offer of $4500. The matter is settled on February 22 when Hemingway agrees to accept $5000 for the serial rights from *Scribner*'s. That Ernest is now a full-blown celebrity is reflected by the fact that his house at 907 Whitehead Street is now listed on area tourist maps. He continues, however, to frequent Sloppy Joe's Bar, where he meets some of the war veterans who are in Florida as part of the Civilian Conservation Corps. Rumors abound that this particular group, working on the roads and bridges in the Florida Keys, were sent to an out-of-the-way location because they are an embarrassment to New Deal programs. "Remembering

Shoot-Flying: A Key West Letter" and "Program Notes," Ernest's appraisal of Luis Quintanilla's etchings, are printed in *Esquire* during February. "Bread" Pinder is trained as a helmsman for the *Pilar* in March to replace Arnold Samuelson, who has returned to Minnesota. On March 17, Ernest hears that Gerald and Sara Murphy's son, Baoth, has died of tuberculosis. He writes a letter of condolence to the Murphys on the 19th. "Sailfish Off Mombasa: A Key West Letter" appears in the March issue of *Esquire*.

April–July: On April 7, Ernest leaves Key West for Bimini. Accompanying him on the trip are Katy and John Dos Passos, Bread Pinder, Sacker Adams, and Mike Strater. While shooting at a shark he has hooked, Ernest accidentally hits himself in both legs. He is immediately taken back to Key West, where he remains for a week under the care of Dr. William Warren. On April 15, after his gunshot wounds have improved somewhat, Ernest and the group, with Charles Thompson replacing Mike Strater, return to Bimini. Pauline flies over to join them in late April. *Gattorno*, a publication containing 38 reproductions of the artist's work and commentary by Hemingway, appears in a Cuban and English edition in Havana during April. (The text will be reprinted in the May 1936 issue of *Esquire*.) "The Sights of Whitehead Street" is published in *Esquire* in April. Mike Strater travels to Bimini in May. Hemingway meets William B. Leeds who owns a yacht named *The Moana*. Leeds also owns a tommy gun, which he sells to Hemingway. Ernest uses the gun in an attempt to keep sharks away from a marlin Strater has caught. He ends up destroying the marlin with his gunfire and a quarrel erupts between him and Strater. The incident is recounted in his Esquire article "The President Vanishes" (July 1935) and further exacerbates the tension between the two old friends. Ernest's overtly aggressive behavior during the trip also results in a fistfight between him and a man named Joseph Knapp. On May 31, Ernest flies back to Key West to see his family. When he arrives, he is told about an imposter appearing as Ernest Hemingway, who has been in Chicago and New York and on a national speaking tour of Ladies' Clubs. News about F. Scott Fitzgerald is relayed to Ernest by Max Perkins. Fitzgerald, now working on a novel set in the Middle Ages and carrying a working title of *Phillippe, Count of Dark-*

ness, is living in Asheville, North Carolina, and has stopped drinking. Ernest also learns that the central character is based on him. *American Big Game Fishing*, containing "Marlin Off Cuba," a revised version of Hemingway's *Esquire* article from *Esquire*'s Autumn 1933 issue, is published by the Derrydale Press in May. Ernest flies back to Bimini on June 5. Shortly afterwards, he lands a 785-pound Mako shark, just 12 pounds under the world record. He spends most of the month fishing. "On Being Shot Again: A Gulf Stream Letter" appears in *Esquire* in June. Interest in boxing is rekindled now and Ernest's had several bouts with locals and an exhibition fight with Tom Heeney, a heavyweight who had once fought Gene Tunney. On July 17, Hemingway mails his completed article, "Notes on the Next War," to Arnold Gingrich. He predicts that a second world war will break out in 1937 or 1938. Ernest begins to read the page proofs of *Green Hills of Africa* and expresses optimism about the sales of the book. "The President Vanishes: A Bimini Letter" appears in the July issue of *Esquire*.

August–October: Hemingway stays in Bimini until August 14. The following day, he arrives back in Key West. Ivan Kashkeen sends Hemingway a copy of his article, "Ernest Hemingway: The Tragedy of Craftsmanship," and correspondence between the two begins. Criticism mounts about Hemingway's keeping a distance between himself and leftist political groups, about his activities, such as safaris and fishing, and his apolitical writing. Ernest's response is to widen the gap and take a firmer stand about remaining independent and not openly affiliated with any leftist group. Hemingway finishes a rough draft of his story "The Snows of Kilimanjaro" on September 1 and begins preparing the *Pilar* for a hurricane that is approaching the Florida keys. The next day he readies his house for the storm. On September 3 the hurricane hits Florida, but Key West escapes the brunt of the damage. Hardest hit are Islamorada and the Upper and Lower Matecumbe Keys. Approximately 1000 of the Civilian Conservation Corps workers are drowned during the storm. Hemingway goes with Bra Saunders and J. B. Sullivan to assist on the site of the drownings. In a subsequent letter to Maxwell Perkins, Ernest comments that he sees more casualties at the location than during the war. On September 16, Hemingway decides to dedicate

Green Hills of Africa to Philip Percival, Charles Thompson, and J. B. Sullivan. The following day, Hemingway's article "Who Murdered the Vets?" written shortly after the Florida hurricane, appears in the *New Masses*. He blames the United States bureaucracy for the death of the Civilian Conservation Corps workers. This piece of journalism is considered the point at which Hemingway moves to the left politically, an interpretation which he denies. Ernest criticizes the editorial policies of the magazine in his article as well as the United States government. On September 18, Ernest, Pauline, Bumby, and Patrick begin a drive north. The family disperses at Columbia, South Carolina, where Bumby leaves for Chicago and the rest travel by train to New York. Hemingway covers the Joe Louis–Max Baer prizefight for *Esquire* on September 24. "Notes on the Next War: A Serious Topical Letter" is published in *Esquire* in September. Ernest goes back to Key West for a brief period and returns to New York for the publication of *Green Hills of Africa* on October 25. The book is published by Charles Scribner's Sons in New York. While in New York, Ernest stays at the Westbury Hotel on East 69th Street. The immediate reviews on his book are an almost equal split of positive and negative. "Monologue to the Maestro: A High Seas Letter," an article in which Hemingway answers questions of Arnold Samuelson, his young writer friend, appears in *Esquire*'s October issue.

November–December: "The Malady of Power: A Second Serious Letter" is included in the November issue of *Esquire*. Ernest is back in Key West where he remains through the close of 1935. A review of *Green Hills of Africa* appears in the Briefer Mention column of the *American Mercury* in December. Although favorable, Ernest is angered that the review was placed in the column and given so little space. Correspondence begins between Hemingway and Abner Green after the latter wrote an open letter to Ernest in *The American Criterion* in which he criticized him for his choice of subjects in writing. This is another instance in which Hemingway is urged to write on more topical and pertinent issues. Hemingway finishes "The Tradesman's Return," the second Harry Morgan story, and sends it to Arnold Gingrich on December 10. The story indicates a slight lean towards the left politically. Ernest begins the third

Harry Morgan story in mid-December. By the end of the year, Hemingway sees an advance copy of F. Scott Fitzgerald's *Esquire* article, "The Crack-Up." Bothered by the content, Ernest feels that Fitzgerald is wallowing in his own defeat. Hemingway's article on the veterans killed in the Florida hurricane is translated into Russian and printed in *Internatsionalnaya Literatura*'s December issue under the title "Kto ubil veteranov voiny vo Floride?" "Million Dollar Fight" and "Death in the Afternoon Cocktail" appear in *Esquire*'s December issue. *The Third New Year/An Etude in the Key of Frankness* is published by Esquire, Inc., in Chicago and New York and includes the first book appearance of Hemingway's "Notes on the Next War."

1936

Green Hills of Africa (British edition)

"The Snows of Kilimanjaro" (short story)

"The Short Happy Life of Francis Macomber" (short story)

"Wings Always Over Africa: An Ornithological Letter" (article)

"The Tradesman's Return" (short story)

"On the Blue Water: A Gulf Stream Letter" (article)

"There She Breaches! or Moby Dick off the Morro" (article)

"The Horns of the Bull" (short story, later retitled "The Capital of the World")

"The Man with the Tyrolese Hat" (excerpt of *Green Hills of Africa*)

Portraits and Self-Portraits (includes autobiographical sketch by Hemingway)

An Approach to Literature (includes reprints of "In Another Country" and "The Killers")

An Anthology of Famous American Stories (contains "The Gambler, the Nun, and The Radio" and "The Killers")

Stories for Men ("The Undefeated" included)

American Points of View ("Notes on the Next War," winner of a $200 prize for best article or essay for 1935, is reprinted)

Farvel til våbrane (*A Farewell to Arms* translated into Danish by Ole Restrup)

Proshchai oruzhiye (*A Farewell to Arms* translated into Russian by Kalashnitkova)

January–March: Stephen Spender's *The Destructive Element: A Study of Modern Writers and Beliefs* is among the seven books published during the year which discuss Hemingway's work. The others are *Seven Years' Harvest: Notes on Contemporary Literature* by Henry Seidel, *Forays and Rebuttals* by Bernard De Voto, *Phoenix: The Posthumous Papers of D. H. Lawrence*, George Slocombe's *The Tumult and the Shouting*, *Parody Party*, and Walter F. Taylor's *A History of American Letters*, which contains a bibliography of Hemingway criticism compiled by Harry Hartwick. The year opens badly for Hemingway as he struggles with a three-week bout of depression. Working and physical exercise in Key West get him out of the state. Hemingway's January article in *Esquire*, "Wings Always Over Africa," discusses Mussolini's attack on Ethiopia. (The piece is reprinted in *Reader's Digest* in February.) At the end of January, Ernest writes "The Horns of the Bull," his short story later retitled "Capital of the World." Visitors, including actress Nancy Carroll and the Waldo Pierce family, upset Hemingway's regimen of work. When news that Carroll is staying at the 907 Whitehead Street home is circulated around Key West, the Hemingways are forced to lock their gates to keep her fans away. In mid-February, Ernest breaks his toe when he angrily kicks the gate while fans stand outside. "The Tradesman's Return" is published in *Esquire*'s February issue. Harry Payne Burton of *Cosmopolitan* visits Ernest in Key West at the end of March to negotiate serial rights for future fiction. Burton offers $40,000 for first serial rights for a new novel, $7500 for a long short story, and $3000 for a short story. He is not interested in publishing Ernest's newest story, "The Horns of the Bull." "The Tradesman's Return" is reprinted in the March issue of *Fiction Parade*.

April–June: Jonathan Cape publishes the British edition of *Green Hills of Africa* on April 4. Hemingway completes "The Happy Ending" on April 19. The story, later renamed "The Short Happy Life of Francis Macomber," is bought by *Cosmopolitan* for $5000. The white hunter in the story, Robert Wilson, is based on Philip Percival. Poet Wallace Stevens is vacationing in Key West. An unfriendly encounter between Stevens and Hemingway turns into a fistfight and the poet ends up with a black eye. Towards the end of April, Pauline leaves for Piggott, Arkansas, and Ernest goes to Havana with Joe Russell and Jane Mason for a fishing trip, which lasts through most of May. The trip is unsatisfactory, with few marlin in the waters and Carlos Gutiérrez nearly blind. After Joe Russell returns to Key West in May, the tension increases aboard the *Pilar*. Hemingway is verbally abusive to Carlos Gutiérrez. "There She Breaches! or Moby Dick off the Morro," an article about Hemingway's sighting whales off the Cuban coast, is published in the May issue of *Esquire* along with a reprint of his "Gattorno: Program Note." *Reader's Digest* republishes Hemingway's "Notes on the Next War" in its May issue. On June 2, Hemingway takes the *Pilar* to Miami for a new engine and two days later leaves aboard it for the Bahamas. Tom and Lorraine Shevlin, the Kip Farringtons, Richard Cooper, Nonie and Margaret Briggs, and Jane Mason are in Bimini when Ernest and his party arrive. While there Hemingway and writer Marjorie Kinnan Rawlings are introduced. Ernest catches a 514-pound tuna. Late in the evening, he uses his catch as a punching bag as he is drunkenly showing off. Arnold Gingrich advises Ernest to publish the three Harry Morgan stories as a trilogy and not to include them in his upcoming collection of short stories. (Hemingway and his editor, Max Perkins, are now corresponding about the stories to include in the collection which will later be called *The First Forty-Nine Stories*.) "The Horns of the Bull" is published in *Esquire*'s June issue. A letter written in response to a questionnaire appears in *Outdoor Life*'s June issue under the title "Hemingway on Mutilated Fish." "The Man with the Tyrolese Hat," an excerpt from *Green Hills of Africa* which recounts Ernest's encounter with Vasili Kandinsky, is published in English in the German magazine *Querschnitt* in June.

July: Ernest returns to Key West on July 16. Shortly afterwards, he meets Professor Harry Burns from the University of Washington in Seattle and nicknames him Professor Mac-Walsey. The advance copy of *Esquire*'s August issue containing "The Snows of Kilimanjaro" arrives. In revising, Hemingway has changed the title, originally "A Budding Friendship," and the name of the central figure from Henry Walden to just Harry. F. Scott Fitzgerald contacts Hemingway to tell him of his irritation with the reference to "poor Scott Fitzgerald" in the story and that he would like it omitted when it is published in book form. On July 17, the Spanish Civil War begins. The Republican government, which had controlled Spain for the preceding five years, was ousted in February when the Popular Front defeated it in a general election. Manuel Ažano became president of the Spanish Republic. On July 13, Calvo Sotelo, the monarchist parliamentary leader, is arrested and murdered as an act of vengeance for the Falangist (fascist) assassination of a Liberal policeman. The murder expedites a revolt which had been in the planning stages for a year. The military, under the leadership of General Francisco Franco, pronounces itself against the Republican government on July 17 and begins to take over local governments. President Ažana gives an order to arm proletarian organizations and union members. This action stops a military takeover and begins the prolonged civil war in which the Nationalists, the right-wing party, supported by the church and the landed class, is given military aid by Benito Mussolini and Adolf Hitler. Hemingway, now 37 years old, leaves for the Nordquist Ranch in Wyoming on July 27 with Pauline, Bumby, and Patrick, and Virginia Pfeiffer and Harry Burns who will travel with the group as far as New Orleans.

August–October: The Hemingways arrive at the Nordquist Ranch on August 10 and move into a nearby cabin owned by Bill Sidley. Ernest receives news from John Dos Passos that Luis Quintanilla is now an officer in the Spanish Republican army. He also hears from several friends, including Katy Dos Passos, Arnold Samuelson, Marjorie Kinnan Rawlings, and Jane Mason, who send their praise of "The Snows of Kilimanjaro." The long story is published in the August issue of *Esquire*. By the middle of the month, Ernest has begun reworking his three stories into *To Have and Have Not*. In September, Hemingway begins to consider going to Spain. Tom and Lorraine Shevlin arrive in Wyoming for a grizzly-bear hunt. Before leaving for the hunting trip, Tom Shevlin reads *To Have and Have Not* and criticizes the novel. Ernest reacts angrily and throws his manuscript into a snowbank outside the cabin. The hunt begins on September 13, the same day Bumby leaves for Chicago to return to school. Hemingway kills two grizzlies within the first four days of the trip. On the 17th, he and Shevlin race each other home on horseback. The stakes are $500. Shevlin wins and adds $900 to his take in a crap game later that day. Ernest, with his competitive nature, is agitated about his losses. The Shevlins leave Wyoming late in the month. Ernest and Scott Fitzgerald have a brief renewal of their friendship when they correspond with each other at the end of September. Fitzgerald is upset about a recent interview he gave to the *New York Post* (on September 25, carrying the headline "The Other Side of Paradise"). Although Hemingway can do nothing for Fitzgerald, their exchange is friendlier than it has been for some time. "The Short Happy Life of Francis Macomber" appears in the September issue of *Cosmopolitan*. By October, Francisco Franco, the head of the Nationalists, proclaims himself *caudillo*, or leader, of Spain. Ernest remains in Wyoming, working on *To Have and Have Not* until late October when he leaves for a short visit to Piggott, Arkansas.

November–December: Ernest arrives back home in Key West during November. He continues his work on *To Have and Have Not*. The novel indicates a shift in Hemingway's political and philosophical outlook. Instead of suggesting that solitude is the answer, he shows some optimism about communal action. The Spanish Civil War is probably most responsible for the change in Ernest. On November 25, he is asked to cover the war by John Wheeler, the general manager of the North American Newspaper Alliance. Hemingway's articles would appear in 60 newspapers served by the news service. Hemingway is receptive to the idea, yet does not agree immediately. Pauline Hemingway and Max Perkins, however, are opposed to Ernest's going to Spain. Bullfighter Sidney Franklin, on the other hand, not only thinks that Hemingway should go but wants to accompany him. At this stage, Ernest remains undecided, but begins to support the Republican side. He pays to send two volunteers to Spain to fight on the Loyalist side and arranges for $1500 to be applied to ambulance-service costs through the Medical Bureau of the American Friends of the Spanish Democracy. Early in December, Ernest meets writer James T. Farrell and the two become friendly. Another new acquaintance is Rexford Guy Tugwell, a member of President Franklin D. Roosevelt's "brain trust," who takes an immediate dislike to the writer. One afternoon at Sloppy Joe's Bar, Hemingway encounters Mrs. Edna Fischel Gellhorn, her son Alfred, and her daughter Martha, who is called Marty. The Gellhorns are vacationing in Florida and are from St. Louis, Missouri. Martha has published a novel, *What Mad Pursuit*, which carries an epigraph borrowed from Hemingway, and a collection of short stories entitled *The Troubles I've Seen*. She is currently working on a new book and plans to return to Europe for this purpose. After her mother and brother leave Key West, Martha stays with the Hemingways. A libel suit has been filed against author Thomas Wolfe. When Ernest learns of it he begins to worry about a similar case being filed against him. He writes to his lawyer, Maurice Speiser, in New York, and to Arnold Gingrich, in Chicago, to ask them to come to Key West to consider the manuscript of *To Have and Have Not* in terms of potential libel suits. When Gingrich arrives, he reports to Ernest that he feels John Dos Passos is libelled in the character of novelist Richard Gordon and Grant and Jane Mason in the figures of Tommy and Helene Bradley. Hemingway feels that he would not be sued by any of these people. He continues to work on the novel through the end of the year. A congratulatory telegram from Ernest is quoted in the *New Masses*' December issue. It appears in a section entitled "Greetings on Our Twenty-Fifth Anniversary." An autobiographical sketch, written in Key West, is published in *Portraits and Self-Portraits* along with a drawing by artist Georges Schreiber. The book is published by Houghton Mifflin in Boston and The Riverside Press in Cambridge, England.

1937

The Spanish Earth (documentary film)
To Have and Have Not (novel)
"The Writer and War" (article)
Numerous articles for the North American Newspaper Alliance
All Good Americans (preface by Hemingway)
"Hemingway Reports Spain" (reprint of NANA dispatches)
"The War in Spain Makes a Movie" (*Life* magazine article, captions by Hemingway)

The Writer in a Changing World (includes reprint of "The Writer and War")

Atlantic Game Fishing (introduction by Hemingway)

"The Spanish War" (reprints of NANA dispatches)

The American Mind: Selections from the Literature of the United States ("The Killers" reprinted)

Woollcott's Second Reader (includes "Big Two-Hearted River")

American Points of View (article "The Malady of Power" reprinted)

The Best Short Stories of 1937 and the Yearbook of the American Short Story ("The Snows of Kilimanjaro" included)

Blow the Man Down/The Yachtsman's Reader (article "On the Blue Water" included)

At have og ikke have (*To Have and Have Not* translated into Danish by Ole Restrup)

Les vertes collines d'Afrique (*Green Hills of Africa* translated into French by Jeanine Delpech)

Különös tarsaság (*The Sun Also Rises* translated into Hungarian by Andor Németh)

"En Espagne, un endroit propre, bien éclairé" ("A Clean, Well-Lighted Place" translated into French by Jeanine Delpech)

"Une belle chasse" (excerpt from *Green Hills of Africa* translated into French by Jeanine Delpech)

"Los cuernos del toro" ("The Horns of the Bull" translated into Spanish)

January–March: In the middle of the month, Hemingway goes to New York to meet with John Wheeler to make arrangements for his work for the North American Newspaper Alliance. He contracts to cover the Spanish Civil War and will receive $1000 for each article sent to Wheeler by mail and $500 for each shorter, cabled piece. Ernest meets with novelist Prudencio de Pereda to help him on his film, *Spain in Flames*. He reworks the commentary which accompanies the film. He returns to Key West by the end of January. "The Killers" is reprinted in *Scribner's* fiftieth anniversary issue. Hemingway is back in New York in February. He joins writers John Dos Passos, Lillian Hellman, Archibald MacLeish and director Joris Ivens in planning a documentary film on Spain. Ernest establishes a corporation, Contemporary Historians, which will raise money to produce and distribute the film. At the end of February, he sails to Europe aboard the *Paris* with Evan Shipman and Sidney Franklin. By March 10, they arrive in Paris, where Ernest stays for over a week. During his stay, he meets artist Luis Quintanilla who has recently been jailed for political reasons in Spain. The artist's work has just been destroyed in the bombardment of Madrid. On March 16, Ernest flies to Spain and drives to Madrid. He checks into the Hotel Florida on March 20 and two days later, while examining the battle sites surrounding the city, meets up with Sidney Franklin and Martha Gellhorn. John Dos Passos arrives near the end of the month. Ernest becomes friendly with correspondents Herbert Matthews and Sefton Delmer. Hemingway writes the following dispatches during March: "Hemingway Wants a Bullfighter to Toss Spain News" (March 13): "Hemingway Finds France Is Neutral" (March 17); "Gay on Their Last Ride" (March 19); "Italians in a Trap" (March 24); and "Brihuega Likened by Hemingway to Victory on World War Scale" (March 29). Among the newspapers carrying the NANA dispatches are the *Kansas City Star*, the *Kansas City Times*, the *New York Times* and the *San Francisco Chronicle*.

April–May: During April, Ernest begins to work on the documentary, later called *The Spanish Earth*. On the 9th, he witnesses a Loyalist offensive against the rebels outside the city of Carabanchel. He and others have set themselves up in a top-floor apartment in a building with a good view of the action. The following day the group is joined by Herbert Matthews, Sefton Delmer, Martha Gellhorn, Sidney Franklin, John Dos Passos, and Virginia Cowles. Ernest and Martha Gellhorn have begun a love affair. He returns to Madrid where he remains until the first week of May. The city is under bombardment throughout the month. On April 22, Martha leaves for a ten-day trip to the central battlefronts. During April, Ernest writes "Heavy Shell Fire in Madrid Advance" (April 10), "A 'New Kind of War'" (April 14), "War Is Reflected Vividly in Madrid" (April 25), and "Shelling of Madrid" (April 11). He arrives in Paris on May 9 and gives a speech to the Anglo-American Press Club at Sylvia Beach's bookshop. The medical needs of the Loyalist army is the subject of his talk. Ernest sails to New York aboard the *Normandie* and arrives on May 18. After a brief stopover he returns to Key West. His articles during the month include "Egging Madrid to Fight" (May 3), and "The Chauffeurs of Madrid" (May 23). The latter was written in New York and printed in the *New York Times*. The *New Republic* reprints a series of Hemingway's dispatches in its May issue under the heading "Hemingway Reports Spain."

June–August: Ernest's brief stay at home is split between Key West and Bimini. On June 2, Joris Ivens notifies him that President and Mrs. Roosevelt have agreed to a showing of *The Spanish Earth* at the White House. Two days later, Hemingway is back in New York to deliver a speech entitled "The Writer and War" to the Second Writers' Congress, held at Carnegie Hall. (The text is reprinted in article form in the *New Masses* on June 22.) Scott Fitzgerald and Hemingway have a short reunion during the conference. Ernest returns to Bimini and begins to make plans to bring out a book containing *To Have and Have Not*, short stories, NANA dispatches and other journalism, and his Writers' Congress speech. He learns that two of his friends have been wounded, one fatally, in the civil war. Leader of the Twelfth Brigade, General Lucasz, has died and his political commissar, Gustav Regler, has been seriously injured. Joris Ivens tells Hemingway on June 19 that the editing is completed on their film. He returns to New York to record a second narration. (An original track had been recorded by actor Orson Welles, but the filmmakers decided to use Hemingway's voice instead.) While there, Ernest decides against the collection of his work being published. After his work is finished, Hemingway returns to Cat Cay in the Bahamas. On July 8, Hemingway, Joris Ivens, and Martha Gellhorn (who is a friend of Mrs. Roosevelt's) are present at the White House for a dinner, followed by a screening of *The Spanish Earth*. Franklin and Eleanor Roosevelt react favorably. On July 10, Ernest and Joris Ivens fly to Los Angeles for a benefit showing of the film. Frederic and Florence March host a party which launches the fundraising drive among film people. Twenty thousand dollars is raised during the evening. The proceeds will allow 20 ambulances to be sent to Spain. Scott Fitzgerald is at the party held on July 12, and this is the last time he and Ernest see each other. The *Los Angeles Times* runs an interview with Hemingway on the same date. Ernest flies on to San Francisco for a brief promotional tour. The *San Francisco*

Chronicle publishes an interview with him on July 15. Hemingway returns to New York to read the proof pages of *To Have and Have Not*. He returns to Bimini in time to celebrate his 38th birthday on July 21. *Life* magazine prints a photo essay using stills from *The Spanish Earth* with captions by Hemingway on July 12. The French translation of Chapter Three of *Green Hills of Africa* appears in *Nouvelle Littéraires* on July 17. Ernest, Pauline, and Bumby leave from Miami for New York on August 3. Ernest encounters Max Eastman in the office of Max Perkins on August 11. A fistfight over Eastman's article "Bull in the Afternoon" ensues. Film reviews of *The Spanish Earth* have now come in and most are favorable. Ernest sails to France aboard the *Champlain* on August 14. He intends to return to Spain. *Blow the Man Down/The Yachtsman's Reader* is published in August.

September–December: Ernest spends the month in and around Madrid with Herbert Matthews and Martha Gellhorn. The three travel through battle zones. By late September, Ernest and Martha begin staying at the Hotel Florida in Madrid. Ernest is again writing articles for NANA. This month he writes: "Americans in Spain Veteran Soldiers" (September 14); "Loyalists Capture Key Centers in Aragon Drive" (September 15); and "Hemingway Doubts Teruel Drive Near" (September 24). In early October, Ernest, Martha, Herbert Matthews, and Sefton Delmer visit the Brunete front. Upon his return to Madrid, Ernest befriends a group of American soldiers, who begin to spend time with him in his room and at the Chicote Bar. *To Have and Have Not* is published by Charles Scribner's Sons in New York on October 15. *Time* magazine devotes its cover story to Hemingway on the 18th. Despite moderate reviews, the novel is ranked fifth on *Publishers' Weekly* bestseller list in its first month of publication and two additional printings are required in October. Ernest writes a play, *The Fifth Column*, while in Madrid. Mostly autobiographical, the lead male character, Philip Rawlings, is similar to Hemingway, character Dorothy Bridges is based on Martha Gellhorn, and their developing love affair is evident in the play. Jonathan Cape publishes the first British edition of *To Have and Have Not* in October. Hemingway's NANA dispatches include "Life Goes on in Madrid" (October 1) and "Loyalists' Drive Seen Progressing as Planned"

(October 7). The *New York Times* reports that Ernest has finished writing his play on November 14. Evan Shipman comes to Madrid in mid-November to recuperate from a war injury. He and Ernest are ill during the month. The Spanish translation of "The Horns of the Bull" is published in *Hoy* on November 4. *The Writer in a Changing World*, containing a reprint of Ernest's "The Writer and War," is published in New York by the Equinox Cooperative Press and the League of American Writers in November. During December, Ernest travels through Spain to various battle sites. He drives from Valencia to the Teruel front with Herbert Matthews and Sefton Delmer on December 17. After returning to Valencia, the group heads back to Teruel and witnesses a successful Loyalist offensive in which they gain the town. On Christmas Eve, Hemingway goes back to Valencia to celebrate the holiday with Martha Gellhorn. Pauline Hemingway has arrived in Paris on the same day. Ernest joins her at the Hôtel Elysée Park for an unhappy reunion. His NANA articles for the month are "Fight in Blizzard" (December 20, from the Teruel front) and "With Army into Teruel" (December 24). *Atlantic Game Fishing* is published by Kennedy Brothers, Inc., during the month.

1938

"The Denunciation" (short story)
"The Old Man at the Bridge" (short story)
The Spanish Earth (transcript of Hemingway's film narration)
Numerous articles for the North American Newspaper Alliance
Numerous articles for *Ken*
"The Spanish War" (NANA articles reprinted in *Fact*)
The Fifth Column and the First Forty-Nine Stories (play and
    short stories)
"The Butterfly and the Tank" (short story)
"Hemingway Reports Spain" (NANA articles reprinted in the
    New Republic)
Quintanilla: An Exhibition of Drawings (folder with preface
    written by Hemingway)
"The Heat and the Cold" (article)

Writers Take Sides/Letters about the war in Spain from 48 American Authors (includes statement by Hemingway)

Just What the Doctor Ordered (excerpts from two *Esquire* articles reprinted)

"A Story from Spain" (reprint of "Old Man at the Bridge")

An Exhibition of Sculpture by Jo Davidson (includes Hemingway's article on Milton Wolff)

Mort dans l'aprés-midi (*Death in the Afternoon* translated into French by René Daumal)

Den ene mot de mange, Statek śmierci, and *Imet' i Ne Imet'* (*To Have and Have Not* translated into Norwegian, Polish, and Russian)

"La Dénunciation" (French translation of "The Denunciation")

January–March: Various works by Hemingway are reprinted in five anthologies through the year. On January 12, Ernest and Pauline sail back to the United States together aboard the *Gripsholm*. At the end of January, Ernest learns that his name is being circulated as one of the editors of a new magazine to be published by David Smart, who also publishes *Esquire*. He writes an official statement from Key West, which denies his affiliation. (The publication is *Ken* and Ernest will begin writing for it during the year.) Adolf Hitler begins his second attempt to combine Austria with Germany on February 12. One month later, the Anschluss, combining the two countries, is passed through a Nazi-controlled plebiscite. Hemingway sends in his first article for *Ken* on March 2, calling for United States aid to the Loyalist forces in Spain. Shortly afterwards, he decides to return to Spain and on March 17 flies to Newark, New Jersey. Two days later he sails to Europe aboard the *Ile de France*. He remains in Paris through the end of the month. His associates while in France are Jim Lardner and Vincent Sheean, both correspondents for the *New York Herald Tribune*. Ernest leaves France on March 31 with a new six-week contract with the North American Newspaper Alliance. *Quintanilla: An Exhibition of Drawings*, a folder published by the Museum of Modern Art in New York with a preface by Hemingway, comes out during the month. "The Heat and the Cold," Ernest's article about the filming of *The Spanish Earth*, is published in *Verve*'s Spring issue.

April–May: Hemingway arrives in Barcelona on April 1. The city has been under siege. On April 3, he and Herbert Matthews begin traveling around the country visiting battle sites. On Easter, Ernest meets an old man in Barcelona. This encounter provides the basis for his first story published in *Ken*, "The Old Man at the Bridge." Later in the month, he meets a young girl named Maria, who has been raped by a Spanish soldier. The character Maria in *For Whom the Bell Tolls* carries the girl's name and is based on her. Ernest is reported to be in a Barcelona theater at a screening of *The Spanish Earth* when an air raid halts the showing for forty minutes. This story, reported in the *New York Times*, notes that upon being recognized Ernest is applauded by the crowd for several minutes. Hemingway's NANA dispatches during April are "Beauty of Spanish Spring Is Chilled by the Menace of Death" (April 4), "Hemingway Tells Rebel Rout of Yanks in Spanish Army" (April 5), "Spanish War Not Over By a Long Shot, Hemingway Reports" (April 7), "Main Rebel Threat Is Deemed in North" (April 11), "Infantry in a New Role" (April 14), "Planes Wreck Tortosa Bridge: Hemingway Witnesses Action in Rebels' Drive to the Sea" (April 16), "Loyalists Await Tortosa Assault" (April 19), "Young Lardner Is Fighting for Loyalist Spain" (April 26), and "Lerida Is Divided by Warring Forces" (April 30). *Ken* publishes its first issue this month. Hemingway's contributions are "The Time Now, the Place Spain" (April 7) and "Dying, Well or Badly" (April 21). The *New Republic* includes Hemingway's NANA dispatches from April 4 through April 6 in its April 27 issue under the heading "Hemingway Reports Spain." Ernest's response to Eugène Jolas' questionnaire entitled "Inquiry into the Spirit and Language of Night" is published in the April-May issue of *Transition*. Early in May, Hemingway visits Marseilles, France, for two days and then returns to Spain until mid-month. He returns to Paris to begin his voyage home. The *New York Times* reports his return to the United States on May 31. John Wheeler of the North American Newspaper Alliance has notified Ernest that he would like more features and less straight reporting from him because of an overlap between his and Herbert Matthews's dispatches. Hemingway writes only two dispatches during May. They are "Leftists at Castellon Heavily Entrenched" (May 9) and "Hemingway Sees Year of War; Madrid Army Strong, Active; 'Moles' Peril

Rebel Position" (May 12). "The Cardinal Picks a Winner" is published in the May 5 issue of *Ken*. Ernest's new short story, "The Old Man at the Bridge," appears in *Ken*'s May 19 issue. *Writers Take Sides/Letters about the war in Spain from 48 American Writers* is published by the League of American Authors in New York during May. A brief anti-fascist statement by Ernest along with a telegram of April 1, 1938, requesting donations for ambulance funds, is included in the collection.

June–September: Ernest arrives in Key West in early June. He divides his time between writing anti-fascist articles for *Ken* and fishing in his off hours. The magazine has put him on a $100 weekly retainer. Three of his pieces appear in *Ken* during June. They are "United We Fall Upon *Ken*" (June 2), "H.M.'s Loyal State Department" (June 16), and "Treachery in Aragon" (June 30). On June 22, Ernest is in New York to cover the Joe Louis–Max Schmeling prizefight for *Ken*. He returns to Key West. After writing the article, Hemingway stops contributing to the magazine.* In June, the *New Republic* reprints his NANA dispatches from April 13 through May 10 in "Hemingway Reports Spain." *The Spanish Earth*, the transcript from the film, is published in a limited edition of 1000 on June 15 by the J. B. Savage Company in Cleveland, Ohio. The introduction is written by Jaspar Wood, a high school student who is the actual publisher of the book. Hemingway, irritated that credit is given to him rather than to director Joris Ivens and photographer John Ferno, telegraphs Wood on July 19 to voice his objections and to tell him that any proceeds from the book alloted to him should be redirected to the estate of Dr. Werner Heilbrun, who was killed in Spain. On July 12, Ernest writes to Max Perkins and encloses "The Old Man at the Bridge," the last story to be added to his new collection. He reports delays in the production of his play, *The Fifth Column*. He is contacted on July 23 by M. J. Olgin, the American correspondent for the Soviet newspaper *Pravda*. Olgin asks Hemingway for an article on fascism in Spain. Ernest's contributions to *Ken*, written in June, are "Call for Greatness" (July 14) and "My Pal the Gorilla Gargantua," his article about the Louis–Schmeling fight (July 28). The London magazine, *Fact*, runs 19 of Hemingway's NANA

*Subsequent articles in *Ken* have been written by the end of June.

dispatches on July 15 under the heading "The Spanish War." On August 1, *Pravda* publishes "Yenobeyectbo otoro he npoctmt." (This article by Hemingway is discovered in 1982 by William Watson. Its first appearance in English, under the title "Humanity Will Not Forgive This," is on November 27, 1982, when it is published in syndicated newspapers across the United States and Canada. The *Toronto Star*, Hemingway's former employer and the flagship newspaper of the Tribune Syndicate, bought the rights to the unearthed article.) Ernest, Pauline, and his three sons leave for Wyoming on August 4. During their drive West, Ernest scratches his left eye, causing recurring soreness and infection, which affects his vision. By August 17, Ernest is at the Nordquist Ranch reading proofs of his new collection of stories. He sends the preface and dedication of the book to Max Perkins on August 20. (In his letter, Hemingway tells Perkins he wants the collection to be dedicated to Martha Gellhorn and Herbert Matthews. The published book, however, does not carry this dedication.) Ernest leaves Wyoming for New York. On August 30, after a meeting with Max Perkins, he sails to France aboard the *Normandie*. Two articles, written before the end of June, are published in *Ken*'s August issue. They are "A Program for U.S. Realism" (August 11), in which Hemingway predicts the outbreak of war within the year, and "Good Generals Hug the Line" (August 25). Ernest spends the remainder of September in Paris with Martha Gellhorn. Sudetenland, a Czechloslovakian state, is taken over by Germany on September 29 as a result of a Munich conference attended by British prime minister Neville Chamberlain, French premier Edouard Daladier, Italian leader Benito Mussolini, and Adolf Hitler. *Ken* publishes Hemingway's "False News to the President" on September 8 and "Fresh Air on an Inside Story" on September 22. Two of his *Esquire* articles, "a.d. in Africa" and "a.d. in America," are reprinted in *Just What The Doctor Ordered*, published by Simon and Schuster during the month, under the title "Running Story."

October–December: Hemingway remains in Paris until November. While there, he writes "Night Before Battle," which he submits to Arnold Gingrich (which is published in February 1939 and turns out to be his last contribution to *Esquire*). He tells Gingrich that he has completed two chapters of a new novel, most likely *For Whom the Bell Tolls. Lilliput* magazine reprints "Old Man at the Bridge" in its October issue under the heading "A Story from Spain." *The Fifth Column and The First Forty-Nine Stories* is published by Charles Scribner's Sons in New York on October 14. The book contains in addition to the play, "The Short Happy Life of Francis Macomber," "The Capital of the World," "The Snows of Kilimanjaro" (with the reference to Scott Fitzgerald altered to "poor Julian" rather than "poor Scott," "The Old Man at the Bridge," "Up in Michigan" (which appears in an American collection for the first time), and all stories from *In Our Time, Men Without Women*, and *Winner Take Nothing*. Despite mixed reviews, sales are brisk. Six thousand copies sell within the first two weeks of publication. On November 4, Ernest travels to Barcelona and then on to Tarragona and Ripoli. He returns to Paris to begin his sea voyage to the United States. On an undetermined date in November, Hemingway delivers a speech over the German Freedom Broadcasting Station. (A portion of the speech will be published in the *Weltbühne* on August 25, 1946.) The *New York Herald Tribune* reports his arrival on November 25. Ernest and Pauline stay together at her apartment on East 50th Street until the end of the month when they return separately to Key West. Benjamin F. Glaser has been hired by the Theatre Guild to adapt *The Fifth Column* for production. "The Denunciation," the first of three short stories set in Madrid, appears in *Esquire*'s November issue. A catalogue, *An Exhibition of Sculpture by Jo Davidson*, is published to benefit the Spanish Children's Milk Fund, a group chaired by writer Dorothy Parker. Hemingway's article, "Major Milton Wolff," is included. Wolff is a member of the Abraham Lincoln Brigade. On December 2, the final evacuation of Loyalists occurs at Ripoli, the town Ernest visited in the previous month, with the assistance of American volunteers in the International Brigade. Ernest is in Key West through December and writes a story, "Nobody Ever Dies." "The Butterfly and the Tank," part of the Madrid series, is published in *Esquire* in December. The French translation of "The Denunciation" appears in this month's issue of *Volontaires*.

1939

"Nobody Ever Dies" (short story)
"Night Before Battle" (short story)
"The Clark's Fork Valley, Wyoming" (article)
"On the American Dead in Spain" (article)
"The Next Outbreak of Peace" (article)
"The Writer as a Writer" (article)
The Fifth Column and The First Forty-Nine Stories (British edition)
"Under the Ridge" (short story)
"Eulogy to Gene Van Guilder" (article)
An Exhibition of Sculpture by Jo Davidson (catalogue reprinted by the Georgian Press, Inc., of New York)
Somebody Had to Do Something/A Memorial to James Phillips Lardner (reprint of "On the American Dead in Spain" included)
Men in the Ranks (foreword of this book published by Friends of the Abraham Lincoln Brigade is written by Hemingway)
All the Brave (book by Luis Quintanilla carrying three prefaces by Hemingway written on March 10, April 18, and May 1938)
"The Fifth Column" (excerpt of play and part of introduction to *The Fifth Column and The First Forty-Nine Stories*)
Five Kinds of Writing (includes "Dispatches from Spain" and short story "A Clean, Well-Lighted Place")
Att ha och inte ha (Swedish translation of *To Have and Have Not* by Thorsten Jonsson)
Pjataja kolonna i Pervye Tridcat' Vosem' Rasskazov (*The Fifth Column* and 38 short stories translated into Russian)
Pyutaya kolonna (preface to *The Fifth Column and the First Forty-Nine Stories* translated into Russian)

January–March: Nine anthologies published during the year contain reprints of Hemingway's fiction. Ernest travels to New York during January to read Benjamin Glaser's adaptation of *The Fifth Column.* Quite displeased with Glaser's work, Hemingway rewrites the play in two weeks. Glaser agrees to his changes. Lee Strasberg is set to direct, and the casting begins. Hemingway is highly agitated with the entire project at this point. He returns to Key West on January 24. The Russian translation of the preface to *The Fifth Column and The First Forty-Nine Stories* appears in the January issue of *Internatsionalnaya Literatura*. An article about Neville Chamberlain, "The Next Outbreak of Peace," is published in *Ken* on January 12. On February 7, Ernest writes to Max Perkins from Key West and tells the editor that he now wishes that he had written *The Fifth Column* as a novel. He also discusses an idea for a story, which is the kernel of *The Old Man and the Sea*. One week later, Ernest begins a month-long stay at the Ambos Mundo Hotel in Havana. He writes the story "Under the Ridge." "Night Before Battle," the last of the Madrid stories, is published in *Esquire*'s February issue. *Vogue*'s February 1 issue contains an article by Ernest entitled "The Clark's Forks Valley, Wyoming." "On the American Dead in Spain" appears in the *New Masses*'s issue celebrating the third anniversary of the Spanish Popular Front victory on February 14. (The article is reprinted in *Somebody Had to Do Something*. The memorial to James Lardner contains work by his father, Ring Lardner, Jr.; Hemingway; Jay Allen; Don Jesus Hernandez; El Camposino; Dolores Ibarruri; and Vincent Sheean and drawings by Castelao. The booklet is published by the James Lardner Memorial Fund in Los Angeles, California. Hemingway is named as sponsor of the fund.) Ernest begins to work on *For Whom the Bell Tolls* on March 1. He returns to Key West to see his son Bumby on March 15, the same day that German troops occupy Prague, making their annexation of Czechoslovakia complete. By March 21, Hemingway has written 15,000 words on his novel. Germany is trying to extend its control over Poland. On the same date, the Polish foreign minister is given a list of demands, which includes the order that the city of Danzig must revert to German control and that the country must ally itself with Germany against Russia. Ford Madox Ford contacts Hemingway about his plans to revive the *transatlantic review*. On March 24, Ernest explains in a letter to Max Perkins that his views on the quality of Scott Fitzgerald's *Tender Is the Night* have changed and confesses that he has always acted with an immature jealousy toward him. Many visitors in Key West prevent Hemingway from accomplishing much work on his novel. "Shipwreck" Kelly is among the people who visit. He arrives on March 24 to discuss a film adaptation of "The Short Happy Life of Francis Macomber" to be directed by Howard

Hawks. On March 31, British prime minister Neville Chamberlain announces England's and France's support of Poland if it should be invaded by Germany. *Cosmopolitan*'s March issue contains Hemingway's "Nobody Ever Dies," a story of a Spanish Civil War veteran in Havana.

April–August: Ernest returns to Havana on April 10 and is soon joined by Martha Gellhorn. She finds the Finca Vigia, located near the village of San Francisco. After they have purchased the house, Martha begins to oversee its renovation while Ernest works on his novel. On April 16, Maksim Maksimovich, Russia's commissar for foreign affairs, presents the Mutual Assistance Pact to the allies. On the following day, the Soviet ambassador talks to Germany about improving German–Soviet relations. The Spanish Civil War ends with the defeat of the Loyalists when Franco and the Nationalists take over Madrid. General Francisco Franco becomes the new leader of Spain. Neville Chamberlain unofficially declines participation in Russia's Mutual Assistance Pact on May 7. Italy and Germany enter into the Pact of Steel on May 22 in which they agree to assist if one or the other becomes involved in a war. On May 23, Hitler tells his military leaders that war with Poland is inevitable. Ernest writes to Charles Scribner and reports that he is on page 199 in his manuscript. "The Writer as a Writer" by Hemingway appears in the May–June issue of *Direction*. The magazine serves as a program for the Third Annual American Writers' Congress in New York in June. Jonathan Cape publishes the first British edition of *The Fifth Column and The First Forty-Nine Stories* in June. An excerpt of the play and the introduction to the collection is published in the Summer 1939 issue of *Now and Then*. By July 10, Ernest has completed 14 chapters of *For Whom the Bell Tolls*, which he mistakenly estimates to be two-thirds of the novel. He turns 40 years old on July 21. In mid-August Ernest stops working on the novel to prepare for a trip west, where he will meet his sons. On August 23, he is in Key West to begin the journey to Wyoming. The Treaty of Nonaggression is signed by Germany and the U.S.S.R. on the same day. This pact, which precipitates World War II, splits Poland between the two countries and gives a free hand to Russia in its dealings with Estonia, Latvia, and Finland, and to Germany in its dealings with Lithuania. Two days later, Britain and Poland sign an agreement and Mussolini notifies Hitler that he will stay neutral in the event of a conflict despite the Pact of Steel. Martha and Ernest reach St. Louis, Missouri, on August 27. She remains there while Ernest continues on to Wyoming.

September: Germany invades Poland at 4:45 A.M. on September 1. Britain and France declare war on Germany two days later. World War II begins. Japan terminates its undeclared war with Russia on September 15 because of the Nazi-Soviet Pact. Japan signs an agreement with the two countries. Russia occupies Eastern Poland on September 17. Hemingway reaches the L-Bar-T Ranch on September 1. His stay is brief. He leaves after Pauline arrives. Ernest travels to Sun Valley, Idaho, to meet Martha Gellhorn. It is his first visit to the town. He and Martha stay in Suite 206 of the Sun Valley Lodge. *Two Kinds of Writing* is published this month.

October–December: Ernest is writing in Sun Valley and spending time with his new friends, Lloyd Arnold, Gene Van Guilder, and Taylor Williams. Arnold and Van Guilder are working on publicity for the fledgling ski resort, and Williams is a hunting guide. By October 2, the Polish resistance is virtually destroyed. The Poles' final attack is defeated on October 6 in the town of Kock. Russia invades Finland on November 30. *Cosmopolitan* publishes Hemingway's "Under the Ridge" in its October issue. Ernest's friend, Gene Van Guilder, is killed in a hunting accident. The eulogy, delivered by Hemingway, is published in the *Idaho Statesman* on November 2. Martha leaves Ketchum (Sun Valley) in mid-November to resume her work as a correspondent for *Collier's* magazine. She is going to Finland to report the war. Hemingway befriends Clara Spiegel who is now staying in Sun Valley. She is married to Fred Spiegel, a friend of Ernest's from the Red Cross ambulance corps in Schio in 1918. Mrs. Spiegel begins to assist Hemingway with his correspondence. He also becomes friends with Tillie Arnold, Lloyd's wife. Ernest writes to Hadley Mowrer, his first wife, on November 24 and tells her that Pauline has just informed him that he is not welcome home in Key West for Christmas if his return is not permanent. On December 7, the *New York Times* reports that Hemingway is co-chairman of the

American Committee for Protection of the Foreign Born Conference. Ernest returns to Key West on December 17. He stays alone during the holidays. His marriage to Pauline Pfeiffer has ended, although no legal action has yet been taken.

1940

The Fifth Column (play produced and first separate edition published)

"Man, What a Sport!" (article)

"War Writers on Democracy" (brief commentary)

For Whom the Bell Tolls (novel)

Henrietta Hoopes Catalogue (evaluation of artist's work by Hemingway and others)

A Stricken Field (novel by Martha Gellhorn carries a 13-line epigraph written by Hemingway)

The Great Crusade (Hemingway writes preface to novel by Gustav Regler)

"The Killers" (reprinted in *Redbook*'s March issue)

The Best Short Stories of 1940 and the Yearbook of the American Short Story ("Under the Ridge" reprinted)

Adiós a las armas (*A Farewell to Arms* translated into Spanish by Héctor Pedro Blomberg)

January–March: Works by Hemingway are reprinted in six anthologies in 1940. Martha Gellhorn rejoins Ernest in Cuba. He has written 24 chapters of *For Whom the Bell Tolls*. He continues to work on the novel through the winter months. On March 6, *The Fifth Column* opens at the Alvin Theatre in New York. (The play, produced by the Theatre Guild, Inc., closes in May after 87 performances.) Finland capitulates to the Soviet Union on March 12. A treaty is signed by the two countries in Moscow. Martha Gellhorn's novel, dedicated to Ernest, is published in March.

April–June: Hemingway completes two-thirds of his novel by the first week of April. His protagonist is based in part on himself and in part on Major Robert Marriman, a former professor of economics and a member of the 15th International

Brigade during the Spanish Civil War. Some characters appear under the real names of the people from which they are drawn (e.g., Maria). Ernest leaves Havana to visit Mayito Menocal's plantation, which is located about 300 miles from the city. While there he writes a preface to Gustav Regler's novel, *The Great Crusade*, and continues to work on his own book. Germany invades Norway and Denmark on April 9. Ernest returns to Havana on April 15, the same day that British and French troops land and then almost immediately evacuate the site in Norway. Ernest tells Max Perkins in a letter dated April 21 that he has selected the title for his novel from a passage by John Donne. British and French troops are driven back from Central Norway by German forces on May 2. Winston Churchill becomes Britain's prime minister on May 10. The Germans invade Belgium on the same day, and the Dutch army surrenders within four days. Britain, alarmed at Germany's progress, begins to plan the withdrawal of nine of its ten divisions in France by evacuation at the English Channel. The following day, German tanks arrive at Abbéville on the Channel. British troops are in Dunkirk on May 24 for evacuation and two days later begin the operation while the French are still considering defending the area. The Belgian army surrenders to Germany on May 27. The French begin to evacuate troops on the 28th. Germany begins its *Luftwaffe* air attacks, which continue through June. Hemingway remains in Havana with Martha Gellhorn. He continues working on *For Whom the Bell Tolls*. He and Pauline have made a temporary divorce settlement; he is to pay her $500 a month. His article about fishing in the Gulf Stream, "Man, What a Sport!," is published in the May issue of *Rotarian*. Charles Scribner's Sons in New York publishes the first separate edition of *The Fifth Column* on June 3. The British evacuation at Dunkirk is completed by June 4. This move, which rescues over 300,000 men, keeps the country's military fit to stay in the war. The allied forces leave Narvik on June 8 and the Norwegian army surrenders to Germany the following day. On June 10, Mussolini declares war on France and his troops enter the southern part of the country while the Germans approach Paris. The city falls on June 14, and two days later Premier Reynaud resigns and is replaced by Marshall Phillipe Petain. France surrenders to Germany on June 22. Northern France is occupied by the Germans while the south is under Italian occupation. An Italo-French armistice is signed on June 24, and all fighting ends in the country the next day. Hemingway's response to Archibald MacLeish's comment that contemporary writers are not fighting fascism is published in *Life* magazine on June 24. General Charles De Gaulle is recognized by Britain as the leader of the Free French as of June 27. Ernest, alone in Havana since Martha's departure at the end of May, is nearing completion of his novel.

July–September: The Battle of Britain begins on July 10. The German *Luftwaffe* starts its air strikes against coastal shipping. Hitler's Operation Sea Lion, his plan for the invasion of Britain, continues through September. Hemingway writes Max Perkins on July 13 to notify him that he has finished *For Whom the Bell Tolls*. He has written 43 chapters and a prologue. He takes his manuscript to New York the following week. Ernest stays in the city at the Hotel Barclay for only a few days before returning to the Finca in Cuba. During July, Premier Petain abolishes the constitution of the Third French Republic and establishes a new government in Vichy, which approaches a dictatorship. By August 5, Lithuania, Latvia, and Estonia have been incorporated into the Soviet Union. Ernest spends most of August working on revisions and reading proofs of *For Whom the Bell Tolls*. He sends the majority of the corrected galleys, along with his dedication of the book to Martha Gellhorn, to Max Perkins on August 26. He also learns, during this time, that the Book-of-the-Month Club is interested in his novel as its October selection. In the latter part of August, Hemingway leaves Havana for Sun Valley, Idaho. He and Otto Bruce begin their drive from Key West on September 1. He is reunited with his three sons and Martha Gellhorn in Idaho and resumes his work on the galleys of his novel. The "Blitz," Germany's bombing of Britain, begins on September 7. (This action will continue until May 16, 1941.) Hitler postpones his planned invasion of England on September 17. On September 12, Italy invades Egypt, which has been under British guard to keep open access to the Suez Canal. Between September 23 and 25, Britain and the Free French try, unsuccessfully, to take Dakar, West Africa. Germany, Italy, and Japan sign the Tripartite Pact in which they agree to enter the war if one of the three is attacked by a new enemy.

October: Early in the month, Hemingway is visited in Sun Valley by Donald Friede. His friend from the 1920s offers to act as his agent in selling film rights to his work. German troops enter Rumania on October 12 and five days later Hitler cancels Operation Sea Lion for the winter. Ernest and Martha go on a pack trip through the Middle Fork region of the Salmon River. They return to Sun Valley on October 21, Scribner's official publication date of *For Whom the Bell Tolls*. Seventy-five thousand copies are ordered in the first printing. The novel receives better critical response than any of his other work has in recent years. The *New York Times* reports that film rights to *For Whom the Bell Tolls* have been sold to Paramount Studios for $100,000. This figure is said to be the highest to date paid for film rights to a novel. During October, the agreement is set with the Book-of-the-Month Club as well. (As part of Hemingway's agreement with Paramount Pictures, he will receive an additional ten cents for each copy of the novel which is sold through the Book-of-the-Month Club.) Two hundred thousand copies are ordered by the club. Dorothy Parker and her husband, Allan Campbell, visit Hemingway in Sun Valley. Actor Gary Cooper and his wife, Rocky, are vacationing at the ski resort. Cooper and Hemingway, who first meet this month, become close friends. On October 28, Italy invades Greece.

November: On November 5, Ernest's divorce from Pauline Pfeiffer becomes final. Franklin Delano Roosevelt is elected to his third term as President of the United States. The *New Masses* November 5 issue carries a review of *For Whom the Bell Tolls* which, although not an outright attack, is mainly negative. The reviewer writes a letter, which appears in the *Daily Worker* on the same date, signed also by Milt Wolff, Freddy Keller, and Irv Goff. These former members of the Abraham Lincoln Brigade attack the novel as being false and a misrepresentation of the Spanish Civil War. The letter stirs a controversy and creates a critical split between those in favor of and those against Hemingway's fictional treatment of the war in Spain. Martha and Ernest leave Sun Valley on November 20. They are married the next day in the dining room of the Union Pacific Railroad depot in Cheyenne, Wyoming. A local justice of the peace performs the ceremony. The couple continues on to New York where they stay at the Hotel Barclay.

By November 23, Hungary and Rumania have joined Germany, Italy, and Japan in Tripartite Pact. The Book-of-the-Month Club offers *For Whom the Bell Tolls* as its November selection. Originally set for 200,000 copies, the club changes its order to 135,000.

December: On December 9, Britain makes gains in its campaigns in Libya and Egypt. Fighting will continue through February 11, 1941, when Britain triumphs. The Hemingways remain in New York through mid-December. Martha makes arrangements with *Collier's* to resume her correspondence work, this time travelling to China. Hemingway agrees to cover the war in China for *PM*, a new newspaper published by Ralph Ingersoll. While in New York, Hemingway meets writer H. G. Wells. On their way home, during a stopover in Key West, Hemingway is introduced to Sinclair Lewis. F. Scott Fitzgerald dies of a heart attack in Hollywood, California, on December 21. He was 44 years old. Hemingway learns of Fitzgerald's death in a letter from Max Perkins on December 28. On the same date, the purchase of the Finca Vigia is finalized. The Hemingways pay $12,500 for their home.

1941

Numerous articles for *PM*
For Whom the Bell Tolls (first British edition)
Og solen gar sin gang (*The Sun Also Rises* translated into Danish by Ole Restrup)
Lys og mørk latter (*The Torrents of Spring* translated into Danish by Flemming Helweg-Larsen)
Tare ga tame ni Kane wa naru (*For Whom the Bell Tolls* translated into Japanese by Oi Shigeo)
Klockan Klämtar för dig (*For Whom the Bell Tolls* translated into Swedish by Thorsten Jonsson)

January–April: Nine anthologies published during the year contain reprints of works by Hemingway. On January 10, Germany and Russia sign a renewal on their pact of August 23, 1939. Martha and Ernest return to New York. During their stay at the Lombardy Hotel, they see many old friends, including Gustavo Duran, Solita Solano, and Donald Friede. Friede delivers the check from Paramount Pictures to Ernest. Bumby comes to stay with them on January 25 and 26. Ernest sends a $400 check to Solita Solano on January 26 to help pay expenses for Margaret Anderson, former editor of the *Little Review*, to return to New York from Europe. The next day, the Hemingways fly to Los Angeles, the first leg of their journey to China. They meet with Gary and Rocky Cooper during their stopover. They are in San Francisco on January 30 and are introduced to actress Ingrid Bergman, who is being considered for the role of Maria in the film of *For Whom the Bell Tolls*. Ernest and Martha sail for Hawaii from San Francisco aboard the *S.S. Matsonia*. Ernest meets with his aunt in Waikiki and has two slightly uncomfortable encounters with academics from the University of Hawaii. The Hemingways arrive in Hong Kong in February and remain there through the month. They are introduced to Sun Yat-Sen's widow. On March 1, Bulgaria joins the Tripartite Pact. Jonathan Cape publishes the British edition of *For Whom the Bell Tolls* on March 7. In early March, the Hemingways fly to Namyung and then to the 7th War Zone at Shaokwan where they travel through the surrounding countryside. Writer Sherwood Anderson, helpful in Ernest's early writing career, dies on March 8. Yugoslavia joins the Tripartite Pact on March 25, yet cancels the agreement two days later following a revolution in the country. The United States Congress passes the Lend-Lease Act in March, which empowers the president to provide or lease goods or services to any nation whose defense he considers vital to the security of the United States. The passage of this act is a step towards the United States entry into World War II. By April, the sales of *For Whom the Bell Tolls* have reached 491,000 copies. The Germans, led by Rommel, defeat the British in Benghazi on April 3. Two days later, British Imperial forces liberate Addis Ababa and capture Massawa. Germany invades Yugoslavia on April 6. Ernest and Martha fly to Chunking in early April and meet Chiang Kai-shek. Ernest is invited to visit Chiang Kai-shek's military academy in Chengtu. He accepts the invitation and is flown to the site. The United States occupies Greenland as a caretaker for Denmark on April 10. On April 13, the city of Belgrade falls, and Russia and Japan sign a neutrality pact.

Ernest and Martha travel through various parts of China in mid-April, including Mandalay, Kunming, Lashio, and Rangoon. Ernest returns to Hong Kong, where he stays through the end of the month while Martha travels to Jakarta.

May–August: The evacuation of British troops from Greece is completed on May 2. Ernest begins his return trip to New York on May 6. He travels through Manila, Guam, Wake Island, Hawaii, and San Francisco and then on to the East Coast. He stays alone at the Hotel Barclay. John Miguel De Montijo files a lawsuit in Los Angeles which charges Hemingway with plagiarism. While he is in New York, Ernest learns of the case, which charges that he took portions of *For Whom the Bell Tolls* from a film script written by De Montijo. Martha rejoins Ernest in New York, and the two leave for Washington where they meet with military leaders to discuss the situation in the Far East. Among the people they confer with is Colonel John W. Thomason, Jr., a Naval Intelligence officer who is also a writer and an artist. Germany invades Crete on May 20. The Royal Navy battlecruiser, the *Hood*, is sunk by the *Bismarck* on May 24, and Britain retaliates by sinking the German ship on the 27th. Martha and Ernest stop over in Key West to visit Patrick and Gregory. They are home in Cuba by June 9, one week after Charles Scribner's Sons has been served papers on the De Montijo lawsuit. On June 12, the *New York Times* reports that *For Whom the Bell Tolls* has been banned in Ireland. Germany invades Russia on June 22. Ernest visits the office of the American Vice-Consul in Havana to file a deposition for the De Montijo lawsuit on June 27. Hemingway's articles first appear in *PM* in June. "Ernest Hemingway Interviewed by Ralph Ingersoll," an interview edited by Hemingway, precedes his first dispatches (June 9). The articles are "Ernest Hemingway Says Russo-Jap Pact Hasn't Kept Soviet from Sending Aid to China" (June 10), "Ernest Hemingway Says We Can't Let Japan Grab Our Rubber Supplies in Dutch East Indies" (June 11), "Ernest Hemingway Says Japan Must Conquer China or Satisfy USSR Before Moving South" (June 13), "Ernest Hemingway Says Aid to China Gives U.S. Two-Ocean Navy Security for Price of One Battleship" (June 15), "After Four Years of War in China Japs Have Conquered Only Flat Lands" (June 16), "Ernest Hemingway Says China Needs Pilots as Well as Planes to Beat

Japanese in the Air" (June 17), and "Ernest Hemingway Tells How 100,000 Chinese Labored Night and Day to Build Huge Landing Field for Bombers" (June 18). On July 12, an Anglo-Russian agreement is signed in Moscow. Ernest celebrates his forty-second birthday in Cuba. He and Martha have recently befriended Robert and June Joyce. Robert Joyce is a first secretary assigned to the American Embassy in Havana. The United States and Russia sign an agreement of nonagression on August 1. President Roosevelt meets with Winston Churchill at Placentia Bay in Newfoundland during the month. The two leaders sign the Atlantic Charter, a statement of war aims to eliminate Nazi tyranny (which later become part of the United Nations charter). Although the United States has not yet declared war, its navy is involved in tailing German U-boats and calling in the British for their destruction. Hemingway, much to his dismay, receives a bill for $1000 for legal fees in the ongoing plagiarism suit.

September–December: In the latter part of September, Ernest and Martha go to Sun Valley and are joined by Bumby, Patrick, and Gregory. He hunts through the fall with Taylor Williams and others. Gary and Rocky Cooper are in Idaho as well. Ernest is introduced to director Howard Hawks, who is involved in the upcoming film adaptation of *For Whom the Bell Tolls*. Cooper is set to play Robert Jordan. On November 14, the U.S. House of Representatives votes in favor of Roosevelt's amendments to the Neutrality Acts, which will permit the country's ships to enter war zones. The Limited Editions Club awards its Gold Medal to Hemingway on November 26. The award is given to new books which are likely to become classics. Ernest decides not to go to New York for the ceremony, but sends Charles Scribner in his place. Writer Sinclair Lewis addresses the group and hails Hemingway as one of the six leading contemporary writers. (Theodore Dreiser, Willa Cather, Somerset Maugham, H. G. Wells, and Paul Romaine are the others Lewis cites.) The Hemingways leave Sun Valley on December 3. They plan to stop off at the Grand Canyon during a leisurely drive back to Key West. Ernest is in Texas when he hears the news of the Japanese air attack on the United States fleet in Pearl Harbor, Hawaii, on December 7. Britain joins the United States in declaring war on Japan on the following day.

Two British ships, *Prince of Wales* and *Repulse,* are sunk by
the Japanese on December 10. Germany and Italy declare war
on the United States on December 11. On the same day, Ernest
writes to Max Perkins from the Saint Anthony Hotel in San
Antonio, Texas. He discusses the war and his anger that Scribner's neglected to send a stenographer to the Limited Editions
award ceremony to record Sinclair Lewis's speech. Hong Kong
falls on December 25. Hemingway's earnings during 1941 approach $140,000. Of this amount, over $100,000 will go to the
U.S. Internal Revenue Service.

1942

Men at War (anthology edited by Hemingway)
For Whom the Bell Tolls (Limited Editions reissue, foreword
   by Sinclair Lewis)
Vogue's *First Reader* (reprint of article "The Clark's Fork Valley, Wyoming")
Hemingway Collection (P. F. Collier's six-volume set, which
   includes *The Sun Also Rises, A Farewell to Arms, Death in
   the Afternoon, To Have and Have Not, The Fifth Column and
   the First Forty-Nine Stories,* and *For Whom the Bell Tolls*)
"Remembering Shoot-Flying: A Key West Letter" (*Esquire* article reprinted in the June issue of *American Rifleman*)
"Varldens huvudstad" (Swedish translation of "The Capital of
   the World" by Thorsten Jonsson)
Efter Stormen ("After the Storm" and 15 other short stories
   translated into Danish by Sigvard Lund)
De ubesejrede ("The Undefeated" and 13 other short stories
   translated into Danish by Sigvard Lund)
Adeus ás armas (*A Farewell to Arms* translated into Portuguese
   by Monteiro Lobato)
Por quien doblan las companas (*For Whom the Bell Tolls* translated into Spanish by Eduardo Johnson Seguí)
Snon pa Kilimandjaro och andra noveller ("The Snows of Kilimanjaro" and other short stories translated into Swedish
   by Thorsten Jonsson)

January–April: Nine anthologies which include work by Hemingway are published during the year. Hemingway learns in Havana that the plagiarism suit brought against him by John Miguel De Montijo in Los Angeles has been dismissed. Ernest is still responsible for his legal fees despite the suit's being groundless. Siam declares war against Great Britain and the United States on January 25. By the 27th, Peru, Uruguay, Bolivia, and Brazil have severed diplomatic relations with the Tripartite powers. The British-Soviet-Persian Treaty is signed on January 29. Singapore falls on February 15. On March 3, Hemingway writes to Max Perkins to inform him of an offer he has received from Nat Wartels of Crown Publishers. Wartels asks Ernest to edit and write an introduction to an anthology of war stories. Excerpts of *A Farewell to Arms* and *For Whom the Bell Tolls* would be included. Rangoon falls on March 8. During the month, Hemingway reads Dudley Nichols's screenplay for *For Whom the Bell Tolls* and is disappointed with the adaptation. Ingrid Bergman has been signed to portray Maria in the film. Ernest contacts John Wheeler of the North American Newspaper Alliance and asks to be signed on as a war correspondent again. Wheeler declines the offer and explains that the news service is not sending correspondents to war zones yet. Hemingway becomes involved in plans to prevent Nazis from entering Cuba. Falangist sympathizers in the country have been assisting Nazis in their efforts to infiltrate Cuba. Ernest and Martha visit their friend Nathan Davis in Mexico City for two weeks. (The time of this trip is probably in late April.)

May–July: Mandalay falls on May 1. The Battle of the Coral Sea begins on May 4 and ends with the Japanese retreat on the 8th. Ernest meets with Robert Joyce and American ambassador to Cuba Spruille Braden to discuss his plans to establish a counterespionage network. He requests supplies, which include a cache of small arms. Braden then meets with Cuba's prime minister who agrees to the plan. Ernest begins to ready his network by mid-May. The operation is named the "crime shop" by the embassy, and Hemingway refers to it as the "crook factory." Bumby visits his father during this time. Ernest continues his work on *Men at War*, the anthology he is editing, and, as it proceeds, has a number of disagreements with Crown's editor Nat Wartels over the contents. Towards the end of May, Hemingway presents another plan to the American embassy. He would like to have the *Pilar* equipped as a Q-boat, but disguised as a research vessel working for the American Museum of Natural History. The plan is approved and, despite the bending of a few regulations, Ernest receives the requested equipment. On May 26, an Anglo-Soviet treaty is signed in London and two days later Mexico declares war on the Tripartite powers. The Royal Air Force begins its "1,000-bomber raid" on Cologne, Germany, on May 30. Half a million Germans are left homeless by the next day and 44 RAF planes are lost as a consequence of the air raids. Ernest selects his crew and devises a new name for the operation. He calls it "friendless." Winston Guest, Don Saxon, Juan Dunabeitia, Paxtchi Ibarlucia, Gregorio Fuentes, Fernando Mesa, Roberto Herrera, and Lucas (last name unknown) comprise the crew of the *Pilar*, now equipped with grenades, machine guns, and a radio. Patrols aboard the *Pilar* begin in June. The Battle of Midway Island, located at the western end of the Hawaiian Islands chain, occurs from June 4 through 6. The first American victory since the country entered the war in the Pacific, the battle costs Japan four of its carriers. The Germans invade Egypt on June 24, not quite two weeks after they have taken Tobruk, Libya, in a battle with British forces. In a letter to Max Perkins on July 8 Hemingway proffers his critical estimate of writers Nelson Algren and James T. Farrell, calling the former superior to the latter. Martha Gellhorn is in the Caribbean on assignment with *Collier*'s magazine. Ernest's three sons are visiting, and the boys are allowed to accompany their father on his patrols aboard the *Pilar*. The Finca is the scene of much socializing now as Ernest divides his time between carousing with his friends, editing *Men at War*, and patrolling on the *Pilar*.

August–October: The U.S.–Japanese battle for Guadalcanal gets underway on August 7. (This battle will becomes the focal point of the war between the two countries and will continue until February 1943, when the Japanese evacuate their troops.) Tom Shevlin, who spends about a month with Ernest during the summer, becomes an additional crew member on the *Pilar*.

Hemingway completes his 10,000-word introduction to *Men at War* by August 25. Martha Gellhorn is in Dutch Guiana during September and plans to go to Washington, D.C., before returning home to Cuba. Ernest's youngest son, Gregory, stays on with his father, after the other boys have returned to school. *Men at War* is published on October 22 by Crown Publishers in New York. Ernest's introduction and reprints of chapter 27 of *For Whom the Bell Tolls*, chapters 29 and 30 of *A Farewell to Arms*, and his NANA article "The Chauffeurs of Madrid" are included. The reviews of the book, mainly critical of his introduction, are generally favorable on his choice of material collected in the anthology. In Havana, Ernest makes arrangements for his friend Gustavo Durán to take over the "crook factory."

November–December: British and American forces land in North Africa on November 8. On the 11th, the German forces move deeper into previously unoccupied French territory. Gustavo Durán, who became a U.S. citizen on November 3 and received a passport on the 9th, flies to Havana on the 12th to begin his work with the "crook factory." Durán takes over the operation with some apprehensions. Martha returns to Cuba in the middle of November. Gustavo Durán and his wife Bonte begin to stay with the Hemingways at the Finca. Shortly afterwards, the two couples have a falling out. The friendship comes to an abrupt halt when Hemingway publicly insults Durán at a luncheon held at the American Embassy. On November 19, Russia begins an offensive which will eventually trap the German army in Stalingrad and on the following day starts another against Germany in the Central Caucasus. During November, the Federal Bureau of Investigation takes over the "crook factory" operation and all counterespionage work in the area on orders from President Roosevelt. *Men at War* remains on the *New York Times* bestseller list through the entire month. Hemingway begins to drink more heavily, which seems both cause and effect of his growing marital problems. John (Bumby) Hemingway is now in Officers' Candidate School and making plans to go overseas. Martha Gellhorn's attempts to get her husband to travel to Europe to cover the war increase. *Men at War* heads the *New York Times* bestseller list on December 13.

1943

For Whom the Bell Tolls (film version of novel)
Kilimanjaros sne ("The Snows of Kilimanjaro" translated in
   Danish by Povl Christensen in special illustrated edition)
"Pour qui sonne le glas" (chapter 2 of *For Whom the Bell Tolls*
   translated into French by Robert Lebel)

January–June: Works by Hemingway are included in eight
anthologies during the year. The Casablanca Conference, attended by Churchill and Roosevelt, is held between January
14 and 24. The results of the meeting are U.S. recognition of
Charles de Gaulle as the leader of France; the naming of General Dwight D. Eisenhower as supreme commander of the Mediterranean theater; the decision by the United States and Britain
to invade Sicily; and the terms for "unconditional surrender."
By February 2, the German army in Stalingrad surrenders.
The *New York Times* reports on March 10 that the Spanish
Ambassador to the United States makes public his feelings that
For Whom the Bell Tolls is propaganda against Spain's leader,
Francisco Franco. British and American bombing of Germany
accelerates in the beginning of March and continues at a higher
intensity through May. On April 4, Hemingway first learns
about poet Ezra Pound's pro-fascist radio broadcasts in Italy.
Ernest is informed about them by their mutual friend, Archibald MacLeish. He continues to make his "Q-boat" patrols
aboard the *Pilar*. On May 5, Hemingway writes to Archibald
MacLeish, now the Librarian of Congress, and asserts his opinion that Pound would be better off shooting himself now to
avoid the repercussions of his fascist broadcasts. The friendship
between Hemingway and MacLeish begins to develop again
although it will never return to its previous closeness. Hemingway leaves Havana for a six-week trip at sea in June.

July–December: On July 10, the day that Sicily is invaded
by the United States, Canada, and Britain, the film *For Whom
the Bell Tolls* premieres in New York. Produced and directed
by Sam Wood, the Paramount movie stars Gary Cooper and
Ingrid Bergman. Dudley Nichols is the screenwriter. Hemingway returns to Havana in time to celebrate his forty-fourth
birthday at the Club de Cazadores. Ezra Pound is indicted for

treason by the Grand Jury in the United States District Court in Washington, D.C., on July 26. The charges against Pound stem from his 125 pro-fascist broadcasts made over Rome Radio from December 1941 to July 1943. Two days prior to Pound's indictment, Italian dictator Benito Mussolini is defeated on the Fascist Grand Council and forced to resign. By August 17, the Allied conquest of Sicily is completed. Hemingway writes to MacLeish on August 10 to tell him that he has read the transcripts of Pound's broadcasts and has concluded that the poet should be institutionalized as mentally unbalanced. The proof of his mental disorder is in the very fact of having made the broadcasts, Hemingway notes. Ernest also tells MacLeish that he is planning to leave on a two-month trip aboard the *Pilar* and that he has not done any writing since the previous year's introduction to *Men at War*. Hemingway's friend Robert Joyce leaves his post at the American Embassy to enter the Office of Strategic Services (the O.S.S., which is the forerunner of the United States Central Intelligence Agency). On August 31, Ernest writes to Allen Tate, currently holding the Chair of Poetry at the U.S. Library of Congress, to discuss what the two, along with Archibald MacLeish, can and are obligated to do to prevent Ezra Pound's being punished severely for his radio broadcasts. Hemingway feels they must take a public stand in Pound's defense. British troops land on the Italian mainland at Calabria on September 3, which prompts the country to sign an armistice. A formal surrender follows on September 8. Four days later, French troops land at Corsica. The Allies take Naples on October 1 and Capua on the 7th. Italy declares war on Germany on October 13. Martha Gellhorn leaves Havana bound for London on October 25, the same day that Japan suffers a major defeat at Raboul, located east of New Guinea. Ernest remains in Havana, where he has been repeatedly forced to cancel his trip aboard the *Pilar* because of inclement weather. By the end of October, Germany has lost 60 U-boats in battle. On November 6, Russia recaptures Kiev. The Royal Air Force holds air strikes over Berlin for five consecutive nights beginning November 22. Churchill, Roosevelt, and Chiang Kai-Shek meet during this period and the two Western leaders confer with Joseph Stalin from November 28 to December 1 for the first time. Out of this conference comes a united battle plan against the Germans. Britain and America will invade France while Russia begins an offensive in its homeland to distract the Germans. The R.A.F. continues its air strikes over Berlin in December. Roosevelt and Churchill meet with the president of Turkey in Cairo, Egypt, from December 4 to December 6. Patrick and Gregory visit their father, who is still alone in Havana while Martha is working for *Collier*'s in London. The boys spend Christmas with Ernest. The British sink Germany's ship, the *Scharnhorst*, in the North Cape. This leaves Germany with only one large fighting ship, the *Tirpitz*, the sister ship of the sunken *Bismarck*. Sales on *For Whom the Bell Tolls* stand at 785,000 copies three years after its publication.

1944

Numerous articles for *Collier*'s magazine
To Have and Have Not (film adaptation of the novel)
They Were There/The Story of World War II and How It Came About by America's *Foremost Correspondents* (includes reprints of *New Republic* articles)

January–March: *For Whom the Bell Tolls* is translated into Danish, French, Finnish, Portuguese, and Spanish in 1944. *The Sun Also Rises* is translated into Spanish and Italian. All told, there are 11 translations of Hemingway's work published during the year. This is the point at which translations of his work begin to proliferate dramatically. Reprints of his writing appear in 11 anthologies published in 1944 as well. Ernest is alone in Havana until Martha's return from London in March. The Americans bomb Berlin during daylight hours for the first time on March 4. On this same date, Ernest's first contribution to *Collier*'s, a brief biographical note on his wife, appears in the magazine. Hemingway makes an agreement with *Collier*'s to write about the Royal Air Force.

April–June: Ernest and Martha begin their trip to London in April. Their first stop is New York where they stay at the Hotel Gladstone. The Hemingways meet writer John Steinbeck during a dinner at Costello's restaurant. They are joined by John Hersey and John O'Hara. The Allies begin their offensive against German forces in Italy on May 12. The following day, Martha Gellhorn sails for Europe. Ernest stays on in New York until the 17th when he flies to London on a private plane. He checks into the Dorchester Hotel upon arrival. Hemingway is reunited with old friends Gregory Clark and Lewis Galantière and his brother, Leicester. During the third week of May, Ernest meets Mary Welsh, a researcher for the London Bureau of *Time*, *Life*, and *Fortune*, who is married to journalist Noel Monks. On May 25, Ernest is in an automobile accident, which occurs while he is on his way home from a late-night party. He suffers a head injury and is taken to St. George's Hospital for treatment. He is then taken to the London Clinic where he stays for four days. The effects of his concussion will last for the next few months. Martha Gellhorn arrives in London in time to visit Ernest at the clinic and an argument between the two ensues. Martha is angered by Ernest's raucous behavior which landed him in the hospital. Ernest leaves the clinic on May 29 and checks back into the Dorchester. He and Martha do not stay together. Ernest meets journalist Bill Walton, who is with *Time*, *Life*, and *Fortune*. The two will remain close friends throughout Ernest's life. The Allies enter Rome on June 4 and are victorious over the Germans. British and American forces land in Normandy on June 6 under the command of General Eisenhower. Hemingway has been taken to the transport *Empire Anvil* and watches the British and American battle with the Germans on Omaha Beach. Because he was a safe distance from the action, Ernest is angered when he learns that Martha was ashore during the fight. Both travel back to London. Martha leaves soon afterwards for Italy while Ernest stays and begins to write articles for *Collier*'s and to court Mary Welsh. By mid-June, the Allies are continuing their steady movement into France. Ernest is visiting the 98th Squadron at Dunsford in Surrey when the area is attacked by German bombers. On June 18, a bomb, which narrowly misses the Dorchester, destroys the Chapel of the Horse Guards at Westminster Abbey. Hemingway requests permission to accompany fliers from the 98th Squadron when they strike a German buzz-bomb launch platform. Permission is granted and Ernest flies with the R.A.F. in a Mitchell twin-engine medium bomber. American troops capture Cherbourg, France, on June 26. Ernest goes to the Thorney Island RAF station at the invitation of Captain Wykeham Barnes. He is shown the Mosquito Attack Wing 140, which has been involved in offensive strikes over Gestapo headquarters in various parts of occupied Europe. The following day, June 29, Hemingway accompanies Barnes on two runs in a Mark VI Mosquito, the first a trial, the other in pursuit of a German V-1. Ernest writes an account of the flight upon their return the next morning.

July–September: Ernest is listed as a staff correspondent for *Collier*'s on July 8 and stays on the masthead until May 12, 1945. Around this time, he travels to Cherbourg, France, where he stays with Bill Walton and Columbia Broadcasting System correspondent Charles Collingwood. Ernest is back in London on July 17 and leaves the following day for Normandy. During this period, he writes a poem, "To Mary in London," which remains unpublished until August 1965 when it appears in the *Atlantic*. Colonel Count Claus von Stauffenberg and fellow German officers attempt to assassinate Adolf Hitler on July 20. A bomb is placed in Hitler's headquarters in East Prussia by von Stauffenberg. On July 24, Hemingway is at the press camp of the 4th Infantry Division of the RAF. The division is planning to begin an offensive the next day. After a brief meeting with the commander, General Raymond O. Barton, Ernest is turned over to the public relations officer, Captain Marcus Stevenson. Ernest is in the town of Le Mesnil-Herman on July 28 when he meets Colonel Charles Trueman Lanham, in charge of the American 22nd Regiment. Lanham, called "Buck," and Hemingway will become close friends. Ernest stays with the division for the next nine days as it travels through Le Denisiere, Villabaudon, Hambye, Villedieu-les-Poêles, and St.-Pois. Lieutenant John Hemingway joins the O.S.S. in July. *Collier*'s issues a promotional booklet entitled *Voyage to Victory: An Eyewitness Report of the Battle for a Normandy Beachhead by Ernest Hemingway*. The material in the booklet is a reprint of Hemingway's first article for the magazine, published in the July 22 issue. Ernest turned 45 years old on July 21. On August 3, Hemingway is involved in an incident which constitutes improper conduct for a correspondent but is overlooked. In Villedieu-les-Poêles, he throws three hand grenades into a cellar, which is thought to contain Nazi SS men. The following day, the *New York Times* reports that Hemingway is present during the capture of six German Panzer soldiers in the town. American troops cut off access to the Brittany Peninsula on August 5, the same day that the *Saturday Review of Literature* announces that Hemingway has topped its reader poll of best American novelists. While in St.-Pois with Private Archie Pelkey, his escort, and *Life* magazine photographer, Bob Capa, enroute to see Colonel Lanham, Ernest encounters a German anti-tank gun. He injures his head when he jumps into a ditch to hide from the Germans. On a trip to Mont St.-Michel with Bill Walton, Hemingway joins a group of correspondents staying at the Hotel de la Mère Poularde. The group includes A. J. Liebling, Ira Wolfert, Helen Kirkpatrick, Bob Capa, Lael Tucker Wertenbaker, and Charles Collingwood. Colonel Lanham has set up temporary headquarters in the town at the Chateau Lingeard. Ernest escapes injury when he declines a dinner invitation at the chateau. Heavy casualties are incurred when the Germans bomb the site during the dinner. The division moves south on the following day. The Americans land on the French Riviera on August 15. Two days later, they recapture the towns of Chartres and Orléans, and on August 19 Patton's army reaches the Mante-la-jolise River, just 30 miles from Paris. Ernest arrives at the command post of the American 5th Infantry Division at Chartres. He continues on to Rambouillet where he meets Colonel David Bruce, who has come to lead troops in defense of the town. Hemingway takes over the command of the partisan fighters. He is also involved in the interrogation of prisoners. The Allies liberate Florence, Italy, on August 22. On August 24, Ernest is travelling towards Paris. He arrives in the city during its liberation by American troops and Generals LeClerc and de Gaulle. Mary Welsh joins Ernest at the Ritz Hotel in Paris on August 26. During one of the many celebrations in the city, Ernest meets 25-year-old J. D. Salinger, who has at this time published a number of short stories. "London Fights the Robots" appears in *Collier*'s on August 19. Hemingway writes "Second Poem to Mary" during August. (It is not published until August 1965 when it appears in the *Atlantic*.) On September 2, Ernest leaves Paris to visit battle zones north of the city for two days. The British liberate Brussels and Antwerp on September 3. Hemingway leaves Paris with a group of irregular fighters, other correspondents, and Private Archie Pelkey on September 7. Their destination is

Belgium. Bulgaria declares war on Germany the next day. Ernest is in the town of Hemmeres on September 12 to witness the first American tanks entering Germany. He is with Colonel Lanham. He rejoins the colonel in Schweller, Germany, on September 18 and soon afterwards moves into a farmhouse in the town of Buchet which is jokingly called the "Schloss Hemingstein." Ernest is introduced to artist John Groth. "The Battle for Paris" appears in the September 30 issue of *Collier*'s. The Viking *Portable Hemingway*, edited by Malcolm Cowley, is published on September 18. The collection includes portions of *For Whom the Bell Tolls*, *To Have and Have Not*, and *A Farewell to Arms*; *The Sun Also Rises* in its entirety; *In Our Time*; Chapter 20 of *Death in the Afternoon*; and nine short stories.

October–December: The British land in Greece and liberate Patras on October 4. On the same day, Hemingway reports to the headquarters of the Third Army in Nancy, France, where he faces interrogation by Colonel Park on his activities in Rambouillet from August 18 through 24. He plays down his involvement and, for a time, no further action is taken. Ernest discusses plans for a new novel in a letter to Maxwell Perkins on October 15 from Paris. The story he writes about will later be turned into *The Old Man and the Sea* and *Islands in the Stream*. American troops land on Leyte in the Philippines on October 20. General Charles de Gaulle's administration is recognized as the Provisional Government of France by the Allies on the 23rd. Ernest is spending his time at the Ritz Hotel in Paris with new and old acquaintances, including actress Marlene Dietrich. On October 28, Lieutenant John Hemingway is captured by the Germans on the 7th Army front. "How We Came to Paris" is published in the October 7 issue of *Collier*'s. The movie *To Have and Have Not* premieres during October. This Warner Brothers–First National release stars Humphrey Bogart, Lauren Bacall, and Walter Brennan. Jack Warner is the executive producer of the film, which is produced and directed by Howard Hawks and adapted for the screen by Jules Furthman and William Faulkner. Ernest is in Hürtgenwald, Germany, with the 4th Infantry Division on November 15. The division is set to begin a new offensive the following day. Bill Walton and a bodyguard, Jean Décan, are with Hemingway when he rejoins Colonel Lanham and Lt. Colonel Tom Kenan. Ernest is in this area of heavy fighting between the Germans and Americans until December 3. On November 30, he and Walton visit the town of Grosshau where they see much destruction and heavy casualties. The Allies make great progress against the Germans during the month, including the sinking of Germany's last large fighting ship, the *Tirpitz*, on November 12. "The G.I. and the General" appears in *Collier's* on November 4 and "War in the Siegfried Line" on the 18th. The Hürtgenwald campaign ends on December 3. The following day, while enroute to Luxembourg, Ernest escapes injury during a German air strike. He returns to Paris where he is introduced to writers Jean-Paul Sartre and Simone de Beauvoir. The Germans begin an offensive in Luxembourg on December 16, and Ernest and Bill Walton travel to the city the next day. They stay at Colonel Lanham's headquarters in Rodenbourg. The German offensive Ernest is covering will become known as the Battle of the Bulge. Martha Gellhorn comes to Luxembourg on December 24. She and Ernest are together for the next week in a tension-filled reunion. They, along with Charles Lanham, tour his command stations on Christmas Day. Martha and Ernest close the year together in a New Year's Eve celebration with Bill Walton.

1945

Studio: Europe (introduction by Hemingway)

"Soldier's Home" (reprinted in May issue of *Encore*)

Selected Short Stories (special armed services edition containing 12 stories by Hemingway, distributed free to U.S. servicemen)

"Man versus Bull" (portions of *Death in the Afternoon* reprinted in the January 20 issue of *Hulton*'s *National Weekly Picture Post*)

Golden Jubilee Greetings (brief note published in the Cincinnati Symphony Orchestra Program on March 24 and 25)

Esquire's *First Sports Reader* (contains reprints of "On the Blue Water" and "Remembering Shoot-Flying")

January–March: Thirteen translations of work by Hemingway are published during the year. *To Have and Have Not* is
translated into French, Italian, Finnish, Portuguese, and Spanish. *For Whom the Bell Tolls* is translated into Danish and
Dutch. Other works are translated as well. Hemingway's previously published fiction is collected in 16 anthologies during
1945. Ernest returns to Paris in early January. Among the
people he sees are George Orwell, William Saroyan (with whom
he instigates a fight), and various men from the 4th Infantry.
Late in January, Mary Welsh leaves Paris to return to London.
During January, American troops make advances in the war
in the Pacific and Russia gains ground in its fight against the
Germans in East Prussia. On February 4, U.S. forces enter
Manila. The Yalta Conference, attended by Stalin, Churchill,
and Roosevelt, convenes on the same day and lasts for a full
week. British and Canadian troops begin an offensive against
the Germans along the Maas and Rhine Rivers. Russian troops
capture Budapest on February 13 and, on the same day, renewed Allied bombing occurs over the town of Dresden and
continues through the next day. Mary Welsh rejoins Ernest in
Paris on the 14th. Charles Lanham and Robert Chance visit
Hemingway at the Ritz. During his stay, Lanham presents two
German machine pistols to Ernest. American troops have taken
München-Gladbach, Kiefeld, Trier, and Cologne by March 6,
the day that Hemingway flies back to New York. He stays for
a week. During this time, he meets with Martha Gellhorn, Max
Perkins, and his son, Patrick. On March 13, Ernest and Patrick
begin their journey to Cuba, stopping off in Florida to pick up
Gregory.

April–June: The Hemingway boys leave the Finca on April
1. Ernest is now awaiting Mary Welsh's arrival. The first American troops land on Okinawa, 300 miles from Tokyo, on April
1. Ernest writes to Mary Welsh on April 9 and tells her that
he is now going to concentrate on getting himself back into
condition for writing fiction. By April 13, the Russians have
captured Konigsberg and Vienna, and the Americans have taken
Hanover and Essen. On the previous day, President Franklin
D. Roosevelt died, and Harry S. Truman became the new United
States leader. The Allies capture Bologna on April 20, and four

days later Heinrich Himmler makes an offer of surrender. The San Francisco Conference, out of which the United Nations Charter will come in June, convenes on April 25. Benito Mussolini is arrested and executed by Italian partisans on April 28. The following day, all German armies in Italy and Tyrol surrender. On May 1, Adolf Hitler and his new wife, Eva Braun, commit suicide in a bunker in Berlin. Joseph Goebbels and his family join Hitler in the mass suicide. Mary Welsh arrives at the Finca Vigia the next day, and John Hemingway is released from the German prison camp. The British capture Hamburg on May 3, and two more German armies surrender to the Allies the next day. On May 8, after over 30 million Europeans have died, the war in Europe ends with the official surrender of Germany. The Russians join the Allies in celebrating their own Victory-in-Europe Day on May 9. The three Hemingway boys come to the Finca for a visit with their father and Mary Welsh. Ernest and Mary are in an auto accident on June 21, the day that Japanese resistance on Okinawa ends. Hemingway escapes unharmed, but Mary suffers a facial injury which requires plastic surgery.

July–August: The United States successfully tests an atomic bomb in Alamogordo, New Mexico, on July 16. The British Pacific Fleet joins the United States Third Fleet in attacks against Japan. The Potsdam Conference convenes on July 17 (and continues through August 2). President Truman calls for a Japanese surrender on July 26. Martha Gellhorn's intention to divorce Hemingway is announced in the *New York Times* on July 27. The United States drops an atomic bomb on Hiroshima, Japan, on August 6. Russia declares war on Japan on August 8. The United States drops another atomic bomb over Japan, this time over the city of Nagasaki, on August 9. Russian troops invade Manchuria on the same day and, three days later, enter North Korea. Japan surrenders on August 14, thus bringing an end to World War II. Hemingway learns in mid-August that General Raymond Barton has recommended him for a European Theatre Operations ribbon and Bronze Star for his actions in the defense of Rambouillet, France, in 1944. Mary Welsh leaves Cuba for Chicago where she will stay with her parents and make arrangements for her divorce from Noel

Monks. Ernest stays on in Cuba to fulfill the six-month residency requirement necessary for his divorce from Martha Gellhorn. He completes the introduction for John Groth's *Studio*: *Europe* on August 25.

September–December: Ernest explains to Mary Welsh in a letter of September 1 that he has not returned to Chicago since his father died because he does not want to see his mother. He hesitates, however, to openly insult her by coming to the area and not visiting her. Harry Truman receives Japan's formal surrender from Emperor Hirohito on September 2. Victory over Japan (V-J) Day is celebrated as World War II officially ends, six years and one day after Germany invaded Poland. Hemingway's only writing during September is an introduction for *Treasury for the Free World*, an anthology which will be published in 1946. Charles Lanham and his wife Mary (nicknamed "Pete") come to Cuba on September 22 for a two-week visit. Ernest and Pete do not get on very well. During the fall, the film rights to "The Killers" are sold for $37,500 and those to "The Short Happy Life of Francis Macomber" for $75,000. John Groth's *Studio*: *Europe* is published by the Vanguard Press in October. Ernest is unhappy with descriptive passages Groth has written about him in the book and discusses the matter in letters to General Raymond Barton and Colonel Charles Lanham in November and December. At the end of the year, Ernest's former driver, Jean Décan, is charged as a collaborator in France. Hemingway writes testimony in Décan's defense and convinces Lanham to do so as well. The *New York Times* reports that Hemingway is granted a divorce from Martha Gellhorn on the grounds of abandonment on December 21. The two were married five years and one month. John, Patrick, and Gregory arrive at the Finca to spend the holidays with their father. John, or Bumby, will stay for three months before he resumes his education at the University of Montana.

1946

Treasury for the Free World (introduction by Hemingway)
"The Sling and the Pebble" (book introduction reprinted as article in the *Free World* in March)
The Killers (film version)
"Rede an das deutsche Volk" (portion of speech delivered by Hemingway over German Freedom Broadcasting Station in November 1938 published in *Weltbuhne* on August 25, 1946)
"The Killers" (reprinted along with review and photos from film in *Life*)

January–March: There are 19 translations (into seven languages) of Hemingway's work published during the year. His work is collected in ten anthologies as well. A steady stream of visitors keeps social life at the Finca very active. House-guests include Mr. and Mrs. Gene Tunney, Charles Ritz (of the Ritz Hotel in Paris), Slim (Mrs. Howard) Hawks, and Winston Guest. Ernest begins a new novel during the first two months of the year. *Treasury for the Free World* is published in February. On March 14, Ernest marries Mary Welsh (born on April 5, 1908, in Walker, Minnesota). Gregory and Patrick Hemingway and Winston Guest are present at the ceremony in Havana and at a luncheon which follows. Mr. and Mrs. Richard Cooper hold a reception for the Hemingways in their home after they have made a second trip to a lawyer's office to finalize their vows.

April–August: Ernest has written 700 pages of his new novel by the end of April. The central characters in the book, *The Garden of Eden*, are newly married and the plot revolves around their changing sexual identity in the relationship. (The book remains unpublished and is unavailable for research purposes.) In late June, Hemingway begins to correspond with Konstantin Simonive, a Russian playwright, poet, and novelist. By mid-July, Ernest has written 1000 pages of his manuscript. Mary is now pregnant, and the two begin to make plans to go to Idaho where they will stay through the fall. On August 19, while in transit, Ernest takes Mary to the Memorial Hospital of Natrona County in Caspar, Wyoming. Her fallopian tube has burst and she is seriously ill. Ernest meets his sons in Rawlins, Wyoming, and brings them back to Caspar to await Mary's recovery. Universal Studio's *The Killers* premiers in August. The film, with a screenplay by Anthony Veiller, is produced by Mark Hellinger, directed by Robert Siodmak, and stars Burt Lancaster and Ava Gardner.

September–December: The Hemingways leave Caspar during the first week of September and continue on to Sun Valley, Idaho. Patrick stays in Ketchum after Bumby and Gregory return to school. Hemingway's story, "The Killers," is reprinted in *Life* magazine on September 2 along with reviews and photographs from Robert Siodmak's film. Bumby returns to Sun Valley to celebrate his twenty-third birthday on October 10. As part of the festivities, *The Killers* is screened for the group. Hemingway reacts in a positive way for the first time to a screen adaptation of his work. His companions in Idaho are Mr. and Mrs. Gary Cooper, Colonel Charles Sweeney, Mrs. Dorothy Allen, and Slim Hawks. Mary, Patrick, and Ernest leave Sun Valley on November 10. They travel first to Salt Lake City, Utah, to visit Mrs. Allen and Colonel Sweeney and then to New Orleans, where Ernest meets his mother and father-in-law, Adeline and Thomas Welsh. Patrick leaves for New York on November 28 and Ernest and Mary follow by train two days later. Mark Hellinger and Universal Studios put the Hemingways up at the Sherry-Netherland Hotel when they arrive on December 1. While in New York, Ernest sees Charles Lanham and Ingrid Bergman among others. On December 3, he flies to Gardiner's Island, located at the end of Long Island, for a week's hunting trip with Winston Guest and Charles Lanham. After spending three weeks in New York, the Hemingways return home to Cuba.

1947

"Hemingway in the Afternoon" (response to questionnaire in
    Time magazine on August 4)
The Essential Hemingway (British collection)
The Macomber Affair (film version of story "The Short Happy
    Life of Francis Macomber")

"The Killers" (reprinted in *Ellery Queen*'s *Mystery Magazine* in June)
"The Short Happy Life of Francis Macomber" (reprinted in *Cosmopolitan*'s October issue)

January—June: Seventeen anthologies published during the year contain reprints of Hemingway's work. There are nine translations of various works by Hemingway published during 1946. Ernest resumes his work on *The Garden of Eden*. Patrick is staying with his father at the Finca at the beginning of the year. He and Gregory return to Havana in April to recuperate from injuries sustained in a car accident in Key West. Mary goes to Chicago to assist her mother in taking care of her ill father. Pauline Pfeiffer Hemingway comes to Havana on April 16 to take care of Patrick who has grown worse and shows a propensity towards violence because of a concussion. The film version of "The Short Happy Life of Francis Macomber," called *The Macomber Affair*, premiers in April. Made by United Artists, the movie is produced by Benedict Bogeaus and Casey Robinson, directed by Zoltan Korda, and is adapted for the screen by Robinson and Seymour Bennett. It stars Gregory Peck, Joan Bennett, and Robert Preston. On May 10, after Patrick's condition improves, Pauline returns to Key West. Mary arrives in Havana on May 18. Pauline comes back to the Finca on May 23 and to Ernest's surprise the two women get along very well. During May, Ernest hears about a speech William Faulkner made at the University of Mississippi in which he called Hemingway one of the five best modern novelists but the least experimental. (Faulkner lists himself, John Dos Passos, Erskine Caldwell, and Thomas Wolfe as the other four.) Hemingway interprets Faulkner's comments as meaning that he believes Ernest is a coward. Ernest's anger is likely fueled by the fact that the Associated Press picked up the story for its wire services. He contacts Charles Lanham and asks him to write a letter to Faulkner to tell him about his bravery during World War II, which will disprove the charges of cowardice. Lanham complies and Faulkner writes to both him and Ernest to apologize for the comments which led to Hemingway's misinterpretation. A ceremony is held at the American Embassy in Havana to present Hemingway with the Bronze Star Medal for his activities in World War II. On June 17, Ernest's longtime editor at Charles Scribner's Sons, Maxwell Perkins, dies suddenly.

July–December: Pauline Pfeiffer Hemingway returns to Cuba in July. A joint birthday celebration for her and Ernest is held on July 21, his 48th. Mark Hellinger, producer of *The Killers*, contacts Ernest in late July about buying four more stories for film adaptations. He offers $75,000 plus 10 percent of all profits for film rights to each story. Ernest's health begins to worsen as his blood pressure rises due to overweight. *Time* magazine publishes Ernest's response to being questioned on American writers and writing on August 4. In early September, Ernest and Otto Bruce begin a cross-country drive to Idaho. They alter their route to visit the Hemingway family cabin on Walloon Lake. Ernest's sister, Sunny, is now taking care of the cabin. Mary stays in Cuba while Ernest is in transit to oversee the construction of a tower at the Finca, to be used as an office by Hemingway. Pauline is in Cuba with Mary. On September 12, Katy Smith Dos Passos, Ernest's friend for over 20 years, is killed in an auto accident. Her husband, John, is driving the vehicle she is killed in. Jonathan Cape publishes *The Essential Hemingway* in London during October. The book contains *The Sun Also Rises*, *In Our Time*, excerpts from *A Farewell to Arms*, *For Whom the Bell Tolls*, and *To Have and Have Not*, nine short stories, and the epilogue from *Death in the Afternoon*. Mary arrives in Sun Valley in November but soon leaves to visit Patrick, Pauline, and Bumby in San Francisco. Ernest stays alone in Idaho until her return in December. Early in the month, producer Mark Hellinger dies. Ernest has already received $50,000 from their agreement made in July for the sale of film rights to four stories. The arrangement is now pending until Hellinger's estate is settled. Ernest has been working on *The Garden of Eden*, but puts it aside in mid-December when his friends Juan Dunabeitia and Robert Herrera arrive in Ketchum. Patrick, Bumby, and Gregory come to visit for the holidays. Lillian Ross, working on a *New Yorker* profile on bullfighter Sidney Franklin, appears at the Hemingway cabin on December 24 to interview Ernest for her article.

1948

La Casa Belga (congratulatory note from Hemingway on Havana bookshop's twentieth anniversary reprinted in brochure and published on March 27)

January–June: Seven translations of Hemingway's work are published during the year. Eight anthologies containing reprints of his fiction are published as well. On January 3, Ernest writes to Charles Scribner's Sons for a loan of $12,000 to pay his income tax. He complains about only receiving $50,000 from the film version of "The Killers" since it made a three-million-dollar profit. He appears in an advertisement for Parker Pens that appears in *Life* magazine on January 26. Hemingway leaves Ketchum on February 1 and begins the drive back to Key West. Upon his return to Havana, Hemingway buys a springer spaniel and names it Black Dog. The pet will become one of his closest companions. The tower at the Finca proves too uncomfortable for Ernest to use as an office because of its isolation. Malcolm Cowley comes to Cuba with his wife and son for two weeks. He is interviewing Hemingway for *Life* magazine. Ernest begins to correspond with Lillian Ross and in February sends her a list of his heroes. They are Michael Ney, Napoleon's rear-guard commander during the French retreat from Moscow; Peter Wykeham Barnes of the Royal Air Force; Mary Welsh for the way she behaved when she was seriously ill; his son, Patrick; and writers Gustave Flaubert and James Thurber. Hemingway meets Aaron E. Hotchner in April. The young writer and editor has been sent to Cuba by *Cosmopolitan* to ask him to write an article on the future of literature. Ernest declines an invitation to join the American Academy of Arts and Letters in June. Late in the month, he and Mary take a ten-day cruise aboard the *Pilar* with Patrick, Gregory, Mayito Menocal, and Elicio Arguelles. The group cruises through the Bahamas. Ernest completes a new introduction to an upcoming illustrated edition of *A Farewell to Arms* on June 29.

July–December: After returning to Havana, Ernest goes back out on the *Pilar* for a trip around the time of his forty-ninth birthday. He is accompanied by Mary, Gregory, Gregorio Fuentes, Sinsky, and Mayito Menocal. On August 7, Maurice

Speiser, Hemingway's attorney and friend for 20 years, dies. Alfred Rice begins to represent Ernest. The Hemingways sail to Genoa, Italy, in September. They ship their car for a drive through the country which takes them to Stresa, Como, Bergomo, and Cortina d'Ampezzo. Count Federico Kechler is a new acquaintance. In October, they travel from Cortina to Belluno, Treviso, and Venice. While staying at the Gritti Palace Hotel in Venice, Ernest is given the *Cavaliere di Gran Croce al Merito* in the Knights of Malta. Ernest and Mary revisit the site in Fossalta where he was wounded 30 years ago during World War I. The Hemingways spend most of November at an inn, Locando Cipriani, on Torcello, an island near Venice. Mary is gone on sporadic trips with Alan and Lucy Moorehead. She meets art historian Bernard Berenson at this time. Ernest spends his time shooting and working on an article for *Holiday* magazine entitled "The Great Blue River." During one of his shooting trips at a preserve owned by Barone Nanyuki Franchetti, Ernest is introduced to 19-year-old Adriana Ivancich. He reads galleys of Elio Vittorini's *In Sicily*, to be published by New Directions in 1949, and writes a preface for the book. While in Cortina for Christmas, Ernest and Mary learn that film rights for "My Old Man" have been purchased by Twentieth Century-Fox for $45,000. The news of the sale is welcome because Hemingway is undergoing an audit on his 1944 tax return. His obligation to the Internal Revenue Service is an ongoing irritant to him because of the large portion of his income that he must surrender in taxes. At the end of the year, Ernest tells Charles Scribner that he has begun to work on a section of his planned land, air, and sea novel. He is working on a tale of the sea.

1949

"The Great Blue River" (article)
"The Position of Ernest Hemingway" (two-part article with first part by Hemingway)
In Sicily (introduction by Hemingway)
Joan Miró (includes article by Hemingway)
"The Snows of Kilimanjaro" and "The Short Happy Life of

Francis Macomber" (stories reprinted along with a note by Hemingway)

A Treasury of Great Reporting (reprints of NANA dispatches from April and May 1937)

Game Fish of the World (includes "Cuban Fishing")

January–April: Seven translations of Hemingway's writing, into Dutch, French, German, Greek, and Italian are published in 1949. Previously published work is collected in 16 anthologies. Malcolm Cowley's interview of Ernest appears in *Life* magazine on January 10. It is titled "A Portrait of Mister Papa." Ernest and Mary read the article in Cortina. Mary is offended by some minor biographical details. Ernest thinks the article is adequate, but declines Cowley's request for permission to write a full-length biography. Clement Greenburg's *Joan Miro* includes a reprint of Hemingway's 1934 article on his purchase of the artist's painting, "The Farm." The book is published in January by the Quadrangle Press in New York. Mary has a skiing accident during the month and breaks her arm. Ernest becomes ill and is bedridden during the first two weeks of February. In March, he contracts erysipelas, a disease of the subcutaneous tissue, in his eye and on his face and is sent to a Padua hospital. After leaving the hospital, Hemingway is introduced to Adriana's brother, Gianfranco Ivancich, in Venice. He begins to work on a new novel and incorporates his new acquaintances from Italy into the story. He spends his last month in Italy working on the novel. On April 30, the Hemingways board the *Jagiello* bound for Havana.

May–July: By the end of May, Ernest and Mary are back home at the Finca. Ernest hires a new secretary, Juanita Jensen. In early June, Hemingway puts aside his writing to go on a fishing trip with Charles Lanham, Nanyuki Franchetti, Gregory, Gregorio Fuentes, and a Cuban fisherman named Santiago, who has been hired on to the crew of the *Pilar*. After returning to Havana for a time, Ernest is back on the *Pilar* to celebrate his fiftieth birthday. He returns to the Finca and resumes his work on his new novel. "The Great Blue River," an article on fishing in the Gulf Stream, is published in *Holiday* in July. The *New York Times Book Review* features "The Position of Ernest Hemingway" in its July 31 issue. The article contains "Notes from a Novelist on His System of Work—A Letter from Hemingway" and "Notes from a Critic on a Novelist's Work" by Maxwell Geisman.

August–October: *McCall*'s magazine instructs one of its writers to contact Grace Hemingway for an interview. When Ernest learns of it he threatens to cut off his financial support if his mother grants an interview. Hemingway reports the progress on his novel to Charles Scribner on August 24 and writes that he is now at the stage of contemplating a title. He writes to Bernard Berenson on August 25. This letter begins a correspondence between the two that continues through Ernest's life. Mr. and Mrs. Aaron Hotchner arrive in Havana on September 5. They choose to stay at the Veradero Hotel so as not to disturb Ernest's work. Ernest writes to Charles Scribner on September 21 to report that he has decided on the title for the novel. It is *Across the River and into the Trees* and is paraphrased from the dying words of General Stonewall Jackson. Ernest has written 45,000 words of the book by the end of the month. On September 25, the *New York Herald Tribune Book Review* publishes its twenty-fifth anniversary issue. It contains an article by critic Alfred Kazin in which he names *A Farewell to Arms* as one of the three most memorable books published in the previous 25 years. Aaron Hotchner begins to act unofficially as Ernest's agent in negotiations for the serial rights to *Across the River and into the Trees* which *Cosmopolitan* is seeking. *Esquire*'s September issue contains reprints of "The Short Happy Life of Francis Macomber" and "The Snows of Kilimanjaro" and a brief note by Hemingway on the circumstances surrounding the writing of both stories. Averill Harriman asks Ernest to submit written comments, which will be read at the Roosevelt Memorial Concert, at the Waldorf Astoria in New York on January 30, 1950. He turns down the request. During the month, he writes to Charles Lanham and tells him that his protagonist in *Across the River and into the Trees*, Robert Cantwell, is based on Lanham, Charles Sweeney, and himself. (Renata is drawn from Ernest's new friend, Adriana Ivancich.)

November–December: Gianfranco Ivancich arrives in Havana as Ernest and Mary are planning a trip to New York and

Europe. They fly from Havana and arrive in New York on November 16 where they are met by *New Yorker* writer Lillian Ross. The Hemingways stay at the Sherry Netherland Hotel. A group is assembled for a welcome dinner. It includes Marlene Dietrich, Charles Scribner, George Brown, Virginia Viertel, and Aaron Hotchner. Lillian Ross begins interviewing Hemingway for a *New Yorker* profile when she meets him at the airport. She continues the process through November 18. Ernest, Mary, and Virginia Viertel sail to LeHavre aboard the *Ile de France* on the following day. After their arrival, they drive to Paris and check into the Ritz Hotel. Aaron Hotchner flies from New York to Paris to join the Hemingways. Ernest completes *Across the River and into the Trees* on December 10 at the Ritz. The serial rights to the novel are sold to *Cosmopolitan* for $85,000. On December 24, Ernest, Mary, Virginia Viertel and her husband, and Aaron Hotchner travel to the south of France. The group arrives in Nice during the last week of December. The Viertel and Hotchner return to Paris while Ernest and Mary stay on and then continue their travels, which will take them to Venice.

1950

Across the River and into the Trees (novel and serialized version in *Cosmopolitan*)

The Breaking Point (film adaptation of *To Have and Have Not*)

"Books I Have Liked" (article listing three choices for 1950 published in December 3 issue of *New York Herald Tribune Book Review*)

"Success, It's Wonderful" (article, edited by Harvey Breit, in *New York Times Book Review* on December 3)

Book Find News (letter from Hemingway on Nelson Algren's *The Man With the Golden Arm* included)

Ezra Pound: A Collection of Essays ("Homage to Ezra," first appearance was in *This Quarter*, Spring 1925, reprinted in this British publication)

An Examination of Ezra Pound: A Collection of Essays (American edition of above listing)

"Important Authors of the Fall Speaking for Themselves" (autobiographical note by Hemingway appears in *New York Herald Tribune Book Review* on October 8)

"Hemingway Is Bitter About Nobody—But His Colonel Is" (*Time* magazine prints a cable from Hemingway on September 11)

Under My Skin (film adaptation of "My Old Man")

January–April: Six translations, including Annemarie Horschitz' German translation, are published during the year along with *49 stories* is the title of a German book translated by Herschitz and the inclusion of Hemingway's work in nine anthologies. Ernest spends most of January in Venice. He visits Carlo Kechler in Codroipo for two days. He and Mary are associating with various members of the Italian aristocracy and with Adriana Ivancich. In early February, the Hemingways go to Cortina for a two-week skiing trip. Ernest develops another skin infection and returns to Venice. Mary stays in Cortina and suffers a badly broken ankle while skiing. She returns to Venice where Ernest is revising his novel. The first installment of *Across the River and into the Trees* appears in *Cosmopolitan* in February. The serialized portions appear in the magazine through May. The Hemingways leave for Paris in early March. Charles and Vera Scribner, Adriana Ivancich, and Monique de Beaumont arrive soon afterwards. Ernest and Mary begin their voyage home on March 22 aboard the *Ile de France*. They check into the Sherry Netherland for a week's stay. While in New York, the Hemingways see Ernest's new editor, Wallace Meyer, Patrick, Marlene Dietrich, Charles Sweeny, Evan Shipman, Harold Ross, and Lillian Ross. Ross is still working on her profile of Hemingway. *Under My Skin*, based on "My Old Man," premieres in March. Producer Casey Robinson also writes the screenplay for this film, which is directed by Jean Negulesco and stars John Garfield and Micheline Prelle. *Under My Skin* is released through Twentieth Century-Fox. The Hemingways arrive home at the Finca on April 7.

May–August: Lillian Ross's profile of Hemingway, entitled "How Do You Like It Now, Gentlemen?," is published in *The New Yorker* on May 13. Ernest's initial reaction is positive. Ernest writes a letter to Senator Joe McCarthy on May 8. It is unknown whether the letter was sent to the senator or not. Hemingway criticizes the senator's ongoing campaign against communists and communist sympathizers in the United States. McCarthy's efforts amount to a witchhunt and end up damaging the careers of many writers, actors, directors, and other artists who are believed to have leftist leanings. Ernest's letter is a personal attack on the senator as well. He sends his book dedication to Charles Scribner on June 11. *Across the River and into the Trees* is to be dedicated to Mary Welsh. Ernest also tells Scribner that he has recently written an article, "The Shot." The next day, he and Mary leave for a four-day trip to Bahía Honda and Megano de Casigua on the *Pilar*. Patrick Hemingway marries Henrietta F. Broyles on June 17. The Korean War, which will last 37 months, begins on June 25. The Hemingways, along with Roberto Herrera and Gregorio Fuentes, leave for a three-day cruise on the *Pilar* on July 1. The trip, in celebration of Ernest's having finished checking the page proofs of *Across the River and into the Trees*, turns sour when he falls and injures his head on their first day out. After returning to Havana, Hemingway writes two fables for *Holiday* magazine. They are titled "The Good Lion" and "The Faithful Bull" and are to be illustrated by Adriana Ivancich. Ernest begins to correspond with writer and editor Harvey Breit on July 9.

September: Hemingway turns down Harvey Breit's request to write a biography on September 1. Charles Scribner's Sons publishes *Across the River and into the Trees* on September 7. (Jonathan Cape's British edition preceded Scribner's by three days.) The reviews are generally poor with the exception of the notice written by John O'Hara in the *New York Times Book Review*, which is quite favorable. (Despite the critics, the novel goes on the *New York Times* bestseller list on September 24 and remains there until February 11, 1951.) Ernest begins to have problems with his right leg. It is likely that his old war wound was aggravated by his fall on the *Pilar* in July, but he decides against surgery to remove the last bits of metal left in his limb. Hemingway writes a preface to Lee Samuels's upcoming *A Hemingway Checklist*, the second bibliography of his work. The first major critical collection of essays on Hemingway is published in September. It is *Ernest Hemingway, The Man and His Work*, edited by J. K. M. McCafferty. Portions of Gertrude Stein's autobiography, Malcolm Cowley's *Life* magazine article, and a profile by John Groth are included along with 18 critical essays.

October–December: *Across the River and into the Trees* tops the *New York Times* bestseller list on October 15 and stays in first place through November 26. That his book is selling well helps to diminish Ernest's anger at the mostly negative reviews. Adriana Ivancich and her mother, Dora, arrive at the Finca on October 28. The two will stay with the Hemingways off and on for the next few months. *The Breaking Point*, the second film version of *To Have and Have Not*, opens in October. Ronald MacDougall writes the screenplay for the film produced by Jerry Wald and directed by Michael Curtiz. The Warner Brothers-First National release stars John Garfield and Patricia Neal. Ernest writes a preface for *Pourquoi Ces Bêtes Sont-elle Sauvages* in November. The book by François Sommer is about African animals. During the first three weeks of December Ernest writes one portion of his planned sea-novel series. It carries the working title of *The Sea When Absent*. The others are *The Sea When Young* and *The Sea in Being*. (Part of this work will be published posthumously as *Islands in the Stream*.) The book's protagonist is named Thomas Hudson, and much of the material is drawn from Ernest's life. Guests through the holiday season include Patrick and his wife Henny, Gregory, Gary Cooper, Patricia Neal, Tom Shevlin, and Winston Guest. The Hemingways close the year at home at the Finca. Brief articles by Hemingway appear in New York newspapers in December. They are "Success, It's Wonderful," in which Ernest writes a note about *Across the River and into the Trees* in the *New York Times Book Review* and his choices for the best books of 1950, "Books I Have Liked," in the *New York Herald Tribune Book Review* on the same date.

1951

"Hemingway Rates Charles for *Gazette*" (cable from Hemingway included in article in the *National Police Gazette* in January)

Pourquoi ces Bêtes Sont-Elles Sauvages? (book by François Sommer carries preface by Hemingway translated in French)

"The Good Lion" (fable)

"The Faithful Bull" (fable)

"The Shot" (article)

"On the Books" (letter from Hemingway printed in the *New York Herald Tribune Book Review* column on December 9)

Modern American Literature ("The Snows of Kilimanjaro" included in anthology)

January–June: Seventeen translations of works by Hemingway are published during the year. Charles Fenton contacts Ernest early in the year. He is interested in writing a book on Hemingway's early days as a journalist. Ernest begins to write *The Old Man and the Sea*. He has written 6000 words of the story by January 17. The novel is based on a story told to him by Carlos Gutiérrez in 1935. Carlos Baker writes to Hemingway to inform him of a critical study he has begun of his work. On February 6, Mary and Adriana and Dora Ivancich leave Havana for a trip through Florida. Mrs. Ivancich and her daughter travel to New York and return to Italy on February 23. Writing at a much faster pace than ever before, Ernest almost completes *The Old Man and the Sea* by mid-February, six weeks after the book was begun. He writes a letter to Carlos Baker on February 17 to explain that he does not want a biography written. The following week, after Baker has assured Hemingway that his project is critical and not biographical, he agrees to assist the writer. Ernest begins another story about the sea on March 5. The story, based in part on his submarine hunting in 1942 and 1943, ends with the death of his central figure, Thomas Hudson. Two fables, "The Good Lion" and "The Faithful Bull," illustrated by Adriana Ivancich, are published in *Holiday* magazine's March issue. *Pourquoi ces Bêtes Sont-Elles Sauvages?* is published by Nouvelles Éditions de la Toison d'Or in Paris on March 28. In mid-April, Malcolm Cowley informs Ernest about an upcoming book, which interprets Hemingway's writing as a response to the trauma he suffered in World War I, that he had been asked to read. (Author Philip Young had solicited Cowley's opinion of its accuracy.) After reading the manuscript, he tells Ernest who is upset at the news. Ernest and Cowley correspond on the matter for the next two months. "The Shot," an article about antelope hunting in Idaho, is published in *True* magazine in April. Ernest completes the sea story (working title, *The Sea Chase*) on May 17. The manuscript stands at 45,000 words. He begins to think of expanding the entire project by adding a fourth section. Grace Hall Hemingway, Ernest's mother, dies in Memphis, Tennessee, on June 27 at 79.

July–December: Mary leaves on July 5 to visit her parents. She is away for most of the month. Ernest writes to Charles Scribner on July 8 and tells his publisher that he has turned down an offer from *Cosmopolitan*. The magazine had proposed, through editor Jack O'Connell, to pay Ernest $30,000 to publish the Santiago story in two issues. Later in July, Ernest refers to the story offhandedly as *The Old Man and the Sea* and to the series as *Islands in the Stream* when writing again to Scribner. Hemingway celebrates his fifty-second birthday aboard the *Pilar* in Puerto Escondido. Lee Samuel's *A Hemingway Checklist*, with a preface by Ernest, is published by Charles Scribner's Sons during July. Mary's father's illness necessitates another trip for her to the family home in Gulfport, Mississippi. She is gone from the Finca from August 9 through 20. Pauline Pfeiffer Hemingway dies suddenly on the morning of October 1 at St. Vincent's Hospital in Los Angeles, California. She and Ernest had spoken to each other just hours before she entered the hospital on an emergency basis. The cause of her death was an adrenal medulla tumor. Ernest erroneously believes that problems with Gregory, the subject of their phone conversation, brought on Pauline's death at age 56. In mid-October, Harry Burns, the English professor from the University of Washington, who Ernest had befriended in the 1930s, visits the Finca. D. D. Paige contacts Hemingway on October 15 about signing a petition for the release of Ezra Pound. The document, to be signed by 100 Nobel Prize winners, has been devised by the South American poet, Gabriela Mistral. Ernest is asked to sign despite the fact that he has not won the award. After the signatures have been obtained, the petition is to be given to Harry S. Truman. One week later, Ernest expresses his doubts about the plan's viability in a letter to Paige. Hemingway appears in an ad for Ballantine's ale in *Life* magazine on November 5 (and later on September 8, 1952). The advertisement features photographs taken of Ernest at the Finca Vigia. Juan Dunabeitia, also called "Sinsky," stays with the Hemingways during November to recuperate from his third heart attack. Ernest learns that another old friend, Harold Ross of the *New Yorker*, has died unexpectedly in December. On December 9, he writes to Thomas Bledsoe, Philip Young's editor at Rinehart and Company, to inform him that he will not give his permission for reprinting quotations from any of his work in the proposed book. One week later, Hemingway writes to Charles Scribner and discusses his plan to write a scholarly introduction to his collected works. He considers the possibility of allowing the introduction to be published only posthumously. (The introduction is written in 1959, but remains unpublished.) On December 9, John K. Hutchens includes a letter from Ernest, noting books he would have liked to have seen during 1951 in the "On the Books" column in the *New York Herald Tribune Book Review*.

1952

The Old Man and the Sea (novel)
Reginald Rowe Catalogue (critical appraisal of artist's work by Hemingway included)
"A Tribute to Mamma from Papa Hemingway" (article)
"A Letter from Ernest Hemingway" (printed in column in *New York Post*)
"From Ernest Hemingway to the Editors of *Life*" (printed in the magazine's August 25 issue)
"A Letter from Ernest Hemingway" (printed in *Saturday Review*)
The Snows of Kilimanjaro (film adaptation)

January–August: Eight anthologies published during the year contain works by Hemingway. Twenty-six translations, including the first in Chinese, Croatian, and Serbian, are published in 1952. Ernest and Mary leave Havana in early February to cruise along the Cuban coast on the *Pilar*. On February 11, Charles Scribner dies of a heart attack in New York. Hemingway does not hear of the death until February 16. He returns to Havana the following day. The Wellons Gallery in New York publishes its catalogue for Reginald Rowe's exhibit. Hemingway's appraisal of the artist's work is included. Rowe is one of Ernest's neighbors in Cuba. On March 6, he writes to Philip Young and grants his permission to quote from his works on the condition that the book not cover biographical information. Leland Hayward proposes a plan to have *The Old Man and the Sea* published in one issue of *Life* magazine. Ernest and Mary leave again for a trip along the Cuban coast on March 10. Fulgencio Batista takes over control of the Cuban government on the same day, following a successful military coup. In mid-April, Ernest learns that the Book-of-the-Month Club is interested in offering *The Old Man and the Sea* as an upcoming selection. Leland Hayward is acting on Ernest's behalf in negotiations with *Life* magazine. Herbert Matthews, Ernest's journalist friend from the Spanish Civil War, comes to Cuba to research the ongoing revolution for the *New York Times*. Ernest begins a new Nick Adams short story on April 24. He eventually puts the story aside uncompleted. Arrangements for the publication of *The Old Man and the Sea* are set on May 6. By the middle of the month, Ernest has received $40,000 from the magazine. Adriana Ivancich works on and completes illustrations for the novel by the end of May. Hemingway decides on May 30 that the book will be dedicated to Charles Scribner and Maxwell Perkins. He has by this time relented and given permission to Philip Young to quote from his works. He decides in Young's favor after being convinced that his withholding permission would damage the young academic's career irreparably. Ernest is on the other hand still angry and unwilling to cooperate with Charles Fenton who is researching and planning to write about his early journalism. Photographer Alfred Eisenstadt comes to Cuba to shoot the magazine cover and photo spread for *The Old Man and the Sea* during the middle of June. Anselmo Hernandez, an 80-year-old Cuban fisherman, is used as the model for Santiago. William Faulkner submits a statement on the book to Harvey Breit of the *New*

York Times Book Review on June 20. Faulkner had been asked to review the book, but chose to send a brief statement instead. As in an earlier episode, Hemingway is upset when he reads and misconstrues Faulkner's meaning. Carlos Baker sends Ernest an advance copy of his book, *Hemingway: The Writer as Artist* (published by Princeton University Press in 1952), on August 25. Hemingway responds to the author on the following day saying that, although there are some factual mistakes, he feels it is a decent book. *Life* publishes an article on Marlene Dietrich by Hemingway on August 18 and a letter which discusses details of the writing and publication of *The Old Man and the Sea* on August 25. Columnist Earl Wilson prints a letter from Ernest in the *New York Post* on August 31.

September: *The Old Man and the Sea* first appears in print in *Life* magazine's September 1 issue. Charles Scribner's Sons publishes the book on September 8. Jonathan Cape's British edition appears on the same date. In the autumn issue of *Shenandoah*, William Faulkner speculates that the novel may be the finest single piece of fiction written by any of his contemporaries. Bernard Berenson writes an enthusiastic letter to Ernest on September 6. One week later, Ernest asks the art historian to write a blurb for the book's jacket and on September 21 Berenson complies. The novel goes on to the *New York Times* bestseller list on September 14. (Although never ranking above third, *The Old Man and the Sea* will remain on the list through March 8, 1953.) The Cuban Tourist Institute awards Hemingway its Medal of Honor for the novel. A ceremony is held in Havana on September 23. "A Letter from Hemingway," which Ernest has sent in lieu of granting an interview, appears in *Saturday Review* on September 6. Ernest opts to stay away from New York and the excitement which has been created with the publication of his new novel. Instead, he closes the month in Cuba by spending time fishing for marlin. *The Snows of Kilimanjaro*, starring Ava Gardner, Susan Hayward, and Gregory Peck, premieres in September. The film, produced by Darryl F. Zanuck through Twentieth Century-Fox, is directed by Henry King. The screenplay is written by Casey Robinson.

December: Leland Hayward and Hemingway's attorney, Alfred Rice, come to Cuba to discuss a film version of *The Old*

Man and the Sea. Hayward suggests that actor Spencer Tracy and a young actor, not yet selected, tour the United States with a staged reading of the novel to help promote the upcoming film. Vittorio de Sica is Hayward's choice to direct and production is tentatively set for June 1953. Mary and Ernest begin to make plans for an African safari.

1953

"The Circus" (essay by Hemingway printed in Ringling Bros. and Barnum and Bailey Circus Program)

Salt Water Fishing (preface by Hemingway)

Man and Beast in Africa (English translation of François Sommer's 1951 book with foreword by Hemingway)

La Casa Belga (pamphlet put out by Havana bookshop with note from Hemingway)

The Hemingway Reader (collection of works including short stories, excerpts of novels, and the complete *The Sun Also Rises* and *Torrents of Spring*)

The Little Review Anthology (contains reprints of "Mr. and Mrs. Elliot," and "Valentine" and a short letter from Hemingway)

January–April: Ten new anthologies contain previously published fiction. Eighteen translations of Hemingway's work are published during the year. This includes the appearance of *The Old Man and the Sea* in Chinese, Dutch, Hebrew, Japanese, Turkish, and Spanish. Increased publicity, because of the novel's success, begins to cause more problems for the Hemingways. A burglary occurs at the Finca, and Ernest shoots one of the intruders as he is trying to escape. A young man appears at the door one afternoon and announces angrily that he has come to be tutored by Ernest. The incident ends with Hemingway's sending him off in a cab after a scuffle. Gianfranco Ivancich, Adriana's brother, who has been staying with the Hemingways, leaves for Europe on January 28. Ernest contacts his sister, Sunny, in Memphis about this time after hearing that her husband has died of a heart attack. On February 18, Hemingway writes to Wallace Meyer and Charles Fenton to inform them both that he will not allow his work to be quoted

1954

"Safari" (article)

Library Journal (February 15 issue features letter to Oak Park, Illinois, Public Library from Hemingway)

Wilson Library Bulletin (reprint of above in March issue)

"The Christmas Gift" (article)

"Big Two-Hearted River" (reprinted in *Field and Stream* in May)

"Green Hills of Africa" (excerpts reprinted in *Argosy*'s June issue)

January–February: Hemingway's work is reprinted in 11 anthologies in 1954. Twenty-five translations of his fiction are published during the year as well. Denis Zaphiro arranges for Ernest to be appointed as an honorary game warden of the Kimana Swamp. The Hemingways remain in the area through the first week of January. On the 21st, Ernest, Mary, and pilot Roy Marsh depart from West Nairobi. Following their planned itinerary, they arrive in Entebbe by the end of the next day. They fly over the White Nile on January 23. Later that day, the Cessna they are flying in crashes three miles from Murchison Falls. Mary is in shock and Ernest sustains minor injuries. The three spend the night in the woods. Newspapers around the world report that their plane is missing; some prematurely run obituaries on Hemingway. On January 24, the Hemingways and Roy Marsh are rescued by people aboard the *Murchison*. Dr. Ian McAdam, a British surgeon, has chartered the boat. He and his crew take Ernest, Mary, and Roy to Butiaba. While enroute to Entebbe, the three are involved in another crash as their plane catches fire. The second plane crash on January 24 is far more serious. It occurs 50 miles from Masindi. Marsh and the Hemingways are taken to the town and put up at the Railway Hotel. They are driven to Entebbe the next day and moved into the Lake Victoria Hotel. Patrick Hemingway comes to the city on January 26 to help his father and stepmother. On January 28, Ernest and Roy Marsh fly to Nairobi. Patrick and Mary fly to meet them the following day. Copies of various obituaries are waiting in the city when Ernest arrives. He also gets a more thorough examination. He is suffering from the loss of sight in his left eye, a ruptured kidney, liver, and spleen, loss of hearing in his left ear, a crushed vertebra, sprains in his right arm and shoulder and left leg, a paralyzed sphincter, and first-degree burns on his arms, head, and face. Shortly after his arrival in Nairobi, Ernest begins to write an account of the crashes for *Look* (for which he will be paid $20,000). The magazine published his first African article, "Safari," on January 26. On February 21, Ernest flies to Shimoni with Roy Marsh to meet Patrick, Henny, Philip, and Flora Percival. The group goes on a fishing trip aboard a chartered boat. Late in February, Ernest's condition worsens after a brushfire occurs in their camp in Shimoni. Second-degree burns on his legs, abdomen, chest, and lips and third-degree burns on his left hand and right forearm from the fire are coupled with the still bothersome injuries from the plane crashes.

March–September: The Hemingways sail from Mombasa to Venice aboard the *Africa*. They arrive on March 23 and move into the Gritti Palace Hotel. Ernest begins to receive medical treatment for his many physical problems, internal bleeding now among them. The *New York Times* reports on March 24 that the American Academy of Arts and Letters has awarded Hemingway its Merit Medal. The honor also carries a $1000 prize. In April, Mary travels to Paris, London, and Seville while Ernest opts to stay alone in Venice. *Look* magazine publishes the first part of Hemingway's article on the African plane crashes in its April 20 issue. Aaron Hotchner arrives in Venice on May 2. He and Ernest begin an extended drive to Spain on May 6. By the 10th, they have been through Milan, Nice, Aix-en-Provence, and Carcassonne. They continue on to San Sebastian where they are joined by Juanito Quintana, who accompanies them to Madrid. Writer George Plimpton begins to interview Hemingway for the *Paris Review* at the Palace Hotel. On May 18, Ernest goes to a ranch in El Escorial. He sees actress Ava Gardner and bullfighter Luis Miguel Dominguín. He returns to Madrid the same day and remains there through the end of the month. While there, Ernest is under the care of Dr. Juan Madinaveitia. *Look* publishes part two of "The Christmas Gift" on May 4. On June 6, Hemingway sails from Genoa aboard the *Francesco Morosini*, which is bound for Havana. He arrives home in mid-June. *Life* magazine quotes a cable from Hemingway in an editorial on photographer Robert Capa's death in its June 7 issue. A ceremony is held at the International Yacht Club in Havana on July 21. Ernest is presented with the Order of Carlos Manuel de Cespedes Award, the highest honor given to foreigners by the Cuban government, on his fifty-fifth birthday. He begins to work on short stories based on his experiences in Africa during August.

October: An informal ceremony is held at the Finca Vigia on October 21 in recognition of Hemingway's having been awarded the Nobel Prize for Literature. The Swedish minister to Cuba attends as his country's official representative. The official announcement of the award for 1954 is made on October 28. Ernest gives a speech on Cuban television that day and is interviewed on the telephone by Harvey Breit in New York. The Gold Medal and $35,000 prize are to be presented in Stockholm, Sweden, on December 10. Ernest decides that he will not be able to attend the ceremony because of his ill health.

November–December: Robert Manning, a *Time* magazine writer, comes to Havana to begin interviews with Ernest for a planned cover story. After he has left, the Hemingways leave for a trip aboard the *Pilar* to avoid the publicity surrounding Ernest's Nobel Prize. John Moors Cabot, the American Ambassador to Sweden, reads Hemingway's acceptance speech at the Nobel awards ceremony in Stockholm. (The Gold Medal is eventually presented to Cuba's national saint, the *Virgen de Cobre*, by Ernest and is kept in the shrine of Our Lady at Santiago in Cuba.) *Time* magazine runs a cover story on Hemingway in its December 13 issue. On December 19, the National Broadcasting Company airs an hour-long documentary called "Meet Ernest Hemingway" across the United States. The show features narration by Lester Brown, interviews with Charles Fenton, James T. Farrell, John Mason Brown, Leonard Lyons, Max Eastman, and Malcolm Cowley, a tape of Hemingway reading his acceptance speech, and excerpts of *The Old Man and the Sea* read by actor Marlon Brando.

1955

Les Prix Nobel en 1954 (contains a biographical sketch of Hemingway, his acceptance speech, and the citation to him in French and English)

"Ernest Hemingway's Fillet of Lion" (recipe and commentary included in article entitled "A Christmas Choice of Fair and Fancy Game" in *Sports Illustrated*'s December 26 issue)

Ezra Pound at Seventy (booklet which includes tributes by Hemingway, e.e. cummings, W. H. Auden, T. S. Eliot, Archibald MacLeish, Jose V. de Pina Martins, Marianne Moore, Norman H. Parson, Stephen Spender, and Dame Edith Sitwell)

"The Great Blue River" (article reprinted in *True* magazine in April)

"Africa: Happy is the Dream..." (excerpt from *Green Hills of Africa* reprinted in *Look*'s November 15 issue)

January–May: Twenty-nine translations of Hemingway's work are published during 1955. Seventeen anthologies carry reprints of his fiction. Hemingway's health continues to limit his mobility and interfere with writing. Mary's father, Thomas Welsh, dies in mid-February. She goes to Gulfport, Mississippi, for the funeral and stays with her mother for a short time. Ernest does not leave Havana until he and Mary go on a 17-day cruise on the *Pilar* on April 17. On May 5, the day after their return, Ernest's attorney comes to Cuba for a series of business meetings.

June–December: Leland Hayward and screenwriter Peter Viertel arrive in Havana on June 1. They have come to discuss the filming of *The Old Man and the Sea*. Later in the month, the Hemingways go over to Key West to attend to the house at 907 Whitehead Street which is now being rented. Aaron Hotchner spends the Fourth of July in Havana with Ernest and Mary. Writer Bill Walton and Gianfranco Ivancich are at the Finca for Ernest's fifty-sixth birthday celebration on July 21. Hemingway has agreed to make an endorsement of Pan American Airways. On July 27, company representative Gelston Hardy arrives in Havana with a statement which has been ghostwritten yet is intended to carry Ernest's signature. Hemingway discards this and writes his own statement. The filming of *The Old Man and the Sea* begins in September. George Brown, Ernest's old boxing friend from New York, comes to Havana to train him for the fishing he will be doing during the shoot. A crew of 14, along with Gregorio Fuentes, Elicín Argüelles, and Ernest, works on the fishing scenes for the film. On September 17, Ernest draws his first formal last will and testament and names Mary Welsh Hemingway as executrix of his estate. He has been writing again and by the end of October has completed almost 700 manuscript pages of a book on Africa. Ernest's Nobel acceptance speech is included in *Les Prix Nobel en 1954*, published by Imprimerie Royale P. A. Nordstedt and Soner in Sweden during November. On the 17th, Hemingway receives the Order of San Cristobal during a ceremony held at the Havana Sports Palace. Two days later, he develops an infection in his right kidney which quickly spreads to the other kidney and his liver. By November 20, the illness is serious enough to confine him to bed. He remains inactive, although able to do some work on his African book until January 9, 1956.

1956

"The True Writer" (portion of Nobel acceptance speech reprinted in the *New York Times Book Review* on May 13)
"A Visit With Hemingway: A Situation Report" (article)
"My Life and the Woman I Love" (article)
"Hemingway On the Town" (article)
"Two Tales of Darkness" ("A Man of the World" and "Get Yourself a Seeing-Eye Dog")
Erlebtes Fliegenfischen (book by Charles Ritz on flyfishing with preface by Hemingway)

January–June: During the year, 21 translations of works by Hemingway are published. Eleven anthologies contain reprints of his work. Hemingway's health has improved enough to allow him more mobility and to discontinue the bed rest on January 9. Advertisements carrying his endorsement of Pan American Airlines appear in *National Geographic* and *Holiday* on February 26. The ads include a photograph of Ernest taken by

Aaron E. Hotchner. In mid-March, Hemingway puts aside his work in progress, the African book, and concentrates instead on the filming of *The Old Man and the Sea*. Leland Hayward and Spencer Tracy arrive in Cuba with director Fred Zinneman during the month. In early May, the Hemingways fly to Peru for a fishing trip with Gregorio Fuentes and Elicín Argüelles. They return to Havana at the end of the month. *Look* photographer Earl Theisen comes to Havana to photograph Ernest for an upcoming article in the magazine. Hemingway has been asked to write photo captions and an article for the September issue.

July–December: Ernest sends $1000 to Ezra Pound. (The poet will later tell Hemingway that instead of cashing the check he had it turned into a paperweight.) He also tells Pound that he will be sending him his Nobel Prize medal because, Ernest says, he is the greatest living poet. (Hemingway does not send the medal to Pound, but gives it to the country of Cuba.) His younger sister, Ursula Hemingway Jepson, is in Havana to celebrate Ernest's fifty-seventh birthday on July 21. During the summer, Ernest begins to write again. He produces five short stories. They are "A Room on the Garden Side," "The Cross Roads" (which carries a working title of "Black Ass at the Crossroads," the term "black ass" being one Ernest used to describe depression), "The Monument," "Indian Country and the White Army," and "Get Yourself A Seeing-Eye Dog." In mid-August, Ernest and Mary go to New York for a two-week stay. The Hemingways have a quieter than usual visit. They opt to spend their time in the city at 116 E. 64th Street, in a home owned by Harvey Breit, rather than checking into a hotel. Charles Lanham and Ernest have a brief reunion. Ernest and Mary sail for Paris aboard the *Ile de France* at the end of the month. They stay at the Ritz Hotel until September 17 when they leave for Spain. Mario Casa, a friend of Gianfranco Ivancich, drives the Hemingways to the Gran Hotel Felipe Segundo, located about 20 miles from Madrid. Ernest has been asked to join a committee of writers and artists who are working for Dwight D. Eisenhower's reelection as United States president. On September 30, Ernest writes to J. Donald Adams, editor of the *New York Times Book Review* and chairman of the committee, to decline because of his doubts that Eisenhower will survive another term in office and his refusal to assist in the election of Richard M. Nixon. *Look* magazine publishes "A Visit with Hemingway: A Situation Report" on September 4. The *London Daily Express* publishes two articles by Hemingway in September. They are "My Life and the Woman I Love" (September 10) and "Hemingway on the Town" (September 11). The latter is about the Floridita Bar in Havana. Ernest and Mary travel to Zaragoza, Spain, for the end-of-the-season bullfights. Peter Buckley, Rupert Bellville, and Aaron Hotchner are with the Hemingways as they follow Antonio Ordoñez on the bullfight circuit. Ernest's drinking has increased during his time in Spain. Both he and Mary are suffering from ill health. She is recovering from anemia, and he is once again plagued with high blood pressure, liver problems, and the new ailments of colitis and gastritis. In November, they permanently put aside plans for another trip to Africa when the Suez Canal is blocked on the 14th. On November 17, Ernest is driven back to the Ritz Hotel in Paris where he will stay through the end of the year. He begins to be treated by Dr. Louis Schwartz on November 30. (It is during this stay that Mary and Ernest Hemingway report they are given two trunks that had been stored in the hotel's basement since 1928. The contents of the trunks are the subject of some debate. Some argue that it is unlikely that writings Hemingway claimed to find could have been stored and forgotten for so many years.) Ernest receives a letter from poet Archibald MacLeish on December 15 which tells him of a letter he is circulating on Pound's behalf. MacLeish's idea is to have Pound's case turned over from prosecutors to medical and psychiatric professionals. He is seeking Pound's release from St. Elizabeth's Hospital in Washington, D.C.

1957

The Sun Also Rises (film adaptation)

January–June: Sixteen anthologies published during the year reprint Ernest's writing. Twenty-eight translations, into 18 different languages, are published in 1957. Ernest and Mary sail from Paris to New York aboard the *Ile de France*. During a two-day stay at the Savoy Hotel, Ernest grants an interview to the *New York Herald Tribune*. It appears in the newspaper on January 31. Mary leaves for Minnesota. Ernest and George Brown board the *Ile de France* for a cruise through the West Indies which will eventually take them to Cuba. During the spring, the *Atlantic Monthly* asks Hemingway to write an article on F. Scott Fitzgerald and the early days of their friendship. Ernest begins to work on this but puts the piece aside because of his ambivalence about writing about his writer friends who have died. Instead, he writes a short story, "A Man of the World," for the magazine.

July–December: Ernest, Archibald MacLeish, and Robert Frost have renewed their efforts to get Ezra Pound released from St. Elizabeth's Hospital in Washington, D.C. The two poets ask Hemingway to accompany them to Washington where they will visit the Department of Justice to make a personal appeal. Ernest declines, citing ill health as his reason, but offers to give $1500 to Pound upon his release. The money is intended to help Pound resettle in Italy. Frost and MacLeish travel to Washington, D.C. without Hemingway. John Hemingway, who has moved to Havana, contracts hepatitis and is ill for two months. In the latter part of August, the worsening political climate in Cuba is evident as governmental patrol officers shoot one of Hemingway's dogs on the grounds of the Finca. Ernest decides to take no action and avoid any possible trouble with the Cuban government. The film *The Sun Also Rises* opens on August 27. Peter Viertel wrote the screenplay of the movie, which was produced by Darryl F. Zanuck and directed by Henry King. The Twentieth Century-Fox release stars Tyrone Power, Ava Gardner, Mel Ferrer, and Errol Flynn. In early September, Mary and Ernest go to New York for a short visit. They stay at the Westbury Hotel. Denis Zaphiro, their white hunter on the last African safari, accompanies them on the trip. Ernest is reunited with his old friend Marlene Dietrich. Hemingway begins to write his memoirs when he returns to Havana in the fall. (*A Moveable Feast* will be published posthumously in 1964.) He completes three portions by December. They are about Paris in 1922 and Gertrude Stein. In its December 16 issue, *Newsweek* magazine runs an item about the filming of three Hemingway novels, *The Sun Also Rises*, *A Farewell to Arms*, and *The Old Man and the Sea*. Hemingway's tax bill, a constant source of irritation to him, amounts to $41,000 for 1957. Mary's mother, Adeline Welsh, dies on December 31.

1958

"From the Wisdom of Ernest Hemingway" (excerpts of work by Hemingway reprinted in *Wisdom*'s June issue)

"On the Blue Water" (article reprinted in October in *Jack London*'s *Adventure Magazine*)

The Armchair Esquire ("The Butterfly and the Tank" included along with a checklist of Hemingway's contributions to the magazine)

A Farewell to Arms (second film adaptation)

The Gun Runners (third film version of *To Have and Have Not*)

The Old Man and the Sea (film adaptation)

"Trout Fishing All Across Europe/Spain Has the Best, Then Germany" (Hemingway's November 17, 1923 *Toronto Star Weekly* article reprinted in *Fisherman*'s January issue)

January–June: Thirty-one translations of Hemingway's work are published during the year and 14 anthologies contain reprints of his writing. Ernest continues working on *A Moveable Feast*. "The Art of Fiction, XXXI: Ernest Hemingway Interview" by George Plimpton is run in the Spring issue of the *Paris Review*. On April 18, charges of treason are dropped against Ezra Pound. He is allowed to return to Italy to live with his daughter. Ernest begins to revise *The Garden of Eden* along with working on his memoirs. By the end of June, he has reworked 28 chapters of the novel.

July–December: Ernest turns fifty-nine years old on July 21. Ten days later, he completes his first draft of *A Moveable Feast*. He has worked over one year on the book, which contains 18 sections of his life in Paris in the 1920s. Ernest begins a lawsuit against *Esquire* in August. The magazine's publishers wish to reprint three of his stories on the Spanish Civil War. (The suit will be dropped and only "The Butterfly and the Tank" will be

included in *The Armchair Esquire*, published in October.) By
mid-September, Hemingway has revised 48 chapters of *The
Garden of Eden*. His health is somewhat improved and later
in the month he begins another road trip to Ketchum, Idaho,
with Otto Bruce. *The Gun Runners*, the third film based on *To
Have and Have Not*, premieres in September. Paul Monash and
Daniel Mann share credit for the screenplay of the film, produced by Clarence Greene and directed by Don Siegel. The
Seven Arts/United Artists release stars Audie Murphy and
Eddie Albert. In early October, Bruce and Hemingway meet
their wives in Chicago and the four continue their drive to
Idaho. They arrive on October 6. Ernest and Mary move into
a rental house in the town of Ketchum. Their companions include Taylor Williams, Lloyd and Tillie Arnold, Clara Spiegel,
Forrest MacMullen, Don Anderson, Chuck and Flora Atkinson,
and Dr. George Saviers. Ernest is feeling fit enough to hunt
again. Producer Leland Hayward's film, *The Old Man and the
Sea*, opens in mid-October. Peter Viertel adapts the novel to
the screen. The Warner Brothers release stars Spencer Tracy,
Felipe Pazos, and Harry Bellaver. Bronislaw Zielinski, Hemingway's Polish translator, visits him in Ketchum in early November. After his departure, Aaron Hotchner comes to stay
with Ernest and Mary. He is in the process of writing a teleplay
based on *For Whom the Bell Tolls*. Hotchner accompanies Ernest to Hailey when he addresses a group of schoolchildren.
(A. E. Hotchner recounts this visit to Hailey, Idaho, in *This
Week* on October 18, 1959.) Actor Gary Cooper comes to Idaho
during November. Ernest begins to rework portions of *A Moveable Feast* along with continuing his rewrite of *The Garden of
Eden*. On November 24, Hemingway writes to Bronislaw Zielinski and proposes his plan to establish a $1000 prize and the
royalties from the Polish edition of *Green Hills of Africa* for
the best Polish novel of 1959. The *New York Times* reports
Hemingway's offer on December 3. The Hemingways remain
in Ketchum, Idaho, through the end of the year.

1959

"A Matter of Wind" (article)
Two Christmas Tales (pamphlet)
"Nobody Ever Dies" (story reprinted in *Cosmopolitan*'s April
issue)
"The Worker" (Hemingway's high school poem reprinted in
Chicago Tribune Magazine of Books on May 24 and in *Newsweek* on August 3)

January–March: Twenty-three translations of Hemingway's
work in fifteen different languages appear during the year.
Twelve anthologies containing reprints of his writing are published as well. While the Hemingways are in Idaho, Fidel Castro gains control of Cuba in early January. Ernest receives
word that the Finca Vigia has not been damaged. Hemingway's
attitude towards Castro is approval by default. He feels the
new leader will be an improvement over Batista while he does
not actually support Castro. Ernest and Mary decide to buy a
house in Ketchum from Bob Topping. They begin the process.
Their friend Taylor Williams dies on February 18. On March
16, Aaron Hotchner arrives in Ketchum to drive the Hemingways to New Orleans, Louisiana. During the trip, Ernest sends
a $50,000 check to Chuck Atkinson, who is handling the purchase of the Ketchum house. On March 22, the Hemingways
and Hotchner take a side trip to Juarez, Mexico, for the day.
Hotchner leaves the two in New Orleans. They continue on to
Key West and on March 29 fly to Havana, Cuba.

April–June: Ernest and Mary stay at the Finca for three
weeks during which time he is introduced to playwright Tennessee Williams. The Hemingways travel to New York on April
22. After a short stay, they sail to Spain aboard the *Constitution*. Upon their arrival in Algeciras in May, Ernest and Mary
drive to La Consula, an estate owned by Nathan (Bill) Davis.
The house is located on the Costa del Sol, close to Malaga.
Ernest completes a rough draft of a preface for a school text
edition of his short stories. On May 10, the Hemingways go
into Malaga for the bullfights and, three days later, drive to
Madrid to attend the events at San Isidro. From May 26 through
31, Ernest and Bill Davis travel through Cordoba, Sevilla, Ar-

anjuez, and Granada to follow bullfighter Antonio Ordoñez on his circuit. The matador is badly gored on May 30 while fighting in Aranjuez. Ernest returns to La Consula and reworks his preface, now titled "The Art of the Short Story," on June 13. By the end of June, Ordoñez has recovered, and Hemingway leaves Davis's estate to follow him again. He first travels to Zaragoza and then to Alicante where he is joined by Aaron Hotchner. They continue on to Barcelona and Burgo to watch Ordoñez.

July: Mary and Ernest arrive in Pamplona on July 6. They have come to attend the Fiesta of San Fermín. Aaron Hotchner, Dr. and Mrs. George Saviers, Antonio Ordoñez, and a new acquaintance, Valerie Danby-Smith, are with the Hemingways for the fiesta. Danby-Smith soon becomes Hemingway's new secretary. The group travels a short distance for a picnic by the Irati River, an experience for Ernest similar to one in 1924. Hemingway's health has stabilized somewhat until he develops a kidney infection in Pamplona. After the fiesta, Ernest and Mary return to La Consula. Colonel Charles Lanham arrives at Davis's house on July 18 and presents Hemingway with a copy of the history of the 22nd Infantry Division. Ernest has begun to act more outwardly emotional during this period. When presented with the history, he breaks down in tears. On July 21, a celebration is held in honor of Ernest's sixtieth birthday. The party, attended by Mary Welsh Hemingway, Charles Lanham, Dr. and Mrs. Saviers, Valerie Danby-Smith (who becomes Mrs. Gregory Hemingway not long after Ernest's death), Antonio Ordoñez, Aaron Hotchner, Bill Davis, Mr. and Mrs. Peter Buckley, and Gianfranco and Carmen Ivancich, lasts through the night. Ernest's deteriorating emotional state is manifesting itself in a variety of ways. He is more prone to tears, sentimentality, and anger. In late July, he goes to Valencia with Charles Lanham, the Ivanciches, Valerie Danby-Smith, Mary, and Aaron Hotchner. Another matador and friend, Luis Miguel Dominguín, is badly gored while the group watches. Three days later, Antonio Ordoñez is injured again in a bullfight at Palma de Majorca.

August–October: By the middle of the month, Ernest is in Malaga watching both matadors, who have returned to the arena. His article about the two, "A Matter of Wind," appears in *Sports Illustrated* on August 17. Just days later, both Dominguín and Ordoñez are hospitalized again for serious injuries. Dominguín will be out for the remainder of the season. Ordoñez enters a hospital in San Sebastian, and Ernest stays for a time with his friend. Hemingway and Valerie Danby-Smith drive to Madrid. During their trip, they are involved in a car accident, but neither sustains injuries. They fly back to Malaga. The *New York Times* reports on September 10 that Ernest has been invited by the Moscow newspaper, *Literaturnaya Gazeta* to travel to the Soviet Union, along with United States President Eisenhower. Hemingway declines the offer. Aaron Hotchner contacts Ernest about a business deal he is working on with the Columbia Broadcasting System. Hotchner would adapt selected Hemingway short stories for 90-minute television programs which the network would broadcast. Payment received from CBS and its sponsor, Buick, would be split equally between Hemingway and Hotchner. On October 9, Ernest's growing popularity in the Soviet Union is evident when Ivan Kashkeen presents a lecture on Hemingway to a full house at the Moscow Museum of Literature. Ernest begins to write a lengthy article on bullfighting for *Life* magazine the next day. By October 15, he has written 5000 words. The Hemingways travel to Paris and after a stay at the Ritz Hotel begin their voyage back to the United States. Also aboard their ship, the *Liberté*, is Andrew Turnbull who is researching F. Scott Fitzgerald. On October 31, Ernest agrees to meet with Turnbull to discuss Fitzgerald. He does not, however, offer the writer much information.

November–December: The Hemingways arrive in New York on November 3. They are met by Aaron Hotchner and, to avoid publicity, are taken to an apartment at 1 East 62nd Street. Hemingway gives his manuscript *A Moveable Feast* to Charles Scribner, Jr., on the same day. Three days later, Ernest and Antonio and Carmen Ordoñez fly to Cuba. He is back home after over a year's absence, but stays only a brief time before the three leave for a drive to Idaho. Ernest's winter in Idaho gets off to a bad start as the Ordoñezes leave for Mexico immediately after their arrival because of a family emergency. Mary, who has joined Ernest in Ketchum, breaks her elbow on

November 27 while she, Ernest, and Dr. Saviers are hunting. The severe break makes Mary unable to take care of the house. Ernest has to tend to Mary and to their household. In December, he begins to be troubled by high blood pressure again along with insomnia. *Two Christmas Tales*, a pamphlet published privately is put out during the month by the Hart Press in Berkeley, California. Publishers Ruth and James Hart reprint for the first time two stories which had appeared in the *Toronto Star Weekly* on December 22, 1923. They are "A North Italy Christmas" and "Christmas in Paris." The pamphlet, illustrated by Victor Anderson, is printed by the Harts as well. Only 150 copies are made.

1960

"The Dangerous Summer" (three-part article)
A Fly Fisher's Life (English translation of Charles Ritz's book which carries a preface by Hemingway)
The Collected Poems of Ernest Hemingway (pirated edition)
"Who Murdered the Vets?" (reprint of *New Masses* article in *Mainstream*'s January issue)

January–June: Nineteen translations of Hemingway's work are published during the year. Twenty-two anthologies which include reprints of his writing also appear in this year. A series of pirated editions of his poetry carry 1960 as their publication date. Put out in San Francisco, the book illegally republishes most of the contents of Hemingway's 1923 *Three Stories and Ten Poems* along with "Ultimately," "The Lady Poet with Footnotes," "The Age Demanded," "The Ernest Liberal's Lament" (spelled "Ernest" only in the pirated editions), "The Soul of Spain," (parts one and two), "Neo-Thomist Poem," "Montparnasse," and "Valentine: For a Mr. Lee Wilson Dodd and Any of His Friends Who Want It." (The exact contents vary depending on which pirated edition one encounters. The above listing includes all material reprinted.) On January 16, Ernest and Mary leave Idaho. They travel by train to Miami and continue on from there to Cuba. During February, Valerie Danby-

Smith arrives in Havana to resume her work as Ernest's secretary. In March, journalist Herbert Matthews visits the Hemingways. He has come to Cuba to research the current political climate. Hemingway has written 63,000 words on his bullfight article for *Life* by April 1. The piece is completed on May 28 at nearly double that length. Hemingway had originally been asked for a 10,000-word article. Two days later, *Life* runs an article on the annual Hemingway fishing tournament in Cuba. Fidel Castro is the winner of the 1960 competition. Aaron Hotchner comes to Havana during the latter part of June to help Ernest edit his bullfight article. They cut the piece down to 70,000 words. The magazine decides it is still too lengthy but agrees to buy a portion of it for $90,000 and to pay another $10,000 for Spanish reprint rights.

July–October: In the latter part of July, Ernest, Mary, and Valerie Danby-Smith go to Key West. They stay at the Santa Maria Motel. Ernest flies alone to New York on July 26 and moves into the apartment at 1 East 62nd Street. Mary and Valerie, who have taken the train to New York, arrive on July 29. Aaron Hotchner relays an offer from Twentieth Century-Fox to Hemingway. The film company will pay $100,000 for the rights to Hotchner's stage adaptation of Hemingway short stories. The play is titled *The World of Nick Adams*. In a gesture indicative of Hemingway's mental state, he instructs Hotchner to refuse the offer and hold out for $900,000. Ernest flies to Madrid at the beginning of August. He asserts that the trip is being made reluctantly, that he must go because of Antonio Ordoñez. He drives to Malaga after his arrival in Madrid on August 5. He stays with Bill Davis and his wife, Annie, at La Consula for two days and then returns to Madrid. Ernest complains of depression and nightmares in his letters to Mary, who has remained in New York for a time before returning to Cuba. "The Dangerous Summer" appears in *Life* magazine on September 5, 12, and 19. Ernest is unhappy with the article when he sees it in print and the photograph of him used by the magazine. Valerie Danby-Smith flies to Spain to work for Ernest. In October, Aaron Hotchner joins Ernest at the Hotel Suecia in Madrid. Soon after Hotchner's arrival, Ernest flies back to New York. On October 22, he and Mary leave for Idaho.

Hemingway's emotional state is deteriorating. *Life* magazine publishes its Spanish edition, containing "The Dangerous Summer" on October 31.

November–December: Ernest's depression deepens after he and Mary arrive in Ketchum. His blood pressure problem also gets worse. Mary Hemingway decides that he must be hospitalized for psychiatric treatment. Her decision is reached after consulting with Dr. George Saviers and others. Aaron Hotchner seeks the advice of Dr. James Cottell, a New York psychiatrist. He recommends that Hemingway be sent to the Mayo Clinic in Rochester, Minnesota. On November 30, Dr. George Saviers flies to Minnesota with Ernest. Hemingway is admitted to St. Mary's Hospital under the name of George Saviers to avoid publicity. Mary Welsh Hemingway travels to the clinic by train on the same day. Upon arrival in December, Mary checks into the Hotel Kahler in Rochester and uses the name of Mrs. George Saviers. Ernest is put under the care of Dr. Hugh R. Butt, a liver specialist, and Dr. Howard P. Rome, a psychiatrist. Electro-shock treatments are administered to Hemingway beginning in mid-December. Ernest is allowed to spend Christmas with Mary at the home of Dr. Hugh Butt. (Shortly before his hospitalization, Hemingway became overcome with the fear that the Federal Bureau of Investigation was after him, as well as other law enforcement officers. Hemingway scholar Michael Reynolds discovered in the 1970s that the FBI did in fact have a file on Ernest which the agency began in the 1940s, probably around the time of his submarine searches on the *Pilar*.)

1961

"Hemingway Speaks His Mind" (excerpts of prior interviews and of fiction and nonfiction by Hemingway published in the January issue of *Playboy*)

The Snows of Kilimanjaro and Other Stories (collection of works published by Scribner's Sons in September)

"Pamplona!" (excerpts of *The Sun Also Rises* published in *True* magazine in February)

"After the Storm" (short story reprinted in *Cosmopolitan*'s Diamond Jubilee Issue in March)

January–March: Twenty-five translations in sixteen different languages of Hemingway's work are published in 1961. An equal number of anthologies carrying his previously published writing come out during the year as well. On January 11, the *New York Times* reports that Hemingway has been in St. Mary's Hospital, a part of the Mayo Clinic, since November 30, 1960, for an unspecified illness. The newspaper prints an article on the next day in which hypertension is reported to be the cause of his hospitalization. On January 12, the Hemingways receive an invitation to the inauguration of U.S. president John F. Kennedy. After sending a telegram to Kennedy, Ernest and Mary watch the inauguration in his room at the Mayo Clinic on January 20. Three days later, Hemingway is released from the hospital after a 53-day stay. He and Mary return to their home in Ketchum, Idaho. Ernest resumes his revisions of *A Moveable Feast*. His writing is not going well. He becomes even more reclusive. Dr. George Saviers checks in with Ernest each day to monitor his blood pressure. On February 20, Ernest tries, unsuccessfully, to write a one-line tribute to John F. Kennedy. He is able to complete it one week later on a second try. Dr. Saviers and others around Ernest detect that he is becoming more distraught because of his inability to write. His condition worsens in March as he expresses ungrounded concerns about possible lawsuits against him and fears that he has cancer.

April–June: On April 21, Mary Hemingway finds her husband with a shotgun and tries to keep him under control until Dr. Saviers stops by on his daily rounds. Ernest is taken to Sun Valley Hospital that day. He is flown to the Mayo Clinic on April 25. Mary is instructed to stay behind in Sun Valley. Ernest undergoes further shock treatments after being readmitted to St. Mary's Hospital. On April 27, the *New York Times* reports his return to the hospital, naming hypertension as his ailment. Late in May, Mary Hemingway travels to New York to seek other advice on Ernest's treatment. She goes to Rochester, Minnesota, for a brief time and then returns to New York. Mary starts the process of having Ernest admitted to a private mental health facility in Hartford, Connecticut. Against her wishes, the physicians at the Mayo Clinic recommend Hemingway's release in June. His old friend George Brown flies to Rochester from New York to drive Ernest and Mary back to Ketchum. They arrive in Idaho on June 30 and on the following day Ernest is seen by Dr. George Saviers at the Sun Valley Hospital.

July 2: At approximately 7:40 A.M., Ernest Miller Hemingway dies of a self-inflicted gunshot wound in his home in Ketchum, Idaho. He is 61 years old, two and one-half weeks away from his sixty-second birthday.

July 5: Hemingway's funeral is held. The private service is attended by Don Anderson, Lloyd Arnold, Chuck Atkinson, George Brown, Forrest MacMullen, Leonard Purdy, Alfred Rice, Dr. George Saviers, Charles Sweeny, Mr. and Mrs. William D. Horne, Charles Thompson, Mrs. Clara Spiegel, Gianfranco Ivancich, Ernest's brother and three sisters, and John, Patrick, Gregory, and Mary Welsh Hemingway.

This is a Selected Bibliography, composed of those works which were particularly useful in the preparation of this book. For a more complete bibliography please consult Audre Hanneman, *Ernest Hemingway: A Comprehensive Bibliography* (listed below).

Baker, Carlos. *Ernest Hemingway: A Life Story.* New York: Charles Scribner's Sons, 1969.

Baker, Carlos, ed. *Ernest Hemingway: Selected Letters, 1917-1961.* New York: Charles Scribner's Sons, 1981.

Baker, Carlos. *Hemingway: The Writer as Artist.* 4th ed. Princeton, New Jersey: Princeton University Press, 1972.

Berg, A. Scott. *Max Perkins: Editor of Genius.* New York: E.P. Dutton, 1978.

Brasch, James D., and Sigman, Joseph. *Bibliography of Hemingway's Library.* New York: Garland Press, 1981.

Brooks, Van Wyck. *Writers at Work: The Paris Review Interviews, Second Series.* New York: Viking Press, 1965.

Bruccoli, Matthew J. *Scott and Ernest: The Authority of Failure and the Authority of Success.* New York: Random House, 1978.

Bruccoli, Matthew J. *Some Sort of Epic Grandeur.* New York and London: Harcourt Brace Jovanovich, 1981.

Bruccoli, Matthew J., and Duggan, Margaret, eds. *Correspondence of F. Scott Fitzgerald.* New York: Random House, 1980.

Callaghan, Morley. *That Summer in Paris.* New York: Coward-McCann, 1963.

Cohn, Louis Henry. *A Bibliography of the Works of Ernest Hemingway.* New York: Random House, 1931.

Cowley, Malcolm. *Exile's Return.* New York: Viking Press, 1951.

Fenton, Charles A. *The Apprenticeship of Ernest Hemingway: The Early Years.* New York: Viking Press, 1954.

Haight, Anne Lyon. *Banned Books, 387 B.C. to 1978.* 7th ed. New York: R.R. Bowker, 1978.

Hanneman, Audre. *Ernest Hemingway: A Comprehensive Bibliography.* Princeton, New Jersey: Princeton University Press, 1967.

Hanneman, Audre. *Supplement to Hemingway Bibliography.* Princeton, New Jersey: Princeton University Press, 1975.

Hemingway, Gregory H. *Papa: A Personal Memoir.* Boston: Houghton Mifflin, 1976.

Hemingway, Leicester. *My Brother, Ernest Hemingway.* Cleveland, World Publishing Company, 1962.

Hemingway, Mary Welsh. *How It Was*. New York: Alfred A. Knopf, 1976.

Hotchner, A.E. *Papa Hemingway*. New York: Random House, 1966.

Hotchner, A.E. *Papa Hemingway: The Ecstasy and The Sorrow*. Rev. ed. New York: William Morrow, 1983.

Joost, Nicholas. *Ernest Hemingway and the Little Magazines*. Barre, Massachusetts: Barre Publishers, 1968.

Laurence, Frank M. *Hemingway and the Movies*. Jackson: University Press of Mississippi, 1981.

Miller, Madelaine Hemingway. *Ernie: Hemingway's Sister "Sunny" Remembers*. New York: Crown Publishers, 1975.

Montgomery, Constance Cappel. *Hemingway in Michigan*. New York: Fleet Publishing Company, 1966 (includes three high school short stories from *Tabula* published for the first time).

Oldsey, Bernard, ed. *Ernest Hemingway: The Papers of a Writer*. New York, Garland, 1981.

Reynolds, Michael S. *Hemingway's Reading, 1910-40: An Inventory*. Princeton, New Jersey: Princeton University Press, 1981.

Ross, Lillian. *Portrait of Hemingway*. New York: Simon and Schuster, 1961.

Ryan, Frank L. *The Immediate Critical Reception of Ernest Hemingway*. Washington, D.C.: University Press of America, 1980.

Samuels, Lee. *A Hemingway Checklist*. New York: Charles Scribner's Sons, 1951.

Sanford, Marcelline Hemingway. *At the Hemingways': A Family Portrait*. Boston: Little, Brown, 1962.

Wagner, Linda W. *Ernest Hemingway: A Reference Guide*. Boston: G.K. Hall, 1977.

Wheelock, John Hall, ed. *Editor to Author: The Letters of Maxwell Perkins*. New York: Charles Scribner's Sons, 1979.

Wolff, Geoffrey. *Black Sun: The Brief Transit and Violent Eclipse of Harry Crosby*. New York: Random House, 1976.

Young, Philip. *Ernest Hemingway*. New York: Rinehart, 1952.

Young, Philip. *Ernest Hemingway: A Reconsideration*. Rev. ed. University Park: Pennsylvania State University Press, 1966.

The Posthumous Publications of Ernest Hemingway

Three Novels of Ernest Hemingway: The Sun Also Rises, with an introduction by Malcolm Cowley; *A Farewell To Arms*, with an introduction by Robert Penn Warren; *The Old Man and the Sea*, with an introduction by Carlos Baker. New York: Charles Scribner's Sons, May 1962.

Hemingway: The Wild Years. Edited and with an introduction by Gene Z. Hanrahan. New York: Dell, December 1962 (73 articles by Ernest Hemingway which appeared in the *Toronto Star Weekly* and *Toronto Daily Star* from 6 March 1920 to 12 January 1924).

A Moveable Feast. New York: Charles Scribner's Sons, 5 May 1964 (nonfiction sketches of Paris in the 1920s).

By-Line: Ernest Hemingway. Edited by William White. New York: Charles Scribner's Sons, 8 May 1967 (selected articles and dispatches of four decades).

The Fifth Column and Four Stories of the Spanish Civil War. New York: Charles Scribner's Sons, 13 August 1969 (the title play and "The Denunciation," "The Butterfly and the Tank," "Night Before Battle," and "Under the Ridge"—the first book publication of the "The Denunciation" and "Night Before Battle").

Ernest Hemingway, Cub Reporter: Kansas City Star Stories. Edited by Matthew J. Bruccoli. Pittsburgh: University of Pittsburgh Press, 4 May 1970.

Islands in the Stream. New York: Charles Scribner's Sons, 6 October 1970 (novel).

Ernest Hemingway's Apprenticeship: Oak Park, 1916-1917. Edited by Matthew J. Bruccoli. Washington, D.C.: NCR Microcard Editions, Bruccoli Clark Books, 2 July 1971.

The Nick Adams Stories. Preface by Philip Young. New York: Charles Scribner's Sons, 17 April 1972 (eight previously unpublished stories: "Three Shots," "The Indians Moved Away," "The Last Good Country," "Crossing the Mississippi," "Night Before Landing," "Summer People," "Wedding Day" and "On Writing"—with the previously deleted conclusion of "Big Two-Hearted River" and new material edited by Philip Young).

Three Stories and Ten Poems. Bloomfield Hills, Michigan: Bruccoli Clark Books, 1977 (reprint of first limited edition, 1923, originally published by Contract Publishing, Paris).

Baker, Carlos, ed., *Ernest Hemingway: Selected Letters, 1917-1961*. New York: Charles Scribner's Sons, 1981.

INDEX OF NAMES

INDEX OF PLACES

INDEX OF WORKS